MEETING
DEATH

BOOKS BY HEATHER ROBERTSON

NON-FICTION

Reservations Are for Indians (1970)
Grass Roots (1973)
Salt of the Earth (1974)
A Terrible Beauty: The Art of Canada at War (1977)
The Flying Bandit (1981)
*More Than a Rose: Prime Ministers, Wives and
Other Women* (1991)
On the Hill: A People's Guide to Canada's Parliament (1992)
*Driving Force: The McLaughlin Family and
the Age of the Car* (1995)
Writing from Life: A Guide for Writing True Stories (1998)

FICTION

Willie: A Romance (1983)
Lily: A Rhapsody in Red (1986)
Igor: A Novel of Intrigue (1989)

ANTHOLOGIES

Her Own Woman (1975)
Canada's Newspapers: The Inside Story (1980)
From the Country (1991)

MEETING DEATH

In Hospice, Hospital, and at Home

HEATHER ROBERTSON

M&S

Canadian Cataloguing in Publication Data

Robertson, Heather, 1942–
    Meeting death : in hospital, hospice, and at home

ISBN 0-7710-7562-6

1. Death.   2. Terminal care.   3. Death – Social aspects.   I. Title.

R726.8.R62 2000   362.1'75   C00-931723-6

We acknowledge the financial support of the Government of Canada through the Book Publishing Industry Development Program for our publishing activities. We further acknowledge the support of the Canada Council for the Arts and the Ontario Arts Council for our publishing program.

Typeset in Janson by M&S, Toronto
Printed and bound in Canada

McClelland & Stewart Ltd.
The Canadian Publishers
481 University Avenue
Toronto, Ontario
M5G 2E9
www.mcclelland.com

1 2 3 4 5   04 03 02 01 00

ACKNOWLEDGEMENTS

I acknowledge with gratitude the assistance of the Canada Council's grants to writers program.

Casie Hermansson, a Ph.D student in the department of English at the University of Toronto, saved me an enormous amount of time and energy by thoroughly researching the resources of the university's libraries.

I have been travelling through unfamiliar territory, and I appreciate the assistance of all the medical professionals who opened doors, provided guidance and information, and smoothed my path. I thank hospices and palliative care units for making me welcome, and the team at the Temmy Latner Centre for Palliative Care at Toronto's Mount Sinai Hospital for the gold standard of education and example they provided. Hospice King-Aurora and Hill House Hospice have provided me with opportunities to volunteer in hospice care, and I will continue to do so.

My greatest debt of gratitude is to the patients and their families who so willingly invited me into their homes and told their stories so frankly. I have changed their names when their own privacy, or the privacy of others, needed to be protected.

I

I KNOW MY FATHER will die at dawn, and this certainty, a daughter's intuition, binds me to him as I keep watch in his darkened hospital room. As a child, I would wake in the early morning to hear him coughing and banging pots around in the kitchen. His asthma frightened me, and I would get up to keep him company for breakfast, more for my sake, I think now, than his.

This morning, I sit wrapped in a quilt on a chair by his bed, and I listen to his breathing grow more laboured as fluid fills his lungs. It is just past 3:00 a.m. and the sky outside the hospital window is as black as the bile he began to vomit yesterday afternoon.

"This is the beginning of the end," he said in a loud, matter-of-fact voice. Then his shoulders slumped and he scowled into the steel basin. Harry Robertson is eighty-six in the summer of 1995, a ripe age, but he doesn't want to die, unlike my mother, who planned her suicide for years, and made us promise not to interfere. She washed everything in the house, stocked the fridge with food, then, on a bitter January night, crept outside in her nightgown. In the morning my father found her frozen body on a pile of leaves under the back porch.

That was nearly eight years ago, but in the two weeks since I have been back home in Winnipeg, I have found her scribbled pencilled notes in cupboards and drawers all over the house. The notes are all addressed to me, and they instruct me – with many exclamation marks!! – to care for the old family china and linens she has packed away in faded Eaton's boxes. I am the only child, a privilege and a responsibility that are sometimes hard to bear, and as I read the notes I hear my mother's voice as clearly as if she were in the room. Her big walnut bed is freshly made, unslept in since the day she died.

I have no fantasy of my parents meeting in Heaven, or in Hell for that matter (my mother would be horrified that her escape plan had ultimately failed) but four days ago, when I returned to the empty house after driving my father to the hospital – he hobbled to the car for the last time without a backward glance – I felt my mother's resentful presence. I knew why she was there: Harry was slipping beyond her control, and she was holding on for dear life.

"Let him go!" I shouted. *"Release him! Let him go!"* I paced their bedroom and the upstairs hall, waving my arms and shouting, until I sensed her grudging acquiescence. The violence of my emotions astonished and embarrassed me, but I had, for the moment, exorcized my rage.

Raging against the dying of the light. How apt literary images turn out to be. The light of Harry's life is dying; his flesh is darkening as the shadow of death creeps over his swollen, suffering body with inexorable speed. Only two weeks ago, an oncologist – a young doctor Harry had never seen before – told him bluntly: "You have cancer of the liver. It's terminal."

"How long do I have?" Harry asked.

"Three months."

It was a comfort. He would have the summer.

"Can I stay at home?"

"Certainly," said the oncologist. "I don't see why not."

My father lived alone, happy in the house he'd built himself, and he took great pride in his housekeeping. He had taught himself to cook – rhubarb pie, Scotch broth, and sourdough biscuits were his specialties – and he had fully expected to see in the millennium at the age of ninety-one. He had a strong heart, and his wits were about him.

"What will happen to me?" he asked.

"Oh, nothing to worry about," said the oncologist. "You'll just get weaker and weaker."

My father's voice seemed resigned, almost lighthearted, on the phone, but when I arrived at the airport the next morning, he was not waiting for me in his usual place at the foot of the escalator, arms open to hug me. As I looked around, fearful, I heard a loud whisper: "I'm over here." He was leaning on a baggage cart, a figure so ephemeral that I had not seen him.

We shopped for groceries, as he always did on Saturday mornings, but he had no appetite and ate very little. It worried him. He had lost weight. His shoulders were skeletal, yet his feet had swollen to the point where he could barely put on his shoes. The oncologist had not mentioned these things might happen.

We played cribbage, as we used to do when I was a kid. He could still skunk me, but he was tired and preoccupied. We talked very little. We had never felt the need. "Are you afraid?" I wanted to ask, but I was afraid to ask. "I've had a good life," he said. It was true. It had been an honest, hard-working life: no debts, no old scores left unsettled, no business unfinished, and if he felt any regrets, he kept them to himself.

On Sunday, he phoned his closest friends. "I've bought it," he told them. "I've cashed in." His tone was jocular, but there were friends far away he did not have the heart to call, knowing he would never see them again. We went down the basement to his den, and he opened the filing-cabinet drawers to show me where his will and other important documents were. The cabinets were full of folders, and he began rummaging through them, pulling out birthday cards and letters from friends long dead, minutes he'd kept of organizations he'd once belonged to, receipts for the lumber he'd bought to build this house, and as he went through each file, he told me the stories behind the yellowing pieces of paper.

This inventory of his life calmed us both, and we fell naturally into the relationship we'd had when I was a child. He would chop firewood; I would stack it (neatly too!). I would hold a board while he sawed, and run back and forth to the shed for tools and nails. Now he instructed me how to arrange for his cremation, and the burial of his ashes, next to my mother's, beneath a pink granite boulder on the island where we had spent more than fifty summers. I am to have a bronze nameplate made, and attach it to the granite boulder with cement. "You know how to use cement," he said. He had taught me that too.

Monday morning we went to the bank. The tellers' eyes widened as we walked in the door: my father's skin was acid-yellow. "It's cancer," he told the manager with a rueful smile. "I'm terminal." Her mouth made a shocked little O, and she gazed at him with silent compassion. What was there to say?

He did not complain of pain – he never did – but even though he was taking laxatives, he felt miserably constipated. Every hour or so he rushed hopefully to the toilet – his feet and ankles were swollen into stumps – but passed only a thick yellow liquid. I scrubbed the bathroom daily – he apologized for giving me the extra work – but the sweet, sickly smell clung to everything. "I feel as if I'm six months pregnant," he protested. "You don't know the half of it!" I wanted to laugh, but I bit my tongue. How could I compare giving birth to the final agony awaiting him?

He could not sleep at night, and I would wake at 4:00 a.m. to hear him opening the screen door, looking for the newspaper. He would take it into the kitchen, as he always did, and spread it open on the table, but when I came down, he would be staring at it, head in hands, with unseeing eyes. Once I was up, he would go back to bed and doze, even sleep, for a while.

He asked his doctor, Dr. Murray, to give him a sleeping pill. Dr. Murray prescribed Tylenol 3 and, at bedtime, a tiny red pill called Ativan. Ativan, apparently, was small because it was potent. On Tuesday night, I woke to find my father, in his housecoat, standing by my bed, his trembling hand shaking my shoulder. The upstairs lights were on, and his pale eyes were unfocused, staring.

"Are you all right?" he asked urgently.

"Yes, I'm fine," I said, jumping up.

"Thank god," he said, holding my arm, "I thought I had to rescue you."

He had been hallucinating. I got a chair and sat by his bed, talking softly, as he had used to sit by my bed in the evenings, reading me *Treasure Island*. Now he was lying in my old bed, curled on his side under a thin blanket – a summer breeze, scented with clover, blew in the window – and I wondered whether I should get the battered copy of *Treasure Island* from the bookcase and read to him.

No. He was not a child trying to stay awake, but an old man drifting away, his bed a small, white barque on a darkening sea. His radio was within reach, but he no longer listened to it. He lay with his back to me, unresponsive.

The next night, the phantoms were worse. He did not weep or cry out; he is a reserved man. He blamed the Ativan. "It's the pill from hell," he said. "I won't take it any more." The nightmares confirmed my father's deepest suspicions about drugs, and it began to dawn on both of us that the oncologist had been wrong. If Harry was not going to "pass away peacefully," as they say in the obituaries, how *was* he going to die? We did not know. I could not help. Cancer, the crab, a ravenous sea monster, was eating him alive.

Every six months for the last twelve years, Harry had seen Dr. Murray for a checkup. Dr. Murray, director of the Deer Lodge Centre, a long-term care facility that had been, originally, a veterans' hospital, was an expert in geriatrics, and he had examined Harry as an outpatient in the day clinic. My father thought very highly of Dr. Murray, and considered him to be a friend, but now, whenever he phoned the hospital, Dr. Murray's secretary answered. Dr. Murray was on rounds. Very rushed. Off on vacation at the end of the week. Before he left, Dr. Murray agreed, to our great relief, to come to the house.

I met him at the door, a plump, bustling man in the pink of health, and showed him upstairs. In honour of the doctor's visit, my father had showered and shaved, and he had put on the new grey sweatsuit I had bought for him, with a flock of mallards in flight across his chest. I sat in the kitchen, listening to the murmur of their conversation.

Dr. Murray came downstairs, his face ashen. The cancer was progressing with astonishing speed, he said. "My father is having a very bad reaction to Ativan," I said. "He needs a new prescription." Dr. Murray glanced at his shoes, looked out the door, then fixed his gaze at a point beyond my left shoulder. Ativan takes a while to work into his system, he assured me. Harry has to keep taking it.

Hell it would be, then, and I would be here with my father, alone. If I needed help, said Dr. Murray, I could contact his replacement, Dr. Rosenberg, or Deer Lodge's home care service. In a crisis, I could take my father to Emergency at Grace Hospital. *Emergency!* Was I going to deliver my father to die on a stretcher, among strangers, in a crowded public waiting room?

"What if he dies here, at home?" My voice sounded calm.

Dr. Murray looked shocked.

"Call the police," he said, and left.

On Thursday I called Deer Lodge's home care number and left a message on a machine. Neighbours came by with pies and jams. They stood nervously at the door. "I'm sorry, he can't eat much," I apologized. Neither could I, and I put the treats in the fridge. I wasn't up to conversations. People seemed so far away, even when they were standing in front of me, I didn't have the energy to shout. I couldn't hear. There was a terrific roaring noise in my head. The weather was hot, but I was shaking with cold. The sun shone, but I felt that I had fallen off a cliff into a bottomless black abyss.

An old friend, a retired family doctor, dropped in. I almost wept with relief. He was a kind man, and he had cared for Harry for many years. He would help.

He talked with my father for a long time, and comforted him, but afterwards, when I raised the problem of the pill from hell, he became evasive. In a gentle, friendly way, with much cautious circumlocution, he made it clear that since my father was not his patient, he could not intervene.

Diane Sigurdson, a nursing supervisor at Deer Lodge, called my father to assure him that a bed was ready for him any time he wanted it. "We'll make you comfortable," she promised. As children, Diane and I had played together. I remembered her fondly, and my father was grateful that she had come back into our lives at this critical time. Diane's cheerful, confident tone relieved his mind, but he dreaded the hospital. Hadn't the oncologist told him he could stay at home?

When the home care nurse returned my message, she seemed puzzled by my call. Harry could sit up, and get in and out of bed. He could make it to the bathroom, and was able to eat a few mouthfuls of soup. He could get downstairs for a short time every day. I didn't need help with the housework. What did I want? Her tone was abrupt. I felt guilty. Was I being a wimp? A nuisance? "Why don't you call the VON," she said. She didn't give me a phone number, or suggest how a nurse might help. Harry needed a prescription, and nurses don't write prescriptions.

I was tired. I was tired of making phone calls, to no avail, while my father was alone upstairs. I hung up. We could manage, my father and I, as we had managed before. We would trust the neighbours, and rely on his friends.

Never die in Winnipeg in July. Everybody goes to the lake. I had forgotten this, even though we too had intended to be at the lake by now. Most of the neighbours were away, the city virtually deserted. On Friday, two of Harry's dearest friends called to say they were off to the lake for the weekend. They spoke cheerfully of grandchildren, family reunions. "Please don't go!" I wanted to scream. "Stay home, *please*, just this once. *Harry is dying! He needs you! I need you!*" But summer is short, the weather was beautiful, and I am not one to beg.

Cast adrift, I searched desperately for a paddle, a marker to steer by, something to get us safely to the other shore. I phoned the hospital and asked to speak to Dr. Murray's replacement, Dr. Rosenberg. Sorry, Dr. Rosenberg would not be in until Monday.

Diane called again to assure my father that a bed had been reserved for him. I suspected a conspiracy to force him into Deer Lodge. Well, okay, but what sort of care would he get there? As a war veteran, he could expect to get attention, but what exactly did Diane mean by "comfortable"?

It wasn't Ativan. "Ativan?" a friend said, incredulous. "I've taken Ativan. It's a mild tranquilizer, something executives take when they have to make a speech." At least my father wasn't missing much. Wasn't there something better? The word "morphine" floated into my consciousness. Wasn't morphine given to the dying? Morphine triggered a blurred memory that two Winnipeg hospitals, St. Boniface and Riverview, had palliative care units. I grabbed the telephone book. Under St. Boniface Hospital, I saw "pastoral care." St. Boniface was a Roman Catholic hospital, my father a lapsed Presbyterian secular humanist. The prospect of a priest hovering by his bedside was unthinkable. I called Riverview. Sorry, all beds were full, and there was a waiting list.

I stared out the window at the white stucco houses lining the street, curtains drawn against the sun. How many people in these houses were dying? Were they alone too?

I phoned Aaron, my twenty-year-old son in Toronto, and told him to hop on a plane for Winnipeg. Aaron was nervous, but he came. I worried that news of the sudden arrival of his only grandchild would frighten my father, but Grampa wanted Aaron's assurance that when Aaron eventually inherited the family cottage and island, he wouldn't sell it. After they talked, they both seemed relieved.

Harry played cribbage almost every day with Jim Alward, a fellow teacher and navy veteran and a constant friend. Harry enjoyed a glass of cold Moosehead beer, but he refused to touch his half-empty bottle of single malt Scotch. "I don't want to die drunk," he snapped.

For a puritan who could make a bottle of Glenfiddich last a year, liver cancer was a morbid joke. To me, the cancer was his body's way of saying: "Okay, Harry, that's it. Time's up. Time to get outta here."

Because he ate so little, Harry believed that he was starving, as his boyhood hero, Captain Robert Falcon Scott, had starved in the Antarctic, and while he complained that he couldn't sleep, he seemed to doze much of the time. When he was restless, he talked of relatives and friends, praising some and criticizing others with uncustomary frankness, instructing me, in an indirect way, how I should deal with them after his death. I sat for hours by the downstairs phone, screening his calls, so he wouldn't be pestered by certain crêpe-hanging widows.

He was horrified by the changes in his body. The skin on his arms hung loose in yellow, leathery folds; his swollen ankles were mottled purple. He refused to complain of pain, only of discomfort, but at night I could hear him mutter and groan. Sometimes he sat on the edge of his bed, head bowed, and sighed. Once, as I was clearing his night table, he pushed a scrap of paper towards me. On it, printed in pencil, was a single word: *purgatory*. I recognized my mother's handwriting.

On Sunday afternoon, he gave in: he would go to Deer Lodge. He knew that patients were not admitted on weekends, but once his mind was made up, he became impatient. On Monday he was packed before dawn. He dressed, put on his slippers, and we walked down the stairs. I shut the front door behind us, and helped him into the passenger seat of his Honda. I stole a glance at the house, his house, our house, a grey-shingle Cape Cod with cedar bushes framing the door and red geraniums in matching planters he'd made himself. Blinking back tears, I glanced at my father's face as I drove away. His eyes were fixed straight ahead.

We were at the hospital door by eight o'clock on Monday morning. I located a wheelchair and took him up on the elevator. Diane was waiting.

"You're lucky to be here, Mr. Robertson!" she beamed.

"I *deserve* to be here," he replied.

A dark woman, her hair in a braid, strode up beside us. She was wearing a white tunic, white pants, and a haughty expression. Who was she? Nurse? Resident? Intern? I waited for her to introduce herself, but she looked me up and down and smirked: "My, you look even more exhausted than he does!"

I wheeled my father to his private room. It was a sunny room with a picture window looking south over Assiniboine Park. He flinched at the sight of the steel bars around the bed, and looked up at me in alarm. "I don't need these bars," he protested. He seemed pitifully small. The skin stretched translucent over his skull.

Aides and orderlies rushed in to undress him and unpack his things. His clothes were taken away, and he was given a green hospital gown that left him virtually naked. He felt embarrassed. So did I. I was angry too. We had chosen clothes especially for the hospital, and they were clean. Then the mystery woman in white returned to take his history. "Since when did you have this cancer?" she asked. Her English was accented, and my father, in his distress, found her hard to understand.

"When?" he said. "This month. July."

"July when?"

"This July, July 14."

"*Which* July?" She tapped her pen impatiently against her clipboard.

"July 14."

"I mean July *of which year*," she barked.

"July of *this year*," my father retorted.

She drew in her breath, glanced at me, and replaced the sheet over my father's abdomen.

He was given a sedative. I drove back and forth to the house, bringing his mail and a portable television set (he owned three, usually all blaring at once, with the radio on). I made calls to tell people where he was (he refused to have a phone) and arranged to have the *Free Press* delivered to his room. I was glad to be useful, and grateful for the orderlies' help, but he rejected the TV with a wave of his hand, and never turned it on.

At 11:00 a.m., a chirpy young woman in a canary-yellow uniform dashed in with a steaming plate of stew and french fries. Harry had eaten almost nothing for two weeks. Revolted, he waved it away.

"He can't eat much," I explained. "Perhaps the dietician can think of something. A glass of beer?" Okay.

His name, H. Robertson, was posted on a white card outside his door. His door had to be always open, and he sat on the edge of his bed, looking out into the hall. An old man with a missing leg wheeled himself slowly to the elevator, then back again. His friend shuffled along beside him, an inch at a time, leaning on a walker. All day, patients wandered up and down, their eyes glazed. "Thank god it's not Alzheimer's," my father said.

His youngest sister, Kathleen, arrived from Victoria. Kathleen is a warm-hearted, down-to-earth retired nurse and we were both glad and grateful that she came. Kathleen has a good sense of humour, and she perked Harry up. Dragging himself along the steel bar that led to the bathroom, he joked: "I'm going Via Rail." When we turned and waved as we left for the night, he responded with a full naval salute.

My father was going down with his ship, all flags flying. He is a brave man, I thought, and the knowledge lightened my heart. He received his visitors, hunched over in his skimpy gown, as proudly as an ancient chieftain at a gathering of his clan. His eyes were red and sunken, his lips nearly black, but if he noticed the grief and terror on his visitors' faces, he gave no hint. He was glad to see them, and they were brave to come. "It's not something I do well," his friend Marjorie Gillies confessed. But she did. Well.

My father and I played our last game of cribbage on Wednesday. "I'm afraid I can't any more," he apologized, and I put the cards and board away in his drawer. Kathleen sat by the bed and held his hand, but he tossed unhappily from side to side, or sat up, hunched over, his head in his hands. I had no idea what medication he was being given – no one had told me – but if this was the nurses' definition of "comfortable," I wanted to know why.

A doctor's name was posted over the head of his bed: Dr. Blakely. Whatever had happened to Dr. Rosenberg? I went to the nursing station and asked to speak to Dr. Blakely. Dr. Blakely came only twice a week. She would be in the next day, Thursday. She would see me at noon.

Dr. Blakely was a tall, pale young woman who looked more exhausted than I did (I didn't tell her so). Why did I want to see her? she asked. Why didn't I talk to the doctor on duty, Dr. X?

Dr. X? I had never heard of Dr. X.

She nodded towards Dr. X, in her white tunic and black braid, glaring at us from the end of the hall.

"I'm sorry," I said. "I didn't know who she was. She hasn't introduced herself to me. Nobody has told me."

Dr. Blakely looked sceptical, as if it were my fault, but then her expression softened. I took a deep breath: "It seems to me that my father doesn't have three months to live. He may have three weeks, or three days. Can you tell me?"

Dr. Blakely contemplated the ceiling, her hands, the window, then began a nervous, rambling speech about how hard it is to know these things, isn't it, patients are different, aren't they, age, medical history and so on, did we have family who needed to fly in from out of town, a pastor, last rites? "No pastor," I said, "and the family that will be here, is here."

She looked sympathetic, and folded her papers to go.

"Is he getting morphine?" It was all I could do to utter the word.

Dr. Blakely quickly explained that she was only filling in for Dr. Murray while he was on vacation. She had five or six hospitals to cover during the week, and she came here only on Tuesdays and Thursdays. Dr. Murray had left a prescription . . .

She glanced at me. I waited.

". . . however, under the circumstances, due to the nature of the case, it might be possible. . . ."

"My father has a living will. I am his next of kin."

Our eyes met. My father had reread his living will before coming to Deer Lodge and given a copy to Diane on admission. It clearly stated that while he did not wish to be kept alive by artificial means, "I do ask that medication be mercifully administered to me to alleviate suffering even though this may shorten my remaining life." Dr. Blakely will not have to take responsibility for my father's death.

The morphine was offered to my father in a tiny cup the size of a teaspoon. He listened as the nurse explained what it was, nodded, and drank it down. It had little effect, except that the effort of drinking it annoyed him, and he vomited continually. The black fluid that trickled from the sides of his mouth terrified us all. Old blood, from the bottom of his stomach, said the nurses. Nothing to worry about. My father knew better.

Dr. Blakely, as I understood, had prescribed five milligrams of morphine every four hours. Was it a huge dose, or tiny? I had no idea. I did know that he couldn't drink it, and it didn't work. "We have to leave ourselves a window of opportunity to increase it," Diane explained. At 3:30 p.m. Diane said good-bye: she was taking Friday off. At four o'clock, my father reached eagerly for the tiny cup. He spilled most of it, and vomited the rest.

I knew one thing: my father was going to die *with no pain relief at all*. I accosted the new supervisor, a big blonde nurse with a commanding manner. What was she going to do? She looked taken aback – who was this wild woman? – but she hurried into Harry's room and came back moments later, more agitated than I. Dr. Blakely had left a standing order to increase my father's medication as needed, she said, but another doctor had to write a new prescription.

Ellen – her name was pinned to her uniform – picked up the desk phone and dialled, and dialled, and dialled. No answer. The doctors had all gone to the lake. At 4:15, she located the doctor on call. He authorized the prescription, but the hospital's pharmacy had closed.

I stood there while Ellen phoned the duty pharmacist at home. As they spoke, I gathered that he was hosting a barbecue, and resented being interrupted. I pictured him in his backyard, guests laughing, burgers smoking, his car in the driveway. The cadence of Ellen's voice was powerful, calm, insistent. Ellen looked at me. I had clenched my fists. I visualized the pharmacist's car. It was a small car, red or blue, a fast little car that would get him here in ten minutes. *Walk to your car*, I whispered. *Walk to your car now. Drive here now. You must come. Now.*

"He's on his way!" Ellen was jubilant. But it was half an hour before the pharmacist, a surly young man with a small child in tow, slouched off the elevator. He slammed the prescription on the desk, gave us both a dirty look, and left. Several more minutes passed before my father was given a morphine suppository. He relaxed, his breathing became easier, he slept.

Kathleen and I were gathering our things to go home for dinner when Ellen took me aside. "I think you should stay," she said slowly, emphatically. She looked me in the eye and repeated: "It might be a good idea to think about staying the night."

So there it was. How long? I asked. Hours. Not morning.

I brought blankets and bread and cheese from home – the cafeteria was closed – and we sat by his bed, Kathleen and I, his hand in both of hers, keeping watch. He grew restless from time to time, and struggled to turn over, but his legs had become so heavy and numb we could hardly lift them for him. Kathleen pointed to his feet: they were turning white.

We rang the buzzer for help. No one came. "They've all gone to the lake," Kathleen quipped. We laughed to keep from crying. I peered into the hall. The nurses were at the far end, cajoling residents into bed. I looked at the white nameplate outside my father's room: H. ROBERTSON. By this time tomorrow, I thought, someone else will occupy my father's bed (who had been there before?) and a new nameplate will be posted by the door. In the end we are lugged off, a bag of guts.

Twilight fell, and we sat in semi-darkness. Suddenly, my father sat bolt upright and swung his legs over the side of the bed. He stared intently into space, and asked, in an urgent voice: "Who is of our party?"

Kathleen and I looked at each other, mystified. It was the sort of question he might ask a tour leader, or a guide, and I pictured him standing on a crowded station platform, or a pier, waiting to embark.

"Are you going by ship," I asked, "or by train?"

He did not answer, but repeated: "*Who is of our party?*"

I thought for a moment and said: "I am, Father. Kathleen is here. We are going with you." He seemed content, and lay down and closed his eyes. As the room grew dark, I imagined my father standing in a ghostly crowd at the edge of the inky river Styx, waiting to embark for the underworld. Had he been questioning the boatman, Charon?

The image gave me comfort. We were not alone. Others had passed this way before, and had told their stories to be our guides. I could, like Orpheus, descend to the underworld and return. My fear left me. I was calm and wide awake. I walked up and down the hospital corridor, the tile cool on my bare feet. The walls were pale, the lights dim, the quiet broken only by a high, quavery man's voice calling plaintively, "Ernie, Erneee . . ." I slept for a while.

The sky is growing lighter now. Dave, the night nurse, comes in with a flashlight and peers into Harry's eyes. Dave has done this several times during the night. I like Dave. He is quiet, capable, and whenever he moves my father, he bends over his ear and tells him, in a strong voice, exactly what he is doing. My father does not raise his head, or open his eyes, but he nods. "He can hear," Dave tells me. "You can talk to him."

I talk about what I see out the window, the black treetops in the park, the brightening sky. It's hard to find the words ("Say something!" he'd snapped at us yesterday, as we'd sat there, grief-stricken) but the sound of my voice seems to relax him a little. I hope he can hear me, and knows that he is not alone. As I listen to the halting cadence of his breathing, I remember that somewhere, in a novel, I have read about an old man dying, and it was *exactly like this*.

His breathing grows shallow. Dave brings me a paper cup with crushed ice and a spoon; the ice will ease my father's thirst. It's hard to spoon the slush into his mouth – the left side of his face is pressed against the pillow – but he sucks at it eagerly. Dave gives him a morphine suppository. "It's a little early," he says, "but I'm going on my break." Kathleen and I sit by the bed.

My father's chest begins to heave, and black blood trickles from the side of his mouth. We tuck towels under his chin, but the flow increases. We buzz for the orderly. No answer. I run into the hall. A pale young man stands at the far end, guarding a trolley full of towels. His fair hair stands on end. I run up, but he won't give me towels. "I've left the supply room door open," he gestures. "You can help yourselves." He's just a kid, and more afraid than I am now.

I bring armloads of towels, but towels are of no help as my father's life's blood ebbs away. His chest heaves, then, with a shudder, he sighs, and does not breathe again. As the light fades from his face, it slowly fills the room. It's morning, the dawn of a perfect summer day.

II

OUTSIDE, THE SKY is a cloudless cerulean blue, Mary's blue, a sky that should be full of cherubs and seraphim blowing golden trumpets as the Virgin, holding Baby Jesus, ascends into the heavens in a halo of sunlight. But the Holy Family is not part of my iconography, and Winnipeg is not the exquisite Italian campagna of Tintoretto and Botticelli. Winnipeg, a flat, prairie city of sand-coloured buildings, is more evocative of Algeria, the contemporary, sun-scorched desert of novelist and philosopher Albert Camus. I read Camus' *The Stranger*, *The Plague*, and *The Myth of Sisyphus* as a student, and for thirty-five years the bleak task of endlessly rolling my rock up a mountain with courage and creativity has been a more satisfying way of ordering my absurd bourgeois life than any philosophy offered by Plato, Epicurus, the Stoics, Zen Buddhism, or the United Church of Canada. Until now.

Driving back from Deer Lodge to my dead father's house in my dead father's car, I feel dissociated, as if I have not yet quite emerged into the sunlight from my long journey to the near shore of the Styx. The monstrous, slimy Crab, satiated, has slouched off, and I am calm, almost happy, strangely comforted by the imagined, invisible, but almost tangible presence of the horde of other travellers who have jostled beside me on the path and at the ferry terminal, as if we were all leaving, or seeing someone off, for a summer at the lake. *Who is of our party?* I will never know what Charon, ferryman to the underworld, replied to my father's question, or with whom Harry shared his last boat trip, but I am convinced that a mythic Charon exists, and my mysterious companions are the multitude who have made this trip before me. I have been on a journey as old as human imagination.

Imagination is the only guide we have. Much as we try to pretend, no one has ever returned from Hades, Hell, Elysium, Heaven, Paradise, the underworld, or the Great Beyond to tell us what death and dying are all about, or what, if anything, lies ahead. Moreover, as Freud pointed out in 1915 in *Thoughts for the Times on War and Death*, it is impossible for us to imagine our own death; whenever we try to do so, we are still present as spectators. Meeting death, we have to rely on shamans and prophets, poets, playwrights, novelists, conjurers, theologians, therapists, astrologers, philosophers, our friends, relatives, neighbours, and whatever images, memories, and scraps of folklore we carry around in our heads.

As I try to conjure up images, I can see old Charon, with his stained fisherman's smock, scruffy beard, and fiery red-rimmed eyes, prodding the dying with his oar, calling out, "Hurry up, climb aboard! It's time." On the way back from the Styx, Orpheus has accompanied me, trudging along, his lyre slung over his shoulder. Orpheus had made it to Hell and back okay, but when he turned to see if his wife, Eurydice, was following, he doomed her to remain in Hades forever. An untrustworthy companion. Who else is there? I wrack my brain. Hercules, the big, tough guy who captured Cerberus, the many-headed dog that guarded the gate to the underworld? Hercules died insane. Odysseus? Odysseus made it home by outwitting women: Circe, the sirens, and the she-monster Scylla. I am a woman, and I need a mythology that reflects my own imaginative descent to the underworld.

All the names I associate with these descents are male. Osiris, Egyptian god of the dead. Virgil's hero, Aeneas, Dante and his *Inferno*. I am ashamed to realize that while these names and their stories seem familiar to me, I have never read the *Divine Comedy* or Virgil's *Aeneid*, and my knowledge of the Osiris myth is based on a vague recollection of Sir James Frazer's *The Golden Bough*. I found Frazer's theory of the ritual sacrifice of a fertility god convincing, but I am sceptical about his argument that the golden bough, the magic talisman, renewed whenever severed, that allowed Aeneas to visit the dead safely and return, was mistletoe. A deadly poison, mistletoe is not a return ticket. In 1960, I found poet Robert Graves's *The White Goddess* a satisfactory mythology, and then it came out that Graves had made it all up. Consequently, I have been leery of crones, witches, and goddess cults.

Who is of our party? Why have my father's cryptic words unexpectedly conjured up these ancient chimeras from my psyche? I do not believe Carl Jung's theory of a collective unconscious. Greek mythology, with its brutality, bombast, and complicated sexual politics, has never held more than academic interest for me, and I have no fascination with mummies, funerals, or cults of the dead. I am not Jewish or Muslim, and I have never believed in a Christian God – certainly not the hairy old Sky God of Michelangelo and William Blake – or in Heaven, Hell, sin, original or not, salvation, resurrection, or the divinity of Jesus Christ. I loved bible stories as a kid in Sunday school because they were great *stories*, like *Bambi*, *Treasure Island*, and *Alice in Wonderland*, but it never crossed my mind that the bible was the Word of God, or that God existed. My mother, raised as a Baptist, valued the New Testament for its ethical teachings – my parents lived by the Golden Rule – but she salted her Christianity with Celtic superstitions about knives and broken mirrors. We did not go to church, contribute to the building fund, or recite the Apostles' Creed, and when I was expelled from Sunday school for these faults at the age of ten or so, I rejoiced in my new nickname,

Heathen. I grew up to become an English scholar, writer, reader, researcher, wife, mother, and humanist atheist feminist. Until now.

Death exists. I have seen death, heard it, smelled it, and it has caught me helplessly off guard. For the first time in my life, I contemplate my own mortality. Am I prepared? For what? What does death mean to me, or life for that matter? I rummage through the rag bag of my memory for other images of death: Socrates drinking hemlock, paintings of martyrs and Christ on the cross, Andrew Marvell's "Times wingèd Chariot hurrying near," "the skull beneath the skin" from T. S. Eliot's "Whispers of Immortality," John Donne's sonnets and his sermon, "Do not send to ask for whom the bell tolls, it tolls for thee." *La Traviata*, Shakespeare for sure – *King Lear, Hamlet, Othello, Macbeth, Romeo and Juliet* – John McCrae's "In Flanders Fields," F. H. Varley's war painting of a cart full of corpses, titled *For What?* Nothing here but snippets and half-forgotten fragments, an incoherent, unintelligible cultural compost heap. And I considered myself educated! I have no idea what I know, or what I believe. I am ignorant. I can't even remember the name of the novel, or the writer, whose realistic deathbed scene had made my father's dying reassuringly familiar. Balzac? Zola? Tolstoy? Tolstoy wrote superb deathbed scenes, including a classic short story, "The Death of Ivan Ilyich," and his own dramatic death at Astopovo, a rural railway station, fleeing from his wife, was perfectly in character.

Where did I get the idea that dying was peaceful? You'll just get weaker and weaker, the oncologist had told my dad. Had he really expected him to lie down, close his eyes, cross his hands over his chest and stop breathing? What a joke! I had witnessed my father restless, agitated, struggling in mortal combat. A death agony, isn't that what they used to call it? I think of the stock phrase in all those obituaries, "Phoebe Bird passed away peacefully. . . ." Did she? Who says? Was her family there when she died? Is dying peacefully something we're now expected to do, like not speaking ill of the dead? There were times when Harry was sad, and mad as hell. What's wrong with that? I'd be sad and mad too. Who wants to die? I remember another book now, *On Death and Dying*, by a doctor, Elisabeth Kübler-Ross. I haven't read it, but I have often heard about her five-stage theory of dying, ending with "acceptance." Was my father an aberration? Or have I completely misunderstood her?

I am stupid about practical things too. My knowledge of medicine is nil, and my formal education in human anatomy has been limited largely to the reproductive organs. Even that is hazy. Where is the liver? Right side? Left? What does it do? As a nurse, I am incompetent. I have no skills, no training. I would not have been able to nurse my father properly during the last week of his life; I wouldn't even have known enough to turn him in bed. In Deer Lodge, he had professional, twenty-four-hour nursing. He enjoyed the nurses' company too. I am grateful, and I have a new respect for nurses. In the circumstances, going to Deer Lodge had been the right thing to do.

As for morphine, my belief that it creates a blissful, dreamlike trance is based solely on Alfred, Lord Tennyson's poem, "The Lotus-Eaters," Coleridge's "Kubla Khan," a poem allegedly written under the influence of opium, and *Confessions of an English Opium Eater*, published in 1821 by Thomas De Quincey, the hippie druggie of his day. What if they, like Robert Graves, had made it all up? The only person I can think of who knows about morphine is Dr. Larry Librach, head of palliative care at Toronto's Mount Sinai Hospital. Our sons had been friends in high school, and one day Aaron had come home, his eyes big and round. "David Librach's dad has a *really interesting* job," he'd announced. "He takes care of dying people." Dr. Librach's macabre job had stuck in my mind, and I had thought of Larry Librach several times during the past two weeks. Too late, now, but not for me. Someday it will be my turn.

I am dreading having to sell my parents' cherished house, but when I walk in the door, I find that, like the grandfather's clock that stopped, short, never to go again, Harry's spirit has departed. The house where I grew up is nothing more than a wooden box. I have the task of cleaning it out, selling stuff, giving things away, packing others to take home. It won't be too hard. My father lived a spartan life, and, apart from her confetti of handwritten notes, my mother has left almost no personal belongings. I retrieve her wooden darning egg and some old spools of thread from a dresser drawer.

Before Harry went to the hospital, he had given his most precious possession to the school down the street where he'd been a volunteer storyteller and historian for many years. It was a scale model, about two feet long, of Christopher Columbus's flagship, the *Santa Maria*, one of two model ships he had built from kits as a teenager in 1928. One of the teachers at the school, tears streaming down his face, had come to carry it away.

Since 1950, the *Santa Maria* had occupied the place of honour on the living-room mantelpiece. It looked like a fifteenth-century antique, and as the years passed, it became antique. The second ship, a man-of-war sailed by Sir Francis Drake, had pride of place over my dad's desk in his basement den. To my childish eye, the ships were beautiful, better than a clock, for instance, or a Dresden shepherdess, but until now it had never occurred to me that these ships might be sacred.

My father's fascination with ships and the sea, Drake, Magellan, the *Kon-Tiki*, *Treasure Island*, mystified me. He'd been born in Winnipeg, and apart from his father, who had worked in the shipyards of the River Clyde before emigrating from Scotland to Canada, there is no seafaring tradition in our family. Harry had joined the naval reserve during the war, becoming an instructor in navigation at King's College, Halifax. He never went to sea. Yet, since the day he took it off in 1945, his navy uniform has been hanging at the back of his bedroom closet. It's there still. What am I to do with it?

I lift the hanger. My god, it's heavy. I can hardly carry it. No wonder naval officers went down with their ships. The greatcoat looks handsome, hardly worn, and the brass buttons, with their anchors, are beautiful. Would it fit me? I try it on, and nearly sink to the floor. No way can I lug fifty pounds of blue serge through

Toronto's icy slush. I feel the disapproving presence of my mother's ghost again. The navy had been a touchy subject with her. She hated old-soldiers-never-die sentimentality – "Let the dead bury the dead," was her favourite aphorism – but there was more to it than that. Something had happened between them, some hurt that had to do with the navy. It seemed odd to me too that my father, a teacher and principal for nearly forty years, enjoyed reliving a short, uneventful wartime interlude.

Harry has left all his legal and financial documents in perfect order, but while we had managed to discard several boxes full of old files before he became too tired, I now face the task of sorting through old insurance policies, receipts for lumber for the house dating back to 1950, a personal letter of commendation from the inspector of schools on his retirement, birthday valentines from his students, university exam marks, circa 1927, and a carrier's certificate of honour from *The Manitoba Free Press*, dated January 31, 1924, certifying that Harry Robertson had "delivered on the average of 52 papers daily without a single complaint being recorded against him."

I open the drawer containing his navy memorabilia. I find exercise books, lessons copied out in my father's neat, schoolteacher's handwriting, and group photographs of solemn-looking officers standing or sitting in front of King's College. They seem to have spent a lot of time dressing up to have their pictures taken, considering there was a war on. Then I find, tucked away, his official certificate of service. It states that Henry Robertson was appointed to active service with the Royal Canadian Naval Volunteer Reserve as a Probationary Sub-Lieutenant on May 15, 1943, and was honourably discharged as Acting Lieutenant on July 5, 1945. With the certificate is a carbon copy of a will, dated January 4, 1943, in which Henry Robertson, of His Majesty's Canadian Ship *Chippawa*, bequeaths his wages, together with all his other estate and effects, to his wife, Margaret Ellen Robertson.

Chippawa, a ship in name only, was the navy's training and recruiting centre in Winnipeg. My father must have enlisted during the Christmas holidays, 1942. I was nine months old. No wonder Christmas was always a miserable time in our house. At age thirty-two, Harry had run away to sea. I can understand why. The Royal Navy was losing the Battle of the Atlantic – German submarines were in the Gulf of St. Lawrence – but I can sympathize with my mother's feelings. I would have felt abandoned too.

Now that they are both dead, I can almost laugh with relief. Whee, I'm free! No more expectations. *No more expectations!* My emotions no longer shock or surprise me. I am in free fall, and like other people who fall off cliffs, my whole life seems to be passing before my eyes. Grief, I am beginning to discover, is not a simple matter of sobbing. I am shaken by anger – *How dare you do this to me!* – and numbed by remorse, elated by freedom, overwhelmed with loneliness. I feel guilty about feeling so ambivalent, and I blame myself for failing to save my parents' lives.

Stupid and irrational, I know, but I *am* stupid and irrational. And tired. Dead tired. Do other people feel this way? How can we be expected to survive a death, and then go back to work as if nothing has happened? Until now, I could never understand the stories of Aboriginal tribes who, after a death, threw away their weapons, destroyed their houses, tore their clothing and mutilated their bodies, but now these violent expressions of grief make perfect sense to me. I remember that for more than a year after my mother's death, my father would fall and injure himself, something he had never done before and stopped doing later, and I can see now how survivors might kill themselves or die of misery. I have to be careful not to go crazy like Heathcliff in *Wuthering Heights*, and I will be thankful to have a few weeks at the lake.

I will bury my father's ashes next to my mother's. He'd had it all planned, down to giving me the receipt from the company that had made her bronze nameplate so I could get his plate made to match. He didn't care about a funeral – we'll have a celebration of his life at the end of August when everyone's back from the lake – but he had *insisted* that the Cropo Funeral Chapel handle his cremation. It made no sense to me. Cropo was way up North Main Street, on the opposite side of the city, but then Harry had been born and raised in the north end and he had taught for many years at a high school not far from the Cropo Funeral Chapel. Perhaps he'd passed it every day on the streetcar.

The next Tuesday, I drive up to get his ashes (how quickly we disappear). A low, windowless beige building, the Cropo Funeral Chapel could be a banquet hall, a bowling alley, or a North Winnipeg interpretation of Lenin's tomb. Inside, it's a blaze of light. Table lamps and crystal chandeliers illuminate wallpaper in dazzling shades of scarlet and pink, and tiny gilt chairs, upholstered in contrasting shades of satin, are placed around the edges of a turquoise carpet patterned with roses and peonies. As a swarthy young man leads me towards the office, I peer into several more brilliantly lit rooms decorated in noisy patterns and clashing colour schemes. It's North Winnipeg, all right, part furniture showroom, part Dracula's castle with touches of Versailles and the Ottoman Empire. My father must have known that Cropo's would cheer me up.

The secretary, a casually dressed, middle-aged woman, gives me a package of documents – the death certificate, their bill – and I'm pleased that her manner isn't weepy or unctuous. With a smile, she hands me a plain, dark green shopping bag, a shiny bag like I would get from a fashionable Toronto boutique. What's this? I peer inside. A black plastic box. My father's ashes. They've put my father in a shopping bag!

Well, why not? My mother's black box had been wrapped in brown paper. On Harry's instructions, this had been a no-frills cremation, plain box, no casket, no embalming (ugh), no viewing, no service. I had even written his obituary myself, a service, I had been informed rather huffily, that Cropo's customarily provided. I was amazed. How would they know what to say? No wonder so many people pass away peacefully after a long/brief illness or a courageous/valiant struggle/battle with cancer. All the funeral directors are working from the same script. As I pick up the shopping bag, a tall, pale, white-haired man in black looms in the doorway and asks, in a sepulchral voice, *Is everything all right?* Yes, thanks, I shriek, and flee.

Harry had fallen sick at the lake, opening up the cottage with Jim Alward, and when my husband, Andrew, Aaron, and I finally arrive, a month later, everything appears to be in place. But when I unlock the kitchen door, I notice that the dark red floor is covered with white streaks, like paint. Vandals. I go in carefully, but apart from white streaks all over the floors, windows, and bedspreads, nothing has been touched. Then I notice, on the veranda floor, the corpse of a merganser duck, and, in front of the fireplace, a second dead duck. Heavenly messengers, but they have started to smell. We bury them quickly.

The ducks had come down the fireplace chimney. Shitting everywhere, they had banged themselves against the windows in a futile effort to escape. Funny thing is, my father *always, always* covered the fireplace chimney with a screen for the summer – it was the first thing he did on opening the cottage – but when I go up on the roof, there is no screen. He didn't forget. I look everywhere, indoors and out. The screen has disappeared.

I put the shopping bag with his ashes on his bed in the boathouse. The boathouse was his favourite place, my mother's too, and he would spend hours there snoozing, playing solitaire, looking at the stars, listening to the lake water lapping with low sound by the shore. As I look around, I notice the varnished wooden box, stencilled on the top, "Lieut. H. Robertson, RCNVR." He'd had it made by a ship's carpenter in Halifax. It's a small box, about two feet long and a foot deep, but it's empty, and a perfect place to store the keepsakes I've saved, his wristwatch, razor and shaving brush, an engraved school bell, a square of Robertson tartan, his principal's certificate, university degrees, passports, a copy of the *Free Press* with his obituary, his treasured cribbage board, the pack of cards we'd played with and the little red and silver ballpoint pen he'd used to keep score until the day before he died. The box has been sitting there for years, but it seems fortuitous, as if, fifty-three years ago, Harry Robertson, facing the prospect that he might be killed, had commissioned his own urn.

He never talked about death, his parents', his brother's, my mother's, his own. Death wasn't taboo – he was a great funeral-goer – it was just *there*, like taxes, and he never dreamed of cheating on his taxes. Stowing his things in the box, I realize that the navy had provided Harry Robertson with rituals and traditions, a masculine code of self-discipline and self-sacrifice and an honourable role to play in a theatre of war. It was as if Harry Robertson had prepared for his death, and had uncannily anticipated how he would die. His navy script wouldn't have worked if he'd died in his sleep, or been hit by a car. Is there a link somewhere, I wonder, between HMCS *Chippawa* and Charon's boat? Who is Charon, anyway, and why a river and a boat?

I could use some rituals of my own right now. I have always liked the way the Norse placed the corpses of their dead chieftains in their ships, seated before the mast, surrounded with all their treasure, then sent the ships, flaming, out to sea. I contemplate our old wooden rowboat, overturned, half-buried in grass. Harry built it the year before I was born, a lovely little boat, light, safe, easy to manoeuvre. I'd rowed that boat all over the lake as a kid, but as the years passed the stern rotted out and it leaked badly. He bought a couple of aluminium boats, and dumped the little rowboat in the brush. My heart ached to see it abandoned, but my father refused to restore it or destroy it.

I am tempted to set it alight, and tow it into the middle of the lake, but I suspect that the other cottagers and the forest fire patrol may not be into my recreating a scene from *Beowulf*. I can, however, burn the boat, in pieces, in a small pyre on the shore.

It takes me hours to remove all the brass screws. Brass screws were sacred to my father, and they must be saved. The wood is dry and easy to break. I carry it in armloads down to a rock ledge by the water, ram newspaper underneath, and light a match. The wood burns quickly, very hot, with oily smoke and a pungent odour of melting paint and varnish. As I gleefully tend my crazy, toxic little bonfire, I feel, for the first time in my life, that I am doing something spiritually satisfying.

Maybe I am a Druid. What *is* a Druid? Julius Caesar gave the Druids a bad rap for human sacrifice when he invaded Britain. Fifty-five years later, in Jerusalem, Roman invaders crucified Jesus of Nazareth. So, who's telling the story? Do I have to admit my ancestors killed and ate people? That's something to think about. But what is the Christian Eucharist but the ritual eating and drinking of the body and blood of Jesus? I don't do that.

I must read *Beowulf* again. I used to joke with my Old English classmates about Grendel's mother, the huge, slimy, snakelike monster who lurked in a murky mere and ate men raw, but Grendel's mother isn't funny any more. I've met her. Grendel's mother is hemorrhage, jaundice, uremia, edema, typhoid, plague, malaria, AIDS, influenza, cholera, cancer, drowning. It puzzles me that she has to be a *woman*. Why do men play warriors and women get to be death? I am going to read Kübler-Ross's *On Death and Dying* when I get home, and I will phone Larry Librach.

III

I FIND *On Death and Dying* to be a disappointing collection of rambling, fragmentary interviews with patients known only as "Mrs. S." or "Dr. G." Their stories are uncorroborated and without context, and dying is discussed with such nervous circumlocution I find it impossible to know what, if any, "stage" these patients are in, or if they're dying at all. Kübler-Ross says that a lot of dying patients feel lonely, unhappy, angry, and manipulated, but I would too if I were sick and in a hospital. And how do we know they're telling the truth? The examples Kübler-Ross offers of "acceptance" of death could as easily be described as defeat, exhaustion, and faith. Her other categories – denial, anger, bargaining, and depression – are just as arbitrary and meaningless. How has this pop psychology come to be *imprinted* on our collective consciousness? Do we believe in a peaceful, "accepted" death because we *want* to believe in it? And is this belief false?

If there is no formula, do those of us who lack the comforting rituals and images of organized religion, who have no belief in salvation, resurrection, reincarnation, or nirvana, each have to meet death in our own way? In recent years we have invented creative and meaningful rituals to honour the dead, but what do we do with the dying? We can't say: You're looking great! Get well soon! Have a good day! Cheer up, you'll be fine! Our clichés fail us. What do we say?

We have no etiquette for dying. We know more or less what to do at weddings and bar mitzvahs, concerts, plays, and dinner parties. We are able to introduce strangers to each other, and we have some grasp of procedure at formal meetings. We are becoming comfortable attending childbirths, but how do we behave at a deathbed? Do we cry, or maintain self-control? Talk, or be silent? Should we maintain vigil by the bedside, or is that being ghoulish? If we keep busy, is that being indifferent? If we ask questions, are we being invasive, and if we laugh, is that inappropriate? What if we do *the wrong thing*? What is the right thing? Ann Landers and Miss Manners don't say much on the subject, and we don't have a collective memory bank of rules and phrases to draw on at a time when our minds are clouded by panic, grief, and fear. Our instinct is to run away, and most of us do.

Doctors aren't much help. "You have three months to live, Harry. Go home. Do not pass Go. Do not collect $200." Do they pick their cards at random, six months, four, one year, from a stack they keep, like a Tarot pack, in their desk drawers? How do they know? Are they pretending? Playing god? Harry had two weeks. The specialist's prognosis misled everyone into thinking we had until September. Had we been told that Harry's time was short, friends and neighbours might have interrupted their vacations to come and say goodbye. I would have wasted less time running around, trying to dig in for a long haul that never came, and we would have been less frightened by the cancer's rapid, catastrophic course. I feel betrayed, and it worries me that my father may have too.

Harry believed in medicare. He supported medicare politically for years before it became law, and contributed thousands of dollars over almost thirty years. Shouldn't he be entitled to medical care at death at least equivalent to the care women and babies receive in childbirth? I had expected my obstetrician to examine me regularly, advise appropriately, calm my fears, and deliver my baby safely. He did, and he had an anaesthetist on hand to administer an epidural that knocked out my pain after a long labour. Love those drugs! I'd done all the fashionable natural childbirth exercises, and I'd failed. If natural childbirth is considered an unnecessary agony, why isn't a natural death? There wasn't a doctor in Deer Lodge when my father died, and had Kathleen and I not stayed, he would have died *alone*. Was this what he had expected, or deserved?

Five years earlier, Harry, on his own initiative, had gone to his lawyer to draw up his living will. It was a brief, boilerplate document addressed to "my family, my physician, my lawyer, and all others whom it may concern." It expressed his wish, if there was no expectation of his recovery, that he be "allowed to die and not be kept alive by medications, artificial means or 'heroic measures,'" and to receive, instead, medication to alleviate his suffering even though this might shorten his remaining life. I had witnessed it – I completely agreed with my father's views – and, as the will instructed, I kept a copy.

I had been surprised that the medical staff at Deer Lodge seemed to show no interest at all in Harry's living will. Now, reading it again myself, I see why. It starts out saying, "If the time comes when I can no longer take part in decisions for my own future. . . ." Harry was perfectly capable of making decisions until the last hours of his life, so the will was irrelevant. As it was, he honourably fulfilled his side of the bargain by dying quickly, with a minimum of trouble or cost to the taxpayer. What about our side of the bargain? Apart from the merciful administration of medication to alleviate suffering, what obligations did the living will place on Harry's family, physician, lawyer, and "all others" concerned?

None, absolutely none. There was no commitment to honour his wish to die at home, or to provide nursing or medical care of any kind. The living will didn't even guarantee him a hospital bed. He *was* lucky. What if Deer Lodge hadn't had the kindness and foresight to reserve a bed for him? What would we have done if there had been no bed available at *any* hospital? If we had ended up in Emergency, how would the doctors there have defined "artificial means" and "heroic measures"? I have no idea what these phrases mean.

How could I have been stupid enough to sign this damn thing? The living will placed no obligation on me, as family, to look after my father, and as for the lawyer, the will ends with this contradiction: "I want the wishes and directions here expressed carried out to the extent permitted by law. Insofar as they are not legally enforceable, I hope that those to whom this will is addressed will regard themselves as morally bound by these provisions."

What's that, a licence to malpractice? An open door for euthanasia? A living will certainly seems a licence to neglect. What does it mean by "medication"? Aspirin? Aspirin would certainly have shortened Harry's life; he was allergic to it and it nearly killed him once. And what does it mean to "alleviate suffering"? Pain might be lessened, but still be excruciating, and suffering is more than pain. Suffering is one of those big, dangerous words. Many Christians regard suffering as punishment for our sins, but if Jesus Christ suffered and died for our sins, does suffering not help us emulate Jesus? Christianity is founded on an ideology of martyrdom, and devout Christians, certainly in my puritan past, believed that suffering builds character and purifies the soul. If suffering wins you jewels for your Heavenly crown, why alleviate it?

Suffering is also angst, anomie, dread, despair, fear and trembling, the sickness unto death, *la condition humaine*. Elisabeth Kübler-Ross thought she had slain Suffering by slicing it up into five labelled pieces, but still it stalks the world by night, and lashes the murky mere with its scaly tail. Even legendary Beowulf, in the end, is killed by a fire-breathing dragon.

After weeks of packing and moving my parents' possessions from Winnipeg to Toronto, unpacking, then packing and moving all our accumulated possessions from Toronto to our new home in King City, Ontario, I wonder if I am being obsessive. Maybe I should forget about all this, get over it, go back to work. But travelling to weird places is my work, and Weird is my ancestors' word for Fate.

The Greeks believed that you needed a guide, Hermes, to go to the underworld. A handsome young man, Hermes, all decked out in monogrammed leather, little golden wings sprouting from his hat or his heels, depending on the storyteller. When Hermes wasn't conducting souls to Hades, he was a messenger, the god of travellers and traders, liars and thieves, the Joker, the Trickster of Cree and Ojibwa legend. His symbol was a staff entwined with two snakes, and in his role as guide to the underworld, the Greeks called Hermes a *psychopompus*.

There is nothing pompous about Larry Librach when, in the fall of 1996, I meet him in his office at the end of a narrow, labyrinthine corridor painted bilious yellow. I had often passed Mount Sinai Hospital, a towering concrete slab on Toronto's University Avenue, and I had expected to find Dr. Librach wearing a white coat, presiding over a sunny, top-floor ward of pale-looking people tucked under crisp white sheets, rather like St. Peter with a flock of angels-in-waiting. But while Librach and his palliative care team look after patients in the hospital as well as at their homes, their headquarters are cramped, crowded offices on the ground floor of a shabby, all-purpose building behind the hospital. Librach, with greying, curly hair and a disarming grin, is wearing a colourful woolly sweater.

I have arrived to a crisis. An elderly leukemia patient, a doctor, has been discharged home with his oncologist's parting words: "There is nothing more we can do for you." The man's family has called in a panic. They had believed he was going to get well. Does coming home mean he is going to die? What are they going to do? One of the team's six physicians, probably Larry, will go to the home and assess the need for medication, nursing, and counselling. Librach is furious.

I am shocked. How can a *hospital* callously throw a dying patient out the door? How incredibly cruel! It must be a blunder, the fault of some young resident. Not at all, Librach says. It happens all the time. *There is nothing more we can do*, he says, is a standard phrase in hospitals, and sending patients home to die is accepted practice everywhere. Dying at home can be a terrible experience.

"There are patients *in agony* whose physicians won't refer them to palliative care, although the care we provide is very good," Librach says. "People are fearful of pain. Nobody likes to talk about it, nobody likes to hear about others' pain. It reminds them of their own mortality. Some cancer specialists may be reluctant to prescribe for pain because it's a symbol of their defeat. We're not curing a lot of people." There are also, he adds, personality issues. "A lot of physicians see themselves as masters. 'I'm in control here. You can't tell me you need more morphine. I'm waiting for the end. You're not ready for palliative care yet.' The patients die a week later. So when are they ready for palliative care? They're dead now."

Only about 5 per cent of Canadians who die of disease each year receive palliative care from a specialized team, Librach estimates, yet more than 60 per cent of the cost of health care is spent on people in the last two years of their lives.

"The hospital is for the dying. Most people in intensive care are palliative. More than 90 per cent of women with metastatic breast cancer are going to die. Alzheimer's patients are palliative, heart disease patients are dying. Yet we tolerate two standards of care. There is a standard, our standard, with good pain control, a good specialist, and a good family physician, and a whole other standard that's horrible. People suffer unnecessarily, and we tolerate that. We wouldn't tolerate an obstetrical service where 50 per cent of the patients died in childbirth, and a service next door where none died. But we tolerate people dying with pain because it doesn't seem to be important." One recent study shows, he says, that 50 per cent of a cancer clinic's outpatients suffer uncontrolled pain, and in another, pain and symptom distress accounted for 30 per cent of re-admissions.

At Mount Sinai Hospital, unlike many other hospitals across Canada, palliative care receives moral support, but the physicians – Librach, Frank Ferris, David Ouchterlony, Stan Zheng, Russell Goldman, and Anita Singh – are not paid a stipend by the hospital. They furnished their offices themselves. They drive their own cars on home visits, and pay for their own gas, repairs, and meals on the road. Most of their referrals come from community nurses, especially St. Elizabeth's Health Care and the Victorian Order of Nurses, many of whom are distraught about trying to care for dying patients abandoned by their doctors.

In Canada, hospital staff physicians generally don't make house calls, and many family doctors refuse to do so as well, even if their patients are too weak to get out of bed (there are doctors, too, who won't return their patients' frantic phone messages). By dying, we reproach our doctors for failing to cure us, and if they neglect us, too bad, we won't be around to complain. House calls take time, and time, in Canada's fee-for-service medical practice, is money. Mount Sinai's palliative care physicians can bill for the time spent with a patient, including counselling sessions with agitated families that sometimes last for hours, but not for the hours they spend driving from house to house, nor for team meetings and frequent telephone consultations with nurses and support staff. They do these things, at considerable financial sacrifice, because they believe that a physician who is unable to treat or cure an illness is obliged to relieve suffering.

I remember that cranky voice on the phone in Winnipeg: "Why don't you call the VON?" Should I have? Yes, Larry says. A VON nurse could have come to our house, explained to us what would likely happen as the disease progressed, discussed our options, and acted as our advocate to get appropriate support. I screwed up. I had this image of a VON nurse as an old, flabby woman with crêpe-soled shoes and her hair in a bun who'd sit in a corner and knit. It was a false image, and I can blame Charles Dickens's Sairy Gamp. "Patients and families don't know how to advocate for themselves," Larry says, trying to make me feel better. "There's no patients' bill of rights up there on the wall that says patients have a right to be free of pain."

That's true, but should the family be responsible for the quality of care given to the patient? As a healthy person of sound mind I can advocate, but why should the dying be expected to beg for care they assume to be part of their cradle-to-grave medicare package? And how can people ask for something they don't know exists? And why

35

should families in emotional turmoil be expected to take on another exhausting, unfamiliar chore? Why should the medical profession download all this stuff on the sufferers?

Doctors, Larry suggests, are more frightened of dying than the rest of us, and it may be their terror that attracts them to medicine in the first place. The practice of medicine is ultimately a doomed struggle against death, with a failure rate of 100 per cent. Doctors are also afraid of killing their patients, as some do from time to time, and when it comes to terminal illness, the bogeyman is morphine.

"When I walk on to a ward, there are doctors who say, 'Here comes Dr. Death,'" Librach says. "There is a doctor who tells me, 'You're killing my patients with morphine.' Sure, if you give enough morphine or any of the other major opioids to anyone you can kill them. It depresses the respiratory centre in the brain. But it takes huge doses given on purpose to do that. If you start with small doses and build up, as we do, people can tolerate it very well. We see very, very few people in respiratory depression."

Five to ten milligrams of morphine, given every four hours, is a starting dose, but patients with severe pain can remain active and alert on fifty milligrams, five hundred, two thousand, or more. Morphine is only one of a number of opioid alternatives. Opium derivatives include codeine, a weak opioid; methadone; and heroin; and there are two popular synthetics, hydromorphone and fentanyl. If one doesn't work, another probably will. Opioids can be swallowed in liquid or capsule form, injected under the skin, absorbed through suppositories or skin patches, or administered continuously via a portable pump. Patients are provided with bolus or "breakthrough" doses to take if pain recurs. Breakthrough pain is usually a signal to increase the dose. There is no upper limit, and people who take opioids to knock out their pain do not become addicted. Librach says: "Heroin users take it for the rush they get, a dazy space, a high that lasts for a few minutes. They're escaping from something. The only thing people in pain are escaping from is pain. I have never seen any of my cancer patients become addicted." For people in pain, narcotics, expertly administered and frequently reviewed, do not cause sleepiness, euphoria, trances, or exotic dreams of Xanadu. "You don't see a lot of dreamy, euphoric terminal cancer patients," Larry says sharply.

I am disillusioned. I had always thought of morphine as a blissful passage to an enchanted land, but Tennyson was writing about the lotus plant, wasn't he, not the opium poppy. I can blame the Greeks too, for calling sleep *narcos* and the god of dreams Morpheus, or is it the fault of the scientists who chose these words for opium derivatives? Much of what I thought I knew about morphine comes from myth, and it is morphine's association with Lethe, the underworld's river of forgetfulness, that gives it its lethal reputation.

"We encounter a host of fears," Larry says. "Patients think that when they're being prescribed morphine, that's it. Uncle George got it just before he died, that's why they're giving me morphine. The other big fear is that if they give me morphine now and it works, what happens later on when my pain gets worse? The answer is that it will work later too, we just have to give you more of it. But the movies have given people an image of a back alley, injecting, images of a narcotic squad, crack cocaine. They think 'I'm going to become an addict. It's wicked, it's evil, it's the end of life.'"

Their fears stem, too, from the fact that morphine, like all narcotics, can legally be prescribed only by a doctor, and many doctors and pharmacists fear that they will be prosecuted for supplying drugs to addicts. In North America, the criminalization of narcotics dates back to 1914, when the United States Congress passed the Harrison Narcotics Act. The act, an attempt to suppress the highly profitable, and legal, international opium trade, merely required doctors, pharmacists, and other licensed dealers to keep records of their drug transactions. In 1919, however, the U.S. Supreme Court ruled that drug addiction was not a disease, but a vice, and doctors who prescribed narcotics to addicts were criminals. The "war on drugs" became a moral issue, part of the Prohibitionists' war on booze and crime, and doctors who prescribed narcotics for patients in pain went to jail.

It was also the first salvo in the Cold War between West and East. Lurid movies, magazines, and newspaper stories blamed opium addiction on the Yellow Peril, Chinese immigrants who lured innocent young girls into white slavery in opium dens. These "Living Dead" stories were illustrated with drawings of dishevelled, curly-haired young women lying semi-comatose in grungy hovels filled with small, Chinese men smoking strange-looking pipes. In fact, the Chinese were the victims. The British had introduced opium into China. Chinese soldiers and labourers were often paid in opium, much of it imported from India, a British colony, and a Canadian girl was at greater risk from opioids prescribed by her doctor for menstrual cramps.

Opium had been considered a benign and beneficial drug since man, or, more probably, woman, first chewed the pod of *papaver somniferum* at a time before human memory. According to Martin Booth's *Opium: A History*, the opium poppy appears to have originated near the Black Sea in Asia Minor, and by 3400 B.C., the highly civilized Sumerians of Mesopotamia knew it as the "joy plant." Poppy seeds and dried opium were easy to transport, and by the second millennium B.C., the use of opium had spread to North Africa and Europe. Egyptian doctors of the time had forty-two potions containing opium, and priests at Epidaurus, the shrine of Asclepius, the Greek god of medicine, may have used opium to induce sleep and healing dreams in their pilgrim patients. In the first century A.D., the Greek physician Galen credited opium with the ability to cure everything, including headache, deafness, leprosy, apoplexy, asthma, kidney stones, and all forms of plague, and Galen's views established the foundation of all medical practice for most of the next two millennia. By the end of the nineteenth century, opium and its chemical derivatives, heroin and morphine, were the staple ingredients in almost every popular patent medicine and over-the-counter remedy, including soothing syrups for crying babies. Mixed with wine, syrup, and spices, opium was sold to adults as laudanum, and opium was consumed in such enormous quantities that wars broke out among rival trading companies (as they do today) over control of the market.

Opium allowed the wounded and injured, surgical patients, and the terminally ill to suffer no pain, but infants died of overdoses and healthy people, fond of a tonic or a pick-me-up, became addicted before they knew what had happened. Isabella, the young first wife of Canada's first prime minister, Sir John A. Macdonald, was an opium addict. Until the law made them criminals, addicts were regarded with a mixture of pity, contempt, and sorrow for their human weakness. If the Americans in 1919 had treated addiction as a drug-induced illness, their compassion would have subsequently saved generations of the sick and dying unnecessary pain.

Larry Librach calls morphine the "gold standard" for pain, *the drug*, THE DRUG, maybe the first drug. Could the opium poppy be the "golden bough"? I wonder. The opium poppy is a magical plant, but Coleridge, an opium addict, didn't write poetry about constipation. Constipation is a major side effect, and if morphine is taken without a laxative, the pain of an impacted bowel can be worse than cancer pain. Coleridge was in such agony he learned to give himself daily enemas. And what happens when, free of pain and perfectly lucid, I am left to contemplate my imminent death? Will I be reduced to gibbering terror?

"When you fall off that cliff, we provide you with a parachute," Larry reassures me. Regular home visits by the doctors give patients psychological as well as physical comfort, and a physician can be reached by telephone twenty-four hours a day, seven days of the week. Even if patients and families never call the number, knowing that help is close at hand if they need it gives them peace of mind. The Mount Sinai team includes social worker Michele Chaban, an experienced counsellor and a clinical thanatologist (a scholar of death and dying), and occupational therapist Lisa Brown. Patients are encouraged to be as busy, independent, and involved in daily activities as possible.

Mount Sinai's palliative practice is founded on the theory of Total Pain. Larry Librach takes pain so seriously he has written a book about it, *The Pain Manual: Principles and Issues in Cancer Pain Management*, a handy, popular reference for doctors and nurses. Successful treatment for pain must include adjuvant drugs and therapies to cope with side effects of medication that may include nausea and vomiting, sedation, dry mouth, confusion and hallucinations, although these symptoms are often caused by the disease, not the drugs. Adjuvant therapies include non-opioid analgesic drugs such as ASA, corticosteroids, antidepressants, tranquilizers, radiotherapy for bone pain and chemotherapy to reduce the size of painful tumours. Getting the mix right requires careful monitoring, pharmaceutical expertise, and sensitivity to each patient's unique needs.

"Pain is always subjective and individual," Librach says. "Pain is what the patient says hurts." In spite of what the politicians say, we cannot feel another's pain, and the words we use to describe it, shooting, stabbing, burning, are inadequate. We tend to say to those who complain, "It's all in your head." That may be true, but the pain is no less real. Total Pain includes the psychological and spiritual suffering caused by grief, loss, anxiety, dread, rage, regret, guilt, fear, panic, and despair. Giving the dying an opportunity to express these emotions in a safe environment, without fear of rejection or blame, helps ease their psychic pain, but even a physician has no prescription. "When people ask, 'Why me?'" Larry says, "What do you say?"

I'd be tempted to be rude and say "Why not?" Even Jesus of Nazareth, dying on the cross, cried out, "My God, my God, why hast thou forsaken me?" If, according to surveys, 80 per cent of Canadians believe in God, and 75 per cent believe in Heaven, why are they so reluctant to meet their Maker? And why believe in a God who, in the end, lets us down? No wonder we portray Death, the trickster, as a grinning skull. We have lost the art of dying, our *ars moriendi*, or did some Christian clerics make that up too? I will have to read John Donne again. That will be a pleasure. And if I'm not going to be reduced to gibbering terror by the prospect of dying, it may be wise to sew and pack my parachute now. I can find nothing ready-made. I will search for silk and string in my cultural rubble, and I will go to the dying to find out how they do it.

IV

I AM IN NO HURRY to do this. I'm scared. Yet, like Christian in Bunyan's *The Pilgrim's Progress*, I feel a burden on my back and a compelling need to explore the land of the dying, a country invisible to the living. My father, to my surprise, has left me enough money to buy a little time and freedom. No destination, no deadline. How long will this trip take, and will I survive it? Superstition reminds me that thinking about a bad thing makes it happen. Where am I going? Am I being intrusive? Exploitive? "People want to talk about their dying," Larry Librach assures me. "When people are told they have cancer, the first thing they think about is dying. It's a relief for them just to talk. My patients have information dehydration. They thirst for knowledge."

It seems we all want to talk about death. When friends and acquaintances ask me the inevitable question, "What are you working on?" I hesitated at first to reply that I am exploring death and dying, or even "palliative care," but as soon as I drop the D word into a conversation, people pour out stories about friends and relatives who had died, and who, with rare exceptions, appear to have suffered from misdiagnoses, pain, neglect, or maltreatment. I am astonished by the vividness of their memories, the vehemence of their language and the horror of their stories. I have no reason to doubt their truthfulness. I am beginning to feel grateful that my father wasn't operated on, admitted to intensive care, resuscitated, or turned into a vegetable. If we, the healthy, knew more about the treatment of terminal illness, could we better protect our mortally sick?

One thing about taking death as my subject, I don't have far to look. In the spring of 1996, I'd learned that Catherine Keachie, a witty, fearless advocate for Canada's community of magazine writers and publishers, had pancreatic cancer. It was a death sentence, and Catherine, I was told, had four months to live. Characteristically, Catherine wanted to attend her own wake, and, not long before the date for her death was due, I found myself among hundreds of her friends and colleagues attending a celebration of her life organized by her employer, the Canadian Magazine Publishers' Association. The event, held at the Toronto Tennis Club, was a benefit, with donations going towards a Catherine Keachie scholarship at the Ryerson University School of Journalism.

What do you do at a party where the guest of honour is the corpse-to-be herself? We stood around in nervous clumps, drinks in hand, waiting for Catherine to arrive. Her ex-husband, Jeff, was there, and Cleo, their fifteen-year-old daughter. How hard it must be for Catherine to leave behind her only child! Yet when Catherine walked in, slim and smart in a black sheath dress, she looked tanned, relaxed, and healthy.

Catherine made her way around the room, saying hello, and goodbye, to each of us in turn, her manner so composed that it seemed cowardly to cry. We drowned our sorrow in drink, and, as the sunlight dimmed, we shouted at each other over the din of frightened conversation. I lost sight of Catherine in the crowd. Was anyone else here feeling as miserable as I was? The speeches were awkward (what *do* you say?) and when this odd, poignant living wake became another raucous party, I left.

Six months later, Catherine was alive, and feeling better. When I called her for a story about morphine, she didn't want to be quoted.

"I intend to come out of this," she said, "and if people know who I am, will they think I'm a former addict?" Her tumours were shrinking (her cancer, she told me, was peritoneal, not pancreatic) and she was weaning herself off morphine. She had a doctor she trusted, a support circle of women friends, and a shaman in Mexico who prescribed a diet based on fresh vegetable juices. Catherine thrived on vegetable juice, and respected morphine:

"On a trip to Mexico, I mislaid my pill box in my luggage. I went thirty hours without morphine, and I found out what lay underneath it. I'd arrange to die pretty quick if I had that kind of pain all the time. It was a real lesson about my illness. I thought about women on the prairies, years ago, when the doctors found the lumps, and how they must have died. With the morphine, I went snorkelling." A few weeks after we talked, Catherine, her cancer in remission, went back to work.

Catherine confronted her cancer with the brisk, down-to-earth capability she brought to all aspects of her life. She didn't define herself as a dying person, and she behaved exactly the way we expect cancer patients to behave: she fought. Catherine's strategy worked for more than a year – she died in December 1997 – but I am as uneasy about the War Against Cancer, declared by United States president Richard Nixon in 1971, as I was about the Vietnam War. In *Close to the Bone: Life-Threatening Illness and the Search for Meaning*, American psychiatrist Jean Shinoda Bolen makes the analogy explicit:

> Cancer patients and AIDS patients are like soldiers were in Vietnam: they are living through uncertainties and risks, they lose their friends to the enemy, perhaps even holding them in their arms as they die, they run into unexpected complications, and the appearance of new symptoms is the equivalent of being ambushed, stepping on mines or being shot at by snipers. The enemy is near, deadly, and for the most part unseen. Patients, like soldiers in Vietnam, are caught up in a war that lasts for years, while contemporaries

go on with their lives as usual. Just as many were blamed for participating in this war, there are patients who are blamed for having the disease, cancer as well as AIDS.

Should the sick be treated like soldiers? Who is winning the war against cancer? Cancer can be beaten, and it can't. Would a Canadian general tolerate an annual casualty rate of 50 per cent of his troops? Would the public? And what happens to the casualties? Are they written off as losers, failures, cowards?

"How we have responded to cancer is extremely revealing of our cultural values," Nova Scotia artist Robert Pope wrote in *Illness and Healing: Images of Cancer*, a collection of drawings and paintings he made as a cancer patient between 1982 and 1992.

> Present treatments reflect the anger and violence of our age. The disease is enveloped in military metaphors. The illness is viewed as an enemy to be fought aggressively. Cancer cells are thought of as "invading" and "colonizing" parts of the body. The three main treatments can be related to human warfare. Surgery can be compared to hand combat with knives and swords, while chemotherapy, like the nitrogen mustard I received as part of my therapy, is synonymous with chemical weapons. Radiation could be associated with the technology of nuclear bombs. With the lack of real improvement in the five-year survival rate for most cancers, the results of the war on cancer bear disturbing similarities to futile colonial wars or our intervention in countries we do not understand.

Robert Pope spoke from the trenches. Diagnosed with Hodgkin's disease, a cancer of the lymphatic system, at age twenty-six, Pope went through seven months of excruciating chemotherapy, followed, four months later, by a second round. "This was the worst period of my life," he wrote. "Any conception of hell I had paled next to what I was living through. The side effects were even more severe. There were times when I was in so much pain from the treatments I felt like dying. My family literally had to force me to go to the hospital for injections. I had fewer visits from friends and came to realize that one of the consequences of cancer was feeling alone."

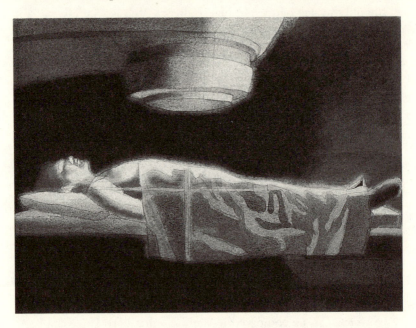

Robert Pope had to spend most of his time in hospital, waiting for tests or undergoing treatment, and, as he looked around, he was struck by the iconography of the cancer ward. In a painting called *Radiation*, based on his own experience, he depicts a young man lying flat on his back on a slab, partially covered by a white sheet, staring up at a menacing machine poised over his groin like a UFO. "There are allusions to religious rituals in this picture," Pope says. "The red lasers which are used for positioning suggest a Christian cross, the table the man lies on is like an altar, he is covered with a white shroud, the machine hovers above him like an idol or faceless god that must be propitiated with bodily sacrifices." In the hospital's ubiquitous television set, with its pale, flickering screen, Pope sees a mindless electronic god, while the temple priests, physicians in white coats, loom over the patient like ominous, threatening ghosts.

Robert Pope incorporated all kinds of religious symbolism into his work – an IV pole, with its tangle of transparent tubes, can look like a Christian cross, or Hermes' staff entwined with snakes – and his allegorical style reflects an artistic tradition that produced Pieter Breughel, Francisco Goya, the Renaissance martyr painters, and the Norwegian modernist Edward Munch, who sketched and painted sad, emaciated girls dying, like his sister, of tuberculosis.

Unlike the others, however, Pope was a participant, and he painted from the bedridden patient's point of view: his own bare feet, motionless on pale sheets; a sombre, white-haired woman, his mother, keeping vigil at the end of his bed; his friends gathered around, healthy, preoccupied with their own lives; a tray of syringes and needles at his bedside. "I began to think about Marx's quote about religion being the opium of the people," Pope observed. "In our age, even though people may not admit it, liberal humanism, with faith in science, has replaced faith in religion." He quoted Dr. Robert Mendelsohn: "Like the communion wafer Catholics receive on the tongue, drugs are the communion wafers of modern medicine. When you take a drug, you're communing with one of the mysteries of the Church: the fact that the doctor can alter your inward and outward state if you have the faith to take the drug."

Robert Pope, who died of his cancer in 1992, foreshadowed his death in a painting called *Elevator*.

"I chose to paint an elevator packed with people to convey an impression of overcrowded, overflowing claustrophobia. In a sense, these people are phantoms. To further this apparition-like quality, I depicted the architecture with a Kafkaesque vagueness, and handled the lighting using a dim, flickering chiaroscuro, overrun by deep shadows. Here are old and young, different races, health care workers, and patients. On the right is Terry Fox, Canada's most public cancer victim. The bursting elevator transports them, like Charon's ferry, through a Homeric underworld, a dark place filled with shadows."

Charon's boat an elevator? In what Pope calls "the ambiguous landscape of cancer," ordinary objects become freighted with symbolism. One of his drawings is dominated by a stark white bathroom sink, a stream of water flowing from the tap. "I understand the sink in two ways," Pope wrote, "first, the moving water as a symbol of life, and second, the drain as a metaphor for life slipping away." Going down the drain, as we say.

We also like to say that we live in a secular, materialistic society, but it dawns on me that we unconsciously invest familiar objects with sacred and mythic significance. When I pick up a copy of *Look Good, Feel Better*, a brochure for cancer patients published by the Canadian Cosmetic, Toiletry and Fragrance Association Foundation, I am amused to find a full-page advertisement for a perfume called Eternity, followed, a few pages later, by Alfred Sung's new fragrance for women, Forever. Is this a sophisticated joke, or did nobody get it? I prefer the plain "before" pictures to the wigs, headscarves, and pencilled eyebrows that make these women look prematurely embalmed. On the other hand, they're putting on their war paint, aren't they, much as my ancestors are purported to have painted themselves blue. What's wrong with dressing up to play your part? On the final page I find an obituary for last year's cover model.

The architecture of Toronto's two new cancer cathedrals, Princess Margaret Hospital and the Regional Cancer Centre at Sunnybrook Hospital, is modelled on Dante's *Inferno*. In both, the waiting room and reception area occupy the ground floor of a towering, glass-roofed atrium, and if you take Charon's ferry up to the top floor and look down, the tiers of floors around the atrium look like the concentric circles of Hell. From up here, the patients in the ground floor waiting room, most of them white-haired – cancer is a disease of the old – now appear to be at the bottom of a pit, but the innermost circle of Hell, the basement, houses, appropriately, the radiotherapy room.

Cancer hospitals are not good places to find people acknowledged to be dying, even when I pass emaciated, comatose patients on stretchers being rushed in the door. A senior oncology nurse at the Sunnybrook Regional Cancer Centre flinches when I say "die" and "palliative." The D word is taboo, and she prefers to talk about "support" care. If all the foot soldiers are going to win their war against cancer, it's the nurses' job to keep up their morale. "Feeling Your Best During Cancer Therapy" is the name of a package of booklets published by the Canadian Association of Nurses in Oncology. It's called a self-help guide, and there's no doubt about where the responsibility for getting better lies:

"The purpose of this brochure is to give you more control over your therapy and your cancer by helping you identify your need to talk to family, friends and your health care team – and their need to hear from you. You will develop a particular relationship with the members of your team based on how they help you, how you use their advice, and how you enable them to help you deal with cancer and cancer therapy."

It is the patient's responsibility to keep a symptom diary, manage the side effects of her treatment, remove emotional barriers to communication with her health care team, and make the most of her consultations. "Being prepared for consultations is the best way you have of making them work for you," the nurses admonish. "Although they may be short, you can get a lot out of a fifteen-minute talk if you know what you want to discuss. Your doctor will appreciate your efforts to streamline your discussion and cooperate with his or her busy schedule. He/she will also respect your willingness to participate fully in your treatment and recovery."

Patient, heal thyself. This approach handily relieves the hospital and the health care team of any obligation. If the patient gets well, she can feel proud; if she dies, she's done something wrong. The ideology reminds me of a conversation I had with CBC broadcaster Barbara Frum shortly after she was diagnosed with leukemia in 1974. Barbara had encountered the emerging theory of "the cancer personality," and she was furious. Elaborated by American psychiatrists Carl Simonton and Lawrence LeShan, the theory had originated with a Jungian analyst, Elida Evans, who believed that cancer was a "symbol" of something that had gone wrong in the patient's life. The psychiatrists defined cancer-prone personalities as passive, repressed, depressed, lonely, and full of self-hatred. I couldn't think of adjectives less applicable to Barbara Frum, and neither could she. "It's bad enough having cancer," Barbara raged, "*but I'm not going to feel guilty about it!*" She didn't, and she enjoyed eighteen years as a celebrated television interviewer before she died in 1992.

"Look at the posters in cancer clinics," says Larry Librach. "There is no information anywhere about pain, or that you might have pain, or that you might even die of your disease." In surveys of cancer patients in Manitoba, Quebec, and Prince Edward Island conducted between 1989 and 1991, Toronto research scientist Dr. Mary Vachon found that more than half of them suffered pain, and the majority described their pain as "distressing, horrible, or excruciating." Most of the patients were frightened, worried about the side effects of their treatments, and in need of practical and emotional support. They also seemed to be in the dark about their disease.

"Similarly to the other two provinces, almost three-quarters of those who were interviewed did not feel they currently had cancer," Vachon stated in her *Final Report on the Needs of Persons Living With Cancer in Quebec*. Yet the Canadian Cancer Society had recommended these patients for her survey precisely because they *did* have cancer; 24 per cent of her Quebec sample had advanced disease, and 6 per cent were palliative. Were the patients deluding themselves, or had their doctors deceived them?

In his 1994 best-seller, *How We Die*, American physician Sherwin B. Nuland admitted to concealing from his brother Harvey the grim truth about Harvey's terminal bowel cancer. "I became convinced that telling my brother the absolute truth would 'take away his only hope,'" Nuland confessed. "I did exactly what I have warned others against. I could not face my brother and speak the words that should have been said; I couldn't tolerate the immediate burden of hurting him, and so I exchanged the possibility of the comfort that may come with an unhampered death for the misconceived 'hope' I thought I was giving him. At no time did I ever consider sharing with him what I knew to be the virtually certain prognosis that he would not survive till summer."

A former board member of Connecticut Hospice, Nuland was an advocate of palliative care, yet, to his later remorse and regret, he sought out a high-risk experimental drug treatment for Harvey that had cured no one and had killed one patient. Only after the chemotherapy failed, and Harvey, suffering terribly from toxic side effects, had been sent home to die, did Nuland arrange for Harvey to die in hospice care.

Nuland was admirably candid about his own mistaken complicity in deception, but while he analyzed the subconscious power of denial, ultimately it was Harvey, not himself, who was responsible: "Again and again I was to be taken aback by the magnitude of his denial, until near his last days. There was something in him that refused the evidence of his senses. The clamor of his wish to live drowned out the pleadings of his wish to know." Harvey Nuland could hardly be blamed for listening to his older brother, the smart doctor, and Kübler-Ross reflects Nuland's patronizing attitude in her advice to physicians: "Never tell patients they are dying, let them tell you."

Rochelle Pittman did exactly that on January 30, 1992, and she did it in front of television cameras and reporters at the Ontario legislature at Queen's Park, Toronto. "Good morning," she told the crowd. "My name is Rochelle Pittman. I don't play basketball. I'm not a rock star and I've never slept with a hockey player. I'm the mother of four, and a grandmother. I had a monogamous relationship for thirty-two years. I am also HIV positive."

In 1984, Rochelle's husband, Ken Pittman, had received a routine blood transfusion during heart surgery. The following year, the Red Cross learned that the blood donor had been infected with the HIV/AIDS virus, but it was not until 1989, after the tainted blood had finally been traced to Ken Pittman, that the hospital notified Ken's doctor, Stanley Bain. Ken was showing all the symptoms of full-blown AIDS – a dry, hacking cough, pain in his legs, diarrhea, nausea, loss of appetite, skin rashes, and extreme fatigue – but Dr. Bain, fearful that Ken was too depressed and his health too fragile to be able to take such bad news, kept the AIDS diagnosis to himself. He assumed that Ken, fifty-eight, and Rochelle, fifty, were no longer having sex.

On March 2, 1990, Ken was admitted to hospital with chills, high fever, profuse sweating, and severe shortness of breath. Diagnosed with pneumonia in both lungs, he was transferred to the intensive care unit and put on a ventilator.

"The next weeks were days of horror for all of us, and certainly for my husband," said Rochelle. "He was unable to communicate with us verbally. He was in constant pain, for which he was receiving morphine. He had days of seizures, nose bleeds, and endured dreadful indignities to his body. Gradually his condition deteriorated until all his major organs, except his heart, had stopped functioning."

Rochelle, urged on by her children, who suspected a tainted blood transfusion was responsible, insisted that Ken be tested for AIDS before he died. On March 20, 1990, Ken was taken off life support and died in Rochelle's arms half an hour later. The next month, in his office, Dr. Bain told Rochelle that Ken's AIDS test was positive. "I looked up at him and said, 'How long have I got to live?'" Rochelle recalled. "He said, 'You weren't having relations, were you?' I said, 'Yes, we were,' and started to cry."

When Rochelle learned that she, too, had AIDS, she felt frightened, contaminated, and ashamed. Convinced she had only a short time to live, she joined a support group for people infected by blood transfusions, and when one of the group was sent home from hospital to die, Rochelle decided to speak out. "I feel terribly betrayed by the whole health system," she said. "They have failed us miserably. I'd like some answers. I want to know how something like this could have happened. Someone has to accept responsibility for these tragedies. I question a society that neglects to safeguard at all costs the safety and well-being of its members. The death of one person is too many. This is not a statistics game."

Rochelle's courage, and the resulting publicity, persuaded other victims of the tainted-blood tragedy to go public. In November

1992, hemophiliac Randy Connors and his wife Janet told their story on CBC television in Halifax, Nova Scotia. Randy, like almost every hemophiliac in Canada, had contracted AIDS from blood that had been improperly screened and tested by the Red Cross prior to 1986. Randy had been reassured by his doctor that hemophiliacs didn't seem to be getting full-blown AIDS, so he needn't worry about practising safe sex. When Janet later developed symptoms she thought were breast cancer, she discovered that she, too, had AIDS.

To see the dying on television was an unusual experience for Canadians, but the public responded with overwhelming sympathy, and the outcry forced the federal government to set up a commission of inquiry into Canada's blood system headed by Mr. Justice Horace Krever. The sordid story of the tragedy is told by André Picard in his book *The Gift of Death*, but I am curious about what the dying had to say to Judge Krever. As I read the witnesses' testimony in the commission's Toronto offices, I find no talk about peace, miracles, or unconditional love. I read about fatigue, oral thrush, throwing up, deception, rejection, anger, depression, dementia, grief, shattered families, isolation, misery, and fear.

Randy Connors, a skeleton in a wheelchair, testified before Judge Krever in March 1994. He had recently been hospitalized for his sixth bout of pneumonia. "I wasn't expected to live," he told the judge. "I am very tired and my voice isn't very good because of the tubes I had down my throat." Randy's T-cell count was zero, his memory was going, and he spent most of his time in bed. Janet, suffering from bacterial infections, was his full-time nurse.

"I am mad as hell that this happened," Randy croaked. "I can't believe that I was given a product that is going to kill me and kill my wife and destroy our family. I just can't get over it. Once I start thinking about it too much, I go crazy. I never wanted to pass this on to my wife. Soon I am going to die, and it will all be over. What is going to happen to Janet when she reaches that point? There is no one there to look after her to the extent that she looks after me now, with some very intimate things like when you mess the bed in the middle of the night. Janet is there to clean it up. What happens when I am gone and I am not there to help her at all? It is just agonizing to think about it."

Randy died in May 1994. The Connors had become powerful AIDS activists and advocates for victim compensation. Rochelle Pittman had successfully sued Dr. Stanley Bain, the Canadian Red Cross, and the Toronto Hospital for $500,000, but her victory brought her no joy. In and out of hospital with colds, diarrhea, and fevers, she had become neurotic about her health and fearful of dying the way Ken had. "I would like to close by commenting on an issue that I realize is very controversial, something I feel strongly about," she told Judge Krever on March 11, 1994. "Speaking as an HIV-infected person and one who has spent much time thinking about my coming death, I would hope that when the time comes and my major organs have shut down and I no longer wish to struggle, that someone could assist me to die with dignity. I know this is a very personal issue, but I truly believe that no one should impose their moral values on others. I feel that Sue Rodriguez was an incredibly courageous woman. I can only hope her fight will not have been in vain."

A month before, on February 12, 1994, Sue Rodriguez of Victoria, British Columbia, had died in bed of an overdose of morphine and Seconal. The drugs had been administered, at Sue's request, by an anonymous doctor, in the presence of NDP member of parliament Svend Robinson. The doctor had committed a crime – it is legal to kill yourself in Canada (who is left to prosecute?) but illegal to counsel or assist in a suicide – yet the police did not press charges. Sue had been near death from amyotrophic lateral sclerosis, ALS, a creeping paralysis with no known cause or cure, and for eighteen months Sue had waged a high-profile campaign to legalize assisted suicide. Her appeal to the Supreme Court of Canada had failed by a narrow vote of five to four, and Sue had gained enormous public sympathy.

The "right to die" movement had surfaced in Great Britain with the Hemlock Society, and Derek Humphrey's how-to book, *Final Exit*, had created a worldwide sensation. In the United States, Dr. Jack Kevorkian was publicizing his services to the terminally ill who wanted a quick end to their lives, and challenging the courts to convict him. Kevorkian favoured using carbon monoxide, a simple, painless solution accessible to anyone who has a car.

Carbon monoxide was the method Saskatchewan farmer Robert Latimer used to murder his severely disabled twelve-year-old daughter, Tracy, in October 1993. Latimer confessed, claiming that Tracy's suffering from cerebral palsy was so intolerable he was acting out of compassion. Advocates for the disabled, however, pointed out that suffering may be in the eye of the beholder, and there was no evidence that Tracy had found her own life unendurable. Robert Latimer was convicted of murder, but his defence raised once more the thorny issue of euthanasia.

What do we mean by "right to die," or "dying with dignity"? Slogans like this, mindlessly repeated, make me uneasy. Rochelle Pittman asked to die with dignity only after all her major organs had shut down. Wouldn't she already be dead? Victoria's Right to Die Society, which organized Sue Rodriguez's media campaign, seems to have consisted of one individual, journalist John Hofsess. In *Uncommon Will*, an authorized biography of Sue Rodriguez, Lisa Hobbs Birnie says that Sue's husband, Henry, watched her relationship with Hofsess with some amazement: "Here was this person, inside my own home, offering to kill my wife, even drawing up a contract to do it – and he'd only just met her."

Do we have the right to kill our child, or anyone else, because we feel compassion? Pity and terror, as Shakespeare knew, go together, like love and hate. And why should dying with dignity be equated with euthanasia? Sue Rodriguez needed to control the exact time and means of her death. Why not just *do it*? She was mobile enough to give interviews, meet with politicians, go out for lunch, spend weekends in Vancouver, and appear as a mystery guest on the CBC's "Front Page Challenge" quiz show. Why not jump off a pier, Sue? Fall overboard on the ferry. Stop eating.

I was angry with Sue Rodriguez because she reminded me of my mother. Incapacitated by degenerative bone disease, my mother had developed a horror of being institutionalized and an unreasonable conviction that she was a burden to the world. The taboo T word, tuberculosis, had never been spoken in my hearing, but from what had been said obliquely over my lifetime, I concluded that the broken back Margaret suffered as a university student, an injury that confined her to bed for two years, was tubercular. She did tell me that as a young woman her doctors had warned her that she did not have long to live, and that she should not think of marrying or having children.

By the age of twenty-four, however, Margaret was well enough to return, part-time, to university night school and fall in love with a classmate, twenty-seven-year-old Harry Robertson. They married in 1938, and I was born, against doctors' orders, four years later. I was always aware that my mother was sick and might die. She might have told me herself. She had a kidney removed, and further surgery, and from earliest memory I was happy to be cared for, from time to time, by an extended family that included Kathleen, my grandparents, babysitters, and a beloved cleaning woman, Mrs. Swedeborg.

I was taught to be an unusually independent, self-sufficient, on-my-own child, but my mother, while she was always going to clinics, seeing specialists, and having surgery, didn't die. Though physically weak, she was so powerful psychologically she often frightened me. Looking back, I think it was the post-war miracle drugs, sulfa and penicillin, that saved her life. When I was in my teens, Margaret, a full-time mother and homemaker, was a part-time mature student completing her B.A. at the University of Manitoba. She graduated, with honours, in 1959. In 1963, when I left home, she was a feminist with a wide circle of intelligent, politically radical friends.

À la recherche du temps perdu. Searching for lost time, a hopeless task. The burden on my back is my mother's suicide. Outwitting death for more than fifty years, she enjoyed, it seemed, a long, happy, successful life: summers at the lake, travel, bridge parties, wonderful friends, financial security, a loving family she had risked her own life to create. But once she had reached her allotted three score years and ten, did death, come, inevitably, to collect her debt?

In her seventies, Margaret's sadness became inexplicable, unfathomable, untreatable, unbearable. She planned her suicide with scrupulous serenity. She told us that she intended to kill herself, but not how, when, or where, and she didn't ask anyone for help. Intellectually, I understood and respected her freedom and determination to make this decision, and the joy she found in making her secret plans fooled me into thinking she was bluffing. She died peacefully, at a time and in a place and manner she chose, but, oh, what grief and guilt she left for the rest of us to bear. What right did Sue Rodriguez have to insist that I, as a citizen, take moral and legal responsibility for *her* death? We don't execute murderers in this country, why ask us to murder the sick?

In *Uncommon Will*, Lisa Hobbs Birnie interprets Sue Rodriguez's crusade as her way of giving meaning to the remainder of her life. According to Birnie, the public Sue, funny, spunky, her hair a blazing red, concealed the private Sue, depressed, narcissistic, manipulative, and hypercritical. Birnie quotes Sue's psychotherapist, Dr. Sandra Elder: "Sue had an aching soul, and never had internal peace. She wouldn't let love in, and when you are starved for love, you sabotage any attempts people make to give it to you. Anger was Sue's foundation. Her identity was based on it."

Rodriguez's model for a televised dying was the AIDS diary of Dr. Peter, a series of vignettes broadcast on CBC television in Vancouver between July 27, 1990, and November 4, 1992. Dr. Peter Jepson-Young had been diagnosed with AIDS in 1988, and by using himself as a clinical case study, he hoped to raise public awareness about the disease. In July, Dr. Peter, a muscular young man with a shock of light brown hair, speaks directly to the camera in a calm, detached voice, showing us the Kaposi's sarcoma on his leg as if his cancer belonged to someone else. He is losing the vision in his right eye, and within months he is completely blind, his face puffy and yellow from chemotherapy. Dr. Peter no longer lectures us about AIDS; he *is* AIDS. Week after week the camera shows us his thinning hair, bloated body, a painful swelling in his leg, and the purple spots of Kaposi's sarcoma spreading over his face, ominous symptoms he cannot see himself. In August 1992, Dr. Peter speaks from his hospital bed, feverish, scared, and fighting for breath. His voice is hoarse, his eyes bruised. His cancer is out of control. "I have some pretty bad days," he admits in October. "The fever is not very easy to tolerate. It's getting to be a real struggle." Dr. Peter died on November 15, 1992.

Dr. Peter's words were playful and charming, honest, unsentimental, and brave. He brought homosexuality and AIDS into family rooms, but his self-portrait was the story of a privileged patient. Dr Peter knew exactly what was wrong with him, and he had immediate access to a hospital bed, drugs, chemotherapy, and radiation, all of which he used to the maximum. He shared a comfortable home with a healthy, devoted partner, Andy Hiscox, and his family was unusually loving and understanding. His status as a doctor opened the door to the CBC, which would not likely have broadcast the diary of an HIV-infected heroin junkie, and television gave Dr. Peter a celebrity status that influenced the way he was treated. His last public appearance was a hilarious star turn at an AIDS benefit. Dr. Peter's experience did not reflect the anger and humiliation of all the young, gay men, shunned by their relatives and doctors, who have been abandoned to die in poverty and degradation, alone.

"I want to be in my own bed," Dr. Peter jokingly tells his family, "a four-poster with lots of down pillows, a red velvet bedspread, and hundreds of weeping relatives around." According to Plato, the dramatic deathbed scene has been around since Socrates drank his hemlock and, as he died, gave a lengthy oration proving the immortality of the soul. Dr. Peter's diary is a modern version of the art of dying.

Dying, like sex and childbirth, was a public event until relatively recently. Overcrowding, with its filth and fleas, was the main reason people died, and family, friends, and neighbours gathered around the deathbed hoping to catch, in the dying patient's last words, a glimpse of the afterlife. The soul, depicted in paintings as a chubby infant or winged cherub, was believed to leave the body with the last breath, but whether or not the soul ascended to Heaven depended on the patient's state of grace. To be saved, Roman Catholics had to make confession and receive absolution from a priest, but Protestants were expected to demonstrate their salvation by rejoicing at the prospect of eternal life. Since death came swiftly and unexpectedly, the art of dying had to be learned from the cradle, and those who died unbaptized, or uncomforted by the church's rituals, were doomed to damnation.

Peter Jepson-Young had lost his Christian faith but he had found a belief. Lying on a rock in the sun at Long Beach on Vancouver Island, listening to the surf, he recited his credo:

"I accept and absorb all the strength of the earth to keep my body hard and strong. I accept and absorb all the energy of the sun to keep my mind sharp and bright. I accept and absorb all the life strength of the ocean to cleanse my body and bring me life. I accept and absorb all the power of the wind to cleanse my spirit and bring me strength of purpose. I accept and absorb all the mystery of the heavens for I am a part of that vast unknown. From these elements I have come, and to these elements I shall return, but the energy that is me shall not be lost."

As I begin to understand that when it comes to mortal illness, modern medicine offers little more than a choice between poppy power and magical thinking, I am not surprised to meet, in a suburban television studio, Lazarus, newly risen from the dead. It's a dark morning in January 1997, the station is Toronto's CFTO, the show, "Canada AM." I am here to talk about electronic copyright, and as I wait, I strike up a conversation with the only other guest, a man in his early forties whose pallor is a shade lighter than his ash-grey suit. His name is Joe Maroon.

Joe tells me he's had AIDS for years, but since he began taking protease inhibitors, a cocktail of experimental, anti-retroviral drugs, his

AIDS has been under control. Joe looks husky, but he moves stiffly, carrying a walking stick. He suffers from neuropathy, a painful degeneration of the nerves in his legs. A year ago, Joe says, he was in Toronto's HIV/AIDS hospice, Casey House, preparing to die. He tells me, with a modest smile, that he is the first man to walk out of Casey House alive.

A few days later, over lunch in his elegant Cabbagetown house, Joe tells me his story. Our gourmet meal is prepared by Joe's partner, Craig, an attractive young South African with curly dark hair and intense black eyes. We are joined, briefly, by Debbie Richard, the visiting nurse from St. Elizabeth Health Care who checks Joe over several times a week. Young, cheerful, efficient, Debbie completely destroys my image of Sairy Gamp. She has to monitor the handfuls of pills Joe takes in various combinations, at specified times, every day. The drugs themselves have toxic side effects, and in addition to his protease cocktail, Joe takes antidepressants, painkillers, and megadoses of vitamin B12. Joe Maroon is not cured, but he views his illness with humorous detachment.

"My red blood cell count was down a while ago," Joe says, "and the doctor said, 'It looks like leukemia.' It didn't matter to me either way. I thought, 'We've got this nice house now. Shucks, I'd like to stick around. No point in being concerned.' I have no terror of death. I've dealt with it."

Joe was a flight attendant with Air Canada before he became too sick to work. Gay male flight attendants, with their international access to sex, have been blamed for bringing the HIV/AIDS virus to North America – Air Canada's Gaetan Dugas was supposedly the first – but new research has traced AIDS deaths back to at least 1930, and the epidemic in Africa emerged in the 1950s.

Joe first noticed spots on his legs in 1981. He shrugged it off until, at a party in Vancouver, he got into conversation with the American playwright Tennessee Williams. "Here I am talking to Tennessee Williams," Joe says, "and he told me about this weird disease where people got spots on their legs. I was concerned. I thought I should buy stock in a condom company, buy more insurance." The disease was labelled Gay Related Immune Deficiency, GRID, and Joe agreed to participate in a study conducted by Dr. Brian Willoughby in Vancouver. Joe was tested for HIV/AIDS in 1985: "Dr. Willoughby gave me the option of knowing. What am I to do? Curl up and die? I said, 'I assume that I am positive, and so is everyone else. I'll do safe sex.'" The next year, Joe was ready to hear the bad news.

"I told my partner," he says. "I didn't tell anybody else. I didn't want to be patronized, treated like an invalid. 'Oh, you poor thing, you're going to die.' I thought it would create psychosomatic problems, bring the illness on." Joe's father and a sister had died young, his mother was dying, friends were dying. "I felt surrounded by death," he says. Joe found a psychiatrist who helped him, and took a leave of absence. He visited Kafarbida, his father's ancestral home in Lebanon, but any ideas he may have had about being buried there vanished when he saw the cliff with the bottomless black hole where the bones of the cemetery's oldest residents were thrown when more space was needed. In France, Joe taught English, did graduate study in psychology, perfected his French, and began to write a family history. "Blood's not thicker than water," he says. "You need history to bond." Joe didn't die, and Air Canada called him back to work.

Joe was living in Vancouver in March 1995, when he fainted in the shower. Nauseous on his next flight to Toronto, he booked off sick and went to the AIDS clinic. The doctors confirmed his worst fears. Craig was in Toronto – they had become lovers but not yet a couple – and together they moved into a house Joe owned and had previously rented out. "I hid out," Joe says. He had to force himself to eat, and he suffered from oral thrush, a painful mouth infection. His hair was falling out, he was losing weight, and his blood count was dropping. He became incontinent, and he was too weak to get out of bed: "Poor Craig was cleaning me in the middle of the night, sometimes three and four times a night."

During the day, Joe was looked after by visiting nurses, a home-maker, a niece, and his older married sister, Helen McArthur. At night and on weekends, Craig, who worked full-time for the Ontario government, was Joe's companion, nurse, cook, secretary, and house-keeper. Craig says little during our lunch, but a week or so later, brimming with emotion, he arranges to speak to me:

"I didn't know Joe was HIV positive. We'd been going out for two years and he hadn't told me. Finally he said, 'I guess this is the last stage of HIV.' I didn't feel angry. I went into auto-caregiver mode. I said, 'We'll just have to concentrate on making you healthy. It will require all our strength, hope, and comfort.' It was absolute hell. You don't know one day from the next. What will happen tomorrow? Things can change overnight. You hear every week of someone dying. It was like being in a time capsule. I had gone to another world."

Outwardly, Craig appeared organized, calm, efficient, but he grew tired and angry. "I'd drag Joe to the bath, then I'd fall asleep on the floor. I fell asleep at my desk, and slept under it at lunch. I did the laundry every night, and the food, day in and day out, and I'd think, 'Does anybody know I'm exhausted?' I remember lying on top of Joe one night he was so cold, writhing, shaking. The bed was wet. I got him bundled up and into the hospital."

Stabilized with blood transfusions and antibiotics, Joe discharged himself to Casey House. Craig and Helen disagreed. They wanted to care for him themselves. "It all felt so final," Craig remembers. "For the first three days I felt so scared for him. Are you ready for this, Joe? Am I ready? Is this what your life really meant? If you don't think so, and you don't have the energy, let me be the energy. I'll get you the hell out of here!"

At Casey House, a hospital-standard hospice with a staff of sixty specialized professionals, Craig was reassured by a funky therapist with rings in her nose, eyebrows, and ears, and by the hospice's open-door policy for visitors. Helen lost her naïveté about gay sex. Puzzled by the contents of a decorative bowl in the reception area, she said to Craig, "That's a funny place to keep tea bags." "Helen," Craig replied, "they're condoms. Would you like a cup of tea?" They rolled about laughing.

Craig slept by Joe's bedside at night, and brought him fresh flowers and tasty tidbits of food every day. Craig and Helen were vigilant about the details of Joe's care and fiercely critical of any staff behaviour they felt was lazy or inappropriate. "I'm going to show these people you don't have to come out of here feet first," Craig promised. When Joe moaned, "This is it, Craig," Craig snapped back, "You're not dead yet for chrissakes, stop playing dead!"

But there was a lot of what Craig calls final talk. Joe, with the help of the hospice social worker, made his will, planned his cremation, and put his financial affairs in order. He was prepared to die, but he was weepy and worried. What would become of Craig? Have you told Craig how much you love him? Helen asked. Why not? If you haven't told him, he will never know. "I made a point of telling Craig," Joe says. "That was my turning point."

Their confession of love transformed their whirlwind romance into a blood brotherhood. Says Craig: "I was doing all Joe's nursing, the IVs, catheters, drugs. I felt this was my mission, my calling. I will *be him* as long as I can be."

On New Year's Eve, 1995, Joe, transferred to hospital, slipped into a coma. His doctors moved him into what Craig calls the death room and suggested that Craig call the family. "Tears were streaming down my face," Craig says, "but I composed myself completely. I was alone in the room. I grabbed Joe's hand. We were consumed in each other spiritually, connected all the way. I truly believe in the Holy Spirit and I said, 'If you need to go, go, Joe, and I'll see you again later. You go. They're all waiting.' I let go myself. There was a sense of relief, a surge of peace. I was conditioning myself to survive. It was a wonderful moment, a fitting finale."

Then the door opened, and Joe's kin, accompanied by a priest, rushed in. Craig stood aside as they gathered around his bed. Craig remembers Helen grabbing Joe's hands and crying, "Fight, fight, fight!" Craig was in awe of Helen's power: "She was *willing* him to live. Then she embraced me, saying, 'You will always be part of my family.' I broke down and sobbed uncontrollably."

At this moment, Joe sat up in bed and said, "Why is everybody here? Am I dying?"

"As a matter of fact, that seems to be the case," Craig replied. Everyone started to laugh.

"I was being given the last rites," Joe says, "and I saw this priest about to send me into the next world. This asshole had refused me communion because I was gay. I thought, 'Hell will freeze over before I die!' It was the *anger* that kept me alive!" Joe lost consciousness. His mourners sent out for champagne. They raised toasts to the New Year and wondered, What do we do now?

Several days later, Joe woke up. "There's this man standing at the end of my bed," he says. "I thought, 'I've gone to Heaven.'" The angel was a counsellor from Casey House who suggested Joe try the new cocktail of anti-AIDS drugs coming out of the United States. What did he have to lose?

"I play with my drugs," Joe says. "I run the show." He tries different things, acupuncture for the pain in his legs, yoghurt, salad, and healthy foods. He forces himself to go out, and his life is a ceaseless round of activities centred on visits to therapists and workouts in the pool at the YMCA. Joe Maroon has lived with HIV/AIDS for fifteen years, possibly much longer. "I have good karma," he smiles. "I always land on my feet, always. I am charmed."

Debbie Richard isn't as mystical. "Joe constructs his fate," she says. "He positions himself so fate can happen. He draws people to him. Joe is somebody who gets what he wants. He goes for that."

After Craig has gone out, Joe admits: "I wouldn't be here except for Craig. He took over everything. He fought for me, he protected me." Joe says he would like his ashes to be mingled eventually with Craig's, and buried, half and half, in Toronto and Capetown, South Africa. Joe has taken a tour of St. James's crematorium at the Toronto Necropolis. He tells gravedigger stories about the "ash pit" where the human remains are boxed, and he was taken aback to see rows of boxes of unclaimed ashes neatly wrapped in brown paper. One box bore a name he knew.

Behind Joe, on a table, I see a colour snapshot of two handsome, tanned young men, one fair, one dark, both in love. I recognize Craig immediately, but it's hard to match the sallow face in front of me with Joe in the picture. Craig says to me later, when we are alone: "This is not the same Joe as before he was ill." Four years later, their whirlwind romance has not turned out the way either had expected.

"My time is monopolized and manipulated by Joe," Craig says. "Joe controls attention. We used to do things together. Now, Joe is steaming ahead and I'm caught in the dust. I became everything for Joe, and I'm angry about it. I was his legs, his arms, his brain. He resented the fact he was so dependent, so he has gone on, he's getting healthy, and I am left behind. I am so consumed by Joe's illness, I am not my own person. I am tired, mentally. I wonder, 'Is there anyone who will take as good care of me?' Or am I going to be one of those people who will be left to die alone?"

V

"BRING OUT YOUR dead! Bring out your dead!" The horrifying images of the Black Death have been imprinted on my mind ever since I read Daniel Defoe's *A Journal of the Plague Year* when I was a student. Defoe describes a scene in London, England, during the Great Plague of 1665:

> People in the rage of the distemper, or in the torment of their swellings, which was indeed intolerable, raving and distracted, and oftentimes laying violent hands upon themselves, throwing themselves out at their windows, shooting themselves; mothers, murthering their own children in their lunacy, others frighted into idiotism and foolish distractions, some into despair and lunacy, others into melancholy madness.
>
> The pain of the swelling was in particular very violent; the physicians and surgeons may be said to have tortured many poor creatures even to death. The swellings in some grew hard, and they applied violent drawing-plaisters or poultices to break them, and if these did not do they cut and scarified

them in a terrible manner, and then they burnt them with causticks, so that many died raving mad with the torment. In these distresses, some broke out into the streets, perhaps naked, and would run directly down to the river, and plunge themselves into the water.

Bubonic plague, with its vomiting, diarrhea, hemorrhages, and gangrenous swellings, was a hideous way to die, but until the nineteenth century, when we started putting the sick, demented, and old into institutions, it was common to see people dying of disease, starvation, and exposure in gutters or by public roadsides. Even today, in cities like Toronto, we pass by, with barely a sideward glance, men and women dying of alcoholism, malnutrition, and mental illness in subways, streets, and parks.

Our attitudes to dying are ambiguous. For most of human history, men who grew to adulthood killed each other in wars or family feuds, women died giving birth. Yet in Canada, within my own roughly fifty-year span of memory, we have dissociated birth from death, developed a collective identity as peacekeepers, and abolished the practice of hanging murderers. We remain preoccupied, however, with murder. Homicides represent a minuscule fraction of the nearly quarter of a million Canadians who die annually, yet we treat murders as significant news. A particularly gruesome or frightening murder may be kept in the public consciousness for years after the culprit has been convicted and jailed, and we spend millions of dollars chasing, prosecuting, and jailing murderers. The murder of a police officer in the line of duty, a rare yet predictable event, causes a mass outburst of sympathy and consternation, yet frequent homicides in Aboriginal communities are ignored by all of us who don't live there. In Rwanda, the failure of UN peacekeepers, including Canadians, to prevent the mass murder of eight hundred thousand Africans in 1994 aroused no public outrage in Canada. Suicides, which outnumber murders ten-to-one, are seldom reported. We are fascinated by airplane crashes, and indifferent to ordinary accidents, especially car accidents, which kill more of us every day. We publish photographs of bodies retrieved from the debris of earthquakes and other natural disasters, but not of bodies dead from cancer or heart disease, however famous the deceased may have been in life. In Hollywood movies, death, especially violent death, has become so predictable we risk being bored to death.

Our fascination with public dying contradicts the prosaic fact that most of us die privately, in bed. When asked, we express an overwhelming wish to die at home, but the odds are that we will die in a hospital. Apart from a select few who manage to die while golfing, giving a toast at a wedding, or, in the case of one man I knew, flying his own single-engined plane (he landed it safely), we are dying in bed because we've been sick for a long time with multiple maladies. We may be taking all kinds of medications, and going back and forth to hospital by ambulance for tests and treatments, but if we become too weak and frail to get to our doctor's office, and our doctor refuses to come to see us, the logical impulse when symptoms become frightening is to call 911 and rush to Emergency. Maybe we don't have a family doctor at all, and if we fall off a medical merry-go-round we have been riding for many years, doctors may perfunctorily pass us from hand to hand, a dead letter, so to speak.

"My God, my God, why hast thou forsaken me?" I am carrying more Biblical baggage on this trip than I thought, and Jesus of Nazareth's terrible, unanswered cry as he died on the cross may explain why, in February 1997, I am driving around the Toronto suburb of North York with Larry Librach, an unorthodox but observant Jew. A doctor can't play God, although many try, or give eternal life, although many try, but a doctor, if only by sitting at a dying patient's bedside, can provide solace, strength, and reassurance. A doctor can also monitor a patient's condition as it deteriorates and adjust the medications appropriately. There may be nothing more for an oncologist to do, but a knowledgeable family physician or a palliative specialist can do a great deal to make a patient's last months or weeks calm, lucid, and pain-free. The philosophy of palliative care is succinctly and eloquently expressed by Dame Cicely Saunders, founder of St. Christopher's Hospice in London, England, in her informative little handbook, *Living with Dying: The Management of Terminal Disease*: "A patient, wherever he may be, should expect the same analytical attention to terminal suffering as he received for the original diagnosis and treatment of his condition. The aim is no longer a cure but the chance of living to his fullest potential in physical ease and activity and with the assurance of personal relationships until he dies."

Larry Librach makes house calls. He firmly believes that home is the best place for the dying to be *if*, and only if, there is strong medical and social support. Since doctors and community health agencies do not customarily provide that safety net, or even know it's needed, his role is to make sure that support is in place for Mount Sinai's palliative patients. Librach visits dying patients at home four days a week, and if he's on call during a crisis, he'll come in the middle of the night or on a weekend. His visits may last a few minutes, or hours, and they account for a small portion of the time he spends talking with patients' nurses, home care workers, and anxious relatives. Librach's income is a fraction of what he could earn in private practice as a family physician, but he believes that compassionate care for the dying is a medical and moral obligation.

"When I was in family practice twenty years ago," Librach says, "I had a patient, a young man, with prostate cancer. I referred him to the cancer hospital and lost track of him. One Friday afternoon, and I'll remember this until the day I die, I got a call from his wife. He had been discharged from the hospital and he was in a lot of pain. Could I come over? I got in the car, leaving my office full of patients, and here I found this young man, completely bald, tumours popping up all over him, in agony, writhing in agony. I gave him a shot of Demerol which I thought should control the pain and ten minutes later he was still in agony. What had happened was, unnoticed by anybody, they had fractured his neck on the way home in the ambulance.

"I sent him back to the hospital. Four weeks later, his wife called again on a Friday afternoon – hospitals try to get rid of people on Friday afternoons – and he was still in agony. They had not treated his pain. I took one look at him and said to myself, *'This man is dying.'* I gave him some morphine. It didn't work. I was afraid to give him a second dose. He died in front of my eyes, right then and there. The first thing that went through my mind was that I'd killed him with morphine. And the second thing was, 'My god, I couldn't help this man!'"

That weekend, at the annual meeting of the Canadian College of Family Physicians, Librach attended a lecture on pain control by Dr. Balfour Mount, a surgical oncologist at Montreal's Royal Victoria Hospital: "Bal Mount said that people do not have to suffer from pain. It was one of those life experiences where I felt the heavens open up and light shine down upon me. Lord, I'm coming! It hit my heart and my soul. I *had* to find a way of dealing with the pain issue."

Dr. Mount's remedy for pain, called the "Brompton mixture," was a liquid combination of morphine, cocaine, ethyl alcohol, flavoured syrup, and chloroform water developed for tuberculosis patients at England's Brompton Chest Hospital. Mount had discovered this narcotic cocktail in 1973 during a week-long working visit to St. Christopher's Hospice. Not only did the Brompton mixture knock out pain, but by prescribing it every four hours, before the effects of the narcotics – the English preferred heroin to morphine – wore off, Dame Cicely could, almost miraculously, prevent her patients' pain from recurring. Dame Cicely, a nurse and social worker as well as a physician, pioneered the practice of caring for dying patients at home, and she reminded doctors that freeing the dying from physical pain did not necessarily relieve their mental or spiritual anguish. It was Dame Cicely who developed the concept of caring for the whole person that differentiated hospice from hospital.

St. Christopher's Hospice is a modern, medically sophisticated teaching facility, but in Quebec the word hospice meant "death house," a sanctuary of last resort for the destitute and incurable.

When Balfour Mount opened his eighteen-bed hospice, modelled on St. Christopher's, in the Royal Victoria Hospital in January 1975, he borrowed a medical word, palliate, to describe his unit's mission to relieve suffering. "Palliative care" was picked up by other Canadian hospitals, including the Toronto Western, where Larry Librach got palliative care up and running in 1978. Librach moved to Mount Sinai in 1988, but it was his colleague, Dr. Frank Ferris, who started the hospital's home visiting program in 1991.

Mount Sinai is a teaching hospital, and since Larry Librach has been on the staff of the University of Toronto Medical School's faculty of family medicine since 1972, I can, with the permission of his patients, accompany him on his daily rounds. Librach's only condition is that I not reveal patients' real names, so I won't. Our first stop is a meeting with Sheila Walker, director of the Jewish Hospice program of Toronto's Jewish Family and Child Service. As Librach puts it: "The family is the patient."

Sheila Walker minces no words: "Dying with dignity is a lot of bullshit. People don't die with dignity. It takes an amazing person to lose all their faculties and still feel dignified." Walker, a feisty, forthright social worker, abhors conventional how-to-die clichés, including Kübler-Ross's five stages. "Denial doesn't bother me," she says, "and nobody has to 'accept' the fact that they're dying." Sheila tells me about a man who boasted, "I don't let anything I can't control worry me," until he began crying. "I tell people it's normal to feel rotten," she says. "I ask them what helps them feel better when they're feeling this rotten. What needs to happen now? People die in a variety of ways. What is their way? I try to go in where they are, fit into it. We'll talk about their sickness, their life history, when they felt stronger, and I'll look for their strengths, try to mobilize their courage, their resources. What things can the family do together? Family members are all in different places. I go with the flow, just *be*."

Sheila Walker believes that soul-searching, however emotionally difficult, ultimately may ease the pain of unresolved grievances, and a simple generous gesture can wipe away years of anger. This is her own story: "I had a horror mother-in-law in California. For twenty-eight years, she wouldn't talk to me. At dinner she'd say to Marshall, my husband, 'Ask Sheila to pass the salt.' She'd ask him, 'How could you have married her? I can't possibly love Sheila.' Then, when she got sick with lung cancer, we brought her to our home in Toronto. I wanted to do that for Marshall, and I found myself feeling very nurturing, worried about her. One day she hugged me. That was weird. She talked to Marshall about 'our Sheila.' One day I put my arms around her and told her I'd take care of Marshall. She put her arms around me, and I found myself crying. I held her hand as she died, and I really grieved her. Dying can do that for people. Dying people can develop a whole different set of priorities."

As Larry Librach smoothly pilots his dark grey Jeep Cherokee through the Toronto traffic, his cellphone rings incessantly. Patients and families are free to call, but most of the messages are from nurses. Mount Sinai doctors work with community nurses from various private agencies, and the nurses change from day to day. Some are practical nurses, not registered nurses, and few of the nurses are expert in end-of-life care. Pain, it appears, is the least of their worries. What do you do with a wife who is forcing food down her husband's throat? "Tell her," Larry says firmly, "that if he eats or not it won't make a bit of difference to his strength. He has no need for solid food."

If we don't eat, we die. But if we're dying, why eat? I discover, to my relief, that it's typical for the dying to be nauseated, unable to swallow, revolted by the sight and smell of food or simply uninterested. Starvation, based on the Arctic adventure stories I've read, has seemed to me an attractive way to go, and I'm taken aback when Larry says that if the dying don't eat, they don't starve. "You don't see any signs of starvation," he says. "No scurvy, no vitamin deficiency. If they suffer from confusion, it has nothing to do with the lack of food. Healthy people can live a long time without food. You use up every bit of fat and muscle. If you have cancer, you may die of your disease with malnutrition, but you won't die of starvation." He does urge his patients to drink water and juices to prevent dehydration. Dehydration may cause confusion.

Daphne, the first patient we see, is a serene woman of seventy or so with soft, snow-white hair. Daphne's in bed, and she has been afraid to get up since she lost feeling in her legs and fell and broke her hip. She has pins in her hip, her bowel cancer has spread to her liver and bones, and she is incontinent. Her husband, who hovers over her with a worried look, has been using diapers, but Daphne's bed is often wet and her sheets have to be changed almost daily. Librach glares at the nurse, a timid young Asian who seems not to understand the conversation, and forcefully suggests that a catheter, attached to a plastic bag, would improve the situation for everyone. He also recommends that a physiotherapist come in to help Daphne regain enough use of her legs to be able to get into a wheelchair. Daphne looks at me with a radiant smile.

"I'm set to go," she says. "I'm going to leave them all." Daphne has children and grandchildren, and one of her daughters had quit her job to come to look after her. "I told her not to come. It made me feel more depressed. I had the church in. It was the most depressing day I ever had. 'Don't bless me!' I said. I get sympathy all the time, but I'm very private. Family are more depressing than anything." Daphne has no pain, but she does have an ugly black ulcer on a hip that has been resting on wet sheets. Librach angrily interrogates the nurse. The nurse clearly knows nothing about treating, or preventing, pressure sores.

Deep, painful skin ulcers can develop almost overnight in bedridden patients who aren't frequently moved or turned. Larry will have to round up a nurse who is expert in wound care and order a ripple-type air mattress to lessen the pressure. There is more to palliative care than pain management, I learn, and these little practical touches, including a hospital bed that can be raised to prop the patient up, are often more effective than drugs. Loss of control over our ability to pee and poop is often one of the great humiliations of dying, and the Herculean task of cleaning up is distressing, even revolting, for the family. Dying incontinent with a catheter isn't dignified, but it's better than dying in a puddle. Glancing fondly at Larry as he packs his satchel to leave, Daphne confides to me in a loud whisper, "We don't have doctors like this any more."

Our next patient, Mrs. Fish, an eighty-eight-year-old woman with bladder cancer, is bent over with pain because she won't take anything stronger than Tylenol 3. Librach has tried his best to change her mind, but she is adamant. "People don't like taking pills," he sighs. There is some hope that radiation might shrink the tumour and ease her pain, but Mrs. Fish resists that too. "I hate going to the hospital!" she shouts. She tells me about being put into "a long dark tunnel." She had to lie on a hard slab, and her head was fixed so she couldn't move. "I had to lie still in this tunnel," she says. "It was claustrophobic. There was no light, and there was a banging noise. I didn't know where I was going. I was screaming." Mrs. Fish is describing an MRI body scan. The hospital has taken a perfect picture of her cancer, but she is terrified to return for treatment. It's common, Larry says, for patients to refuse medication, or for family members to ration it as they see fit. Doctors stubbornly cling to the antiquated notion that patients have to be in pain before they take a painkiller, and nurses instructed to medicate PRN, "as needed," may err on the side of caution. Fear of recurring pain makes the pain even greater.

Unlike Mrs. Fish, Lucia, a middle-aged woman with kidney cancer, has been demanding every therapy, from vitamin A to protein injections, advertised on the Internet. Now she and Jorge, her husband, are insisting that her family doctor prescribe an unlicensed experimental chemical cocktail available in Quebec. The doctor has refused, and he has called Librach in for support. Lucia hovers in the background while the rest of us sit around the kitchen table. "She feels you don't do enough," Jorge says in an accusatory tone. "She has a chance to make it. I don't want to sit around. I am here all day. I can't sleep at night. I take her out. We come home and she says, 'What are we going to do? What can we do about the cancer?' She is mad at *me*!"

Librach softly explains that the drug they are demanding could have damaging or fatal side effects. "It's potentially very toxic," he says. "So is cancer!" says Jorge. "What's the difference?" Jorge, a burly, swarthy man, is used to getting his way. He is mad at his wife for being sick, and mad at the doctors for not curing her. He is taking out on Librach his anger at Lucia's oncologist: "He tells us, 'If you'd had a better surgeon, maybe you could have got the whole thing. It's too late. There's nothing that can be done. I'm running late. Go home.'"

Having got this bitter memory off his chest, Jorge backs down. Librach is used to dealing with irrational demands, but he resents being pressured by relatives to do something harmful or illegal. "Lucia is still alive!" he blurts. "She should *live*. Don't sit and look at the wall and worry!"

Lucia, meanwhile, has been drifting in and out of the kitchen, dancing alone. She looks vague but cheerful, perfectly indifferent to the heated argument about her treatment. "I live on hope," she says. "No negative thoughts are allowed in my mind. I work on it." Lucia has been deeply depressed, and Librach has prescribed Prozac. He estimates that 40 per cent of dying patients suffer from depression severe enough to be medically treated. Lucia smiles sweetly at him as we leave. "The Prozac seems to be working," Larry says as we get in the car, "thank goodness."

Antidepressants are part of a growing pharmacopoeia available to treat the symptoms of terminal disease. Drugs commonly used, in combination, include opioids, anti-inflammatories, corticosteroids, antibiotics, antispasmodics, anticonvulsants, and sedatives. Some problems are solved with simple remedies. Everyday drugs like Gravol help control nausea and vomiting, and the common mouth infection, oral thrush, can be prevented by keeping the mouth clean and moist. It is easily cured. Fresh air and an ordinary fan are as effective as oxygen in treating mild shortness of breath, and opioids are more effective. Relieving a patient's anxiety about suffocation, a common fear, calms panic gasping. Oxygen is dangerous – one patient singed his face when he lit a joint before removing his oxygen mask – and cumbersome. Patients become so dependent they lug their tanks and tubes everywhere.

The philosophy of hospice and palliative care is to enhance the quality of the life remaining to us, not to shorten or lengthen it. Rarely is a patient's pain so intractable it calls for nerve blocks, anaesthesia, or total sedation. The Mount Sinai team, however, is frequently called in to help dying patients whose relatives, and doctors, insist on extreme interventions. Orthodox Jews, for instance, believe that human life must be preserved by any means at any cost, and Larry Librach's next patient, Rachel Benjamin, is an Orthodox Jew.

Mrs. Benjamin, a widow in her seventies, was diagnosed with pancreatic cancer barely a month ago. She was discharged from hospital septic, dehydrated, and in pain. Librach fixed these problems, but her son, with whom she lives, has persuaded the family doctor to put his mother on a course of experimental chemotherapy. He is convinced that if his mother can be kept alive for two months, a better treatment will be available.

Mrs. Benjamin, quiet, but gaunt and yellowish, is lying in bed. In addition to her morphine pump and chemo needle, she is receiving fluid through an IV line and is fed through a G-tube into her bowel. "She has a dismal prognosis," Librach sighs. "She is not a candidate for surgery, and she is not getting stronger." She is not eating or drinking, and her bowel is becoming obstructed by the tumour. Librach has found an excellent nurse, an Orthodox Jew, and the rabbi visits frequently, but Librach cannot persuade the family doctor to discontinue chemotherapy. He is apprehensive. Patients may die of chemical poisoning before they die of their disease, and chemo can make dying a lot more difficult.

"Thirty to 40 per cent of chemotherapy is not necessary or useful," he says. "We rarely see lung cancer patients, although it's the most common cancer, because they're kept in chemo. There's no evidence that it prolongs their lives. In Great Britain, they don't offer chemotherapy for some lung cancers." Librach hates feeding tubes –

"If you have a tumour, you're feeding the tumour" – and he uses IV lines only if extra fluid will do no harm. Recently, at the hospital, he was summoned to the bedside of a woman, dying of breast cancer, who was screaming, "Let me die! Why can't I die? Let me die!" Excess fluid from her IV line had made her body septic and grotesquely swollen. Her doctor had not disconnected the line, and his prescription for antibiotics and diuretics had increased her pain, confusion, and agitation. Librach disconnected the IV and started morphine, but by the time the patient stopped screaming, her family and the three other patients in the ward were traumatized. We naively assume that IV "life lines" are feeding nutrients, but all the bags usually contain is water and salt. Dehydration is a normal part of the dying process. Patients on IVs whose internal organs can no longer process fluids fill up with water. Robert Pope was right to portray hanging IV tubes as intertwined snakes, Grendel and his mother, in their hospital gowns.

Next we visit William, a dignified older man with lung cancer, who is living with his sister in a spacious, comfortable home. William's doctor had told him he had twelve weeks to live, and William is now into week thirteen. William would like Dr. Librach to tell him, please, when, exactly, he is going to die. "I don't know," Larry says with absolute honesty. "Nobody knows." William has some time left, perhaps not much, and because he's been dismally counting the hours until doomsday, he will probably die sooner than if his doctor had not sounded his premature death knell. On the other hand, Luigi, who is lying unconscious, breathing noisily, not many streets away, has outlived his family's expectations to the point where, frankly, they wish the old man would croak.

"You die as you live," Sheila Walker had said at our first meeting. It's not a moral judgement – saints and martyrs die horribly – but a question of culture, genetics, and personality. Her aphorism makes sense, and it sticks in my mind, but what do I make of a popular book on dying by an American rabbi, Harold Kushner, called *When Bad Things Happen to Good People*? According to Kushner, death is bad, people are good. But in my own subterranean Presbyterian culture, death and people are both bad, except for the saved, for whom death leads to Heaven. Driving through the winter wasteland of North York, I ponder the hells of Dante and Milton, and when I meet Irene, who is close to death from liver cancer, I hope Dante and Milton have reserved a particularly dark, cold circle for doctors who mislead, evade, or give false hope.

This is a pain emergency call, and it's Dr. Librach's first visit to Irene. "The pain really grabbed me this morning," she apologizes. "I couldn't even get dressed." Irene and her husband, George, are retired. Their bungalow is small, well-kept, and their yard is neat. Irene, slim and fine-boned in her nightie and dressing gown, says she is in pain from the shunt, or drain tube, in her side. She has been taking Tylenol 3, but, she says, "We're behind the pain. I'm beginning to feel my days. . . ."

There is a pause. We are in the living room. Librach is sitting on an ottoman, leaning forward, tense with concentration. He glances at George in a welcoming way, but he locks his gaze on Irene.

"The cancer is still there," he says. "It's hard to gain strength."

Irene, picking nervously at her nightie, replies: "I don't really know what is what. Maybe we'll be told something. I would like to be told that we've got it under control. How likely do you think this is? A couple of weeks ago, I thought it was quite possible. I thought the antibiotics would do something. Is there a better pill I should take?"

Irene looks down sorrowfully at her ankles. "My feet are swelling," she says, holding them out. "I never have swollen feet." Larry explains softly that decreased protein in the blood can cause fluid buildup. Some treatments, he says, are not very effective with this kind of cancer.

Cancer. The word hangs there in the silence. Irene's oncologist has described Irene's tumour as "masses" in her liver, and has explained to her that these masses are likely the result of tissue scarring due to radiation. Irene, assuming she was getting well, has been looking forward to gardening in the spring.

Until recently, it was standard practice for doctors to conceal a terminal prognosis from their patients. Many still do. They call their strategy "tender subterfuge." They take refuge in incomprehensible textbook terminology, or phrases such as, "There's a significant change in your tumour," which worried patients, grasping at straws, will almost invariably interpret positively. On one cancer patient's chart, Librach found the oncologist's comment, "improved clinically," then, two weeks later, her family physician noted, "deteriorating rapidly." Specialists may order futile tests, treatments, and pills to make it seem that "everything is being done," and they can be reasonably certain that patients, who don't want to hear bad news, will play along. Some doctors may, in all good faith, believe that by evading the truth they give their patients hope and boost their morale, others may simply not know what to say. The easy way out, as the pamphlet *Feeling Your Best During Cancer Therapy* suggests, is to wait for the patient to ask, "Am I dying?"

Silence and subterfuge are major reasons why patients are referred to hospice or palliative care only at an advanced stage of their illness. The referral in itself is a one-way ticket, and Librach finds that, like Irene, his patients have already guessed the truth. Next week, when he visits Irene again, he will explain that her pain, for which he has prescribed Dilaudid, a synthetic morphine, is related solely to her cancer, and he will encourage her to talk about the implications.

Librach's policy is to be honest, but to take his cues from the patient. "I find myself very reticent," he admits. By nature an energetic, optimistic person, Larry tries to establish a mood of calm confidence that encourages people to say what's on their minds. In the Jeep, he can be outraged, gesticulating while barking into the phone, but as soon as he enters a home, he becomes quiet, attentive, and gentle. He never stands over a patient, except for a brief examination, but sits on a chair, preferably a chair slightly lower than the patient's bed or couch. In his casual clothes – he carries his medical supplies in a travel bag – Dr. Librach could be a friend or relative popping in for a chat. The only clue to his profession is his stethoscope.

"I ask people, 'What's going on here?'" he says. "'What do you think is happening?' People *know*. They'll say, 'I'm going to die.' But you have to wait until they're ready." There's no point in bludgeoning people with the truth, he says, or giving them information they don't want or need. He finds that he often has to repeat information four and five times, over several weeks, before his patients hear what he is saying. They may never hear their diagnosis, however bluntly truthful their physician has been, or they may hear only what they want to hear.

In *On Death and Dying*, Elisabeth Kübler-Ross labels psychic deafness "denial," and she, like most people in our noisy, confessional culture, thought denial a bad thing. Denial is, however, a normal defence mechanism, and it can buy people time to pull themselves together. American psychiatrist Robert Kastenbaum believes that patients who appear not to comprehend may simply be distracted by an unfamiliar hospital environment, or they may not want to discuss their disease with doctors who seem more frightened than they are. Unless denial threatens to harm others – children, for instance, may need to be provided for – the inability to hear bad news may be a better way of coping than depression. Nobody at the Jewish Hospice, or on the Mount Sinai team, urges people to "accept" their deaths. The dying can be as upset and hostile as they want, and our last patient of the week is both.

Becky, single, in her late thirties, is a physician with colon cancer that has spread to her lungs, spleen, and pelvis. Wearing black leggings and a sweatshirt, Becky whirls around her apartment, waving her arms, talking with barely a pause in a loud, shrill voice. Becky has been sick for more than a year. Her pain is out of control, and she suffers from nausea, diarrhea, dehydration, exhaustion, and other symptoms she hates. Her legs are so weak she can no longer walk to the end of the street. She blames a self-administered course of experimental chemotherapy, which she insisted on, for poisoning her. She does not see herself as palliative. "I'm trying to think of myself as an active case," she says defiantly. "I pretend that I'm a healthy person."

Doctors are notoriously bad patients, and Becky tells us, with vengeful glee, that she has quarrelled with all the doctors who have been treating her. When her oncologist, who had just delivered bad news, tried to calm her, saying, "You're upset," Becky screamed, "*Shouldn't* I be upset? *I'm scared out of my mind.*" She blames her colleagues at the hospital where she used to work for pulling away from her. "They disappeared very quickly," she says. She has stopped going to church: "People were feeling guilty about me. It was like I was supposed to make *them* feel good. I don't have energy to give to people. So don't abandon me and then say you're sorry."

Librach quietly responds: "We can't look back to find new answers. Let's get after the things we can correct." As soon as he mentions her pain, however, Becky cries, "I'm scared of morphine." She'd had a reaction, years ago, to some samples she had taken, but as she talks, her real fears emerge: "I thought that by taking painkillers I would make my cancer worse. I would not know if it was growing. If the pain was worse, I would try to make it into something positive. I'd see it killing the tumour."

Encountering this kind of attitude in a young doctor makes Larry Librach grind his teeth. Outwardly, he remains cool, and they agree, after more discussion, to try Dilaudid. A difficulty is that Becky has been treating herself, and she will probably continue to do so. She will not be a compliant patient.

I should be feeling compassion for this desperate young woman dying in the prime of her life, but I feel guilty. Becky irritates me. So there. I am not travelling with Larry to feel good. I am tired. He's tired. He was called to the Benjamin home at 6:00 a.m. to pronounce Rachel Benjamin dead. She had vomited blood for twelve hours, then, when she became comatose, her son had wanted her taken to hospital to be resuscitated. Mercifully, the rabbi persuaded him that moving his mother would hasten her death. I wonder if Becky, like a porcupine, has been pushing people away all her life. Do the roles we play dying, as well as living, determine the care we receive, and the memories we leave?

VI

ON BECKY'S COFFEE table, I notice a copy of *The Healing Journey: Overcoming the Crisis of Cancer*, by Alastair J. Cunningham, senior scientist and psychologist at the Ontario Cancer Institute in Toronto's Princess Margaret Hospital. Cunningham conducts a four-step Healing Journey group support program that, according to a Cancer Institute brochure I picked up, improves patients' quality of life. The brochure makes even more optimistic claims: "Psychological self-help work can prolong life, may inhibit the growth of cancer and sometimes brings about unexpected remissions." It also advertises less anxiety and depression, more sense of control, and improved communication. Becky has been attending Cunningham's Healing Journey sessions for several weeks, and she says she has found them beneficial.

I'd heard Cunningham speak at a palliative care conference in April 1996, and his healing journey sounded to me a lot like *The Pilgrim's Progress*. For Cunningham, Bunyan's Slough of Despond is Denial, and his cancer pilgrim's upward zigzag journey is a progress through stages labelled Taking Control, Getting Connected, and Finding Meaning, leading to the Celestial City of Peace Healing.

The healing journey diagram in the workbook that accompanied his lecture reminded me of Snakes and Ladders. What if you struggle all the way up there to Higher Self, and suddenly, zip, you're back down to Self-Help Begins?

Peace Healing seemed to me to be a synonym for Acceptance, another word Cunningham used, and when he talked of "inner healers" and "unconditional love," I heard echoes of two of Kübler-Ross's more recent books, *Death: The Final Stage of Growth* and *Questions and Answers on Death and Dying*. Kübler-Ross has moved into New Age spiritualism, and she takes stories about near-death experiences as proof that there is life after death. "Death," she says, "does not exist." Cunningham doesn't go this far, but by putting his patients through a strenuous course of group exercises including relaxation techniques, meditation, visual imagery, and life writing, as well as, at the fourth level, in-depth psychological therapy, he hopes they will experience spiritual healing, "a transcendent order as a felt sense in the body." He hopes, too, that they will live longer or get well.

Healing is another of those ambiguous, overworked words that means all things to all people. Most of us interpret healing in a physical sense, and Cunningham's work can be traced to a 1989 study by a California psychiatrist, Dr. David Spiegel, that inadvertently and unexpectedly revealed that cancer patients participating in his support group lived on an average eighteen months longer. In his 1993 book, *Living Beyond Limits*, however, Spiegel remained sceptical about the connection between support groups, per se, and longevity. Patients with enough energy and enthusiasm to attend support groups may simply be healthier.

Cunningham's Healing Journey is psychic, and while in his lecture he cited several examples of patients whose cancers had gone into remission, he made no claim to miracles. While patients who are intellectual, introspective, self-disciplined, and looking for challenges might find the Healing Journey productive, Cunningham didn't talk about patients who had fallen by the wayside, and he did not discuss physical symptoms, including pain. Cunningham advocated psychological change, and emphasized the personal nature of this journey. Husbands, wives, children, partners, friends are apparently not wanted on this voyage. I find that scary. Having lived through the rebellious feminism of the 1970s, I know that for many people "finding myself" can be a bad trip. Is this how I want to spend the last months of my life? What if our families and friends are bored to death by our self-preoccupation, estranged by our emotional outbursts, and threatened by the invisible animals, our Inner Healers, who seem to be running our lives? What if they abandon us, or we them? Who else can we turn to when we are frightened and sick? Who else will look after us when we are dying?

Following the publication of Kübler-Ross's *On Death and Dying* in 1969, the public's appetite for positive, uplifting books about dying became insatiable. Since, before 1995, I had never read anything about dying, I had foolishly assumed very little had been published. How could I be so wrong? The University of Toronto libraries have whole sections devoted to books and journals about death and dying, including textbooks for death education courses, and on the self-help shelves of bookstores I have found a bewildering variety of paperbacks about self-healing, living with mortality, and dying gracefully. They all belong to an ancient genre that goes back to the Greek philosophers, who had strong opinions about how to die, and they reflect our continuing preoccupation with achieving "a good death."

In his book *Mortally Wounded: Stories of Soul Pain, Death and Healing*, Dr. Michael Kearney tells of a woman patient, dying of cancer, who asks him, "Should I be reading Kübler-Ross?" Similarly, in 1821, English Romantic poet John Keats, dying, at twenty-five, of tuberculosis, asked for a copy of *Holy Living and Holy Dying* by seventeenth-century Anglican cleric Jeremy Taylor. The book did Keats no good. Keats had lost his Christian faith, and exiled to Rome in the vain hope of a cure, he was separated from his beloved, Fanny Brawne. "I wish for death every day and night to deliver me from these pains," he wrote to his friend Charles Brown, "and then I wish death away, for death would destroy even those pains which are better than nothing . . . The thought of leaving Miss Brawne is beyond everything horrible – the sense of darkness coming over me – I eternally see her figure – eternally vanishing."

The anguish and despair Keats suffered during the last months of his life, meticulously recorded by his paid companion, Joseph Severn, was aggravated by Severn himself, who, fearing Keats might commit suicide, confiscated his morphine; by Keats's deceitful doctor, who put him on a starvation diet for an alleged "stomach complaint"; and by his English friends, who had packed Keats off to Rome, over his protests, to separate him from Fanny, a young woman they considered unsuitable. Keats wrote no poetry during the two years from his diagnosis to his death.

Perhaps because tuberculosis, with its emaciation, hemorrhages, and suffocation, was common and frightful, it was romanticized. Keats's suffering made tuberculosis poetic, the death of composer Frederic Chopin linked it to musical genius, and in Verdi's opera, *La Traviata*, a "tubercular" soprano sings glorious arias before gracefully expiring. Our need to see dying as a creative act was popularized by psychiatrist Carl Jung, who viewed death as a peak experience, and it's no surprise to find that most of the books about death and dying are written by psychiatrists or psychologists, our secular priests.

They are, with rare exceptions, chicken-soup books full of reassuring anecdotes and advice with titles like *To Die Well*, *Living Your Dying*, and *Dying Dignified*. Several are called *The Art of Dying*, including a comprehensive guidebook by American psychologist Patricia Weenolsen, subtitled *The Only Book for Persons Facing Their Own Death*. Weenolsen writes in a breezy, Miss Manners style – this is an etiquette book, after all – and she includes a two-page questionnaire, "Cutting Death Down to Size," for her dying readers to fill out. In answer to questions such as "Do you dread the process of dying?" and "Do you dread the *state* of being dead?" they are to check off, "No problem," "Problem," or "Major problem." There are also multiple choice questions, including, "Do you worry that (a) your death may be meaningless, (b) your life may be meaningless, (c) your life was wasted," and so on and on. The questionnaire reminds me of those "How good is your sex life?" quizzes women's magazines run, and when I picture myself, bald and emaciated, hunched over the page, dutifully reducing the complexity of my life to problem, no problem, major problem, I find the image so funny I buy the book. Would I buy it if I were dying? Would any friend dare give it to me?

Weenolsen's *The Art of Dying* contains a foreword by Bernie Siegel, M.D. A year ago, I had never heard of Bernie Siegel. How could I have missed him? In the netherworld of the dying, Siegel, the author of *Love, Medicine and Miracles*, is ubiquitous. Siegel, a surgeon before he became a therapist, has developed the theory of the Exceptional Patient, the patient who, in spite of a terminal diagnosis, recovers. Siegel's Exceptional Patient program is similar to the Healing Journey – his more recent book is called *Peace, Love and Healing* – and both use meditation, self-awareness, and group therapy to invoke the power of positive thinking.

The belief that the mind can control the body has been around as long as witchcraft, and since there is no medical explanation for spontaneous cures or remissions of terminal disease, love, optimism, and faith might well do. In 1995, on CBC television's "Witness" program, I saw Edmonton filmmaker Joe Viszmeg's story of his own astonishing recovery, "In My Own Time: Diary of a Cancer Patient." Viszmeg, an ordinary-looking, middle-aging single parent, had turned his camera on himself as soon as he was diagnosed with adrenal cancer in 1991. Joe shows us his surgical scar, his bloody tumour, and his naked, bloated body, but most of all we see his own charming, elfin face. We meet Joe's young daughter, Stella, his lovely young second wife, Rachel, who insists on marrying Joe after his cancer is diagnosed, and their infant son, Joe Jr., born in January 1993, after Viszmeg, his body full of cancer, has been given a year to live. Cut to February 1994: Joe is out jogging, waving happily at the camera. Feeling healthy, off drugs and eating well for the first time in years, Joe Viszmeg is impossibly, blissfully, alive.

Viszmeg attributes his miraculous recovery to a healing journey, begun in a Native sweat lodge ceremony in northern Alberta, that took him to the Simonton Centre in southern California, where he learned "to draw upon a great well of love that brings health into my life." Carl and Stephanie Simonton pioneered the mind-over-matter practice of using mental imagery to combat cancer, and their 1978 bestseller *Getting Well Again* became a classic of the self-healing literature. My own bias is that Joe Viszmeg charmed Death into playing a starring role in his home movie.

After more than a year slogging along on this literary death trip, I am getting impatient with Siegel, Simonton, *et al*. Their books form a celestial choir of mutual praise, and I find, to my dismay, that their sacred text appears to be a brief memoir, *Anatomy of an Illness*, published in 1979 by Norman Cousins, the well-known editor of New York's *Saturday Review*. So here I am, a journalist in search of medical truth, finding, at the dead end of this road, a book by another journalist.

How could anybody take *Anatomy of an Illness* seriously? Cousins, hospitalized with a mysterious, debilitating disease, claims to have cured himself by laughing at old Charlie Chaplin movies and ingesting toxic megadoses of vitamin C. Sure, vitamin C was considered a cure-all in the 1970s, but given Cousins's enthusiasm for placebos, I'd guess his doctor had treated him with transfusions of water and salt.

Cousins, the prototype of the patient as consumer, had been influenced by Dr. Hans Selye, a Canadian scientist whose research convinced him that psychological stress could cause, inhibit, and prevent disease, including cancer. This idea has been around since the Roman physician Galen postulated the theory that our health was subject to bodily "humours." In the nineteenth century, the celebrated Canadian-born physician Sir William Osler stated: "Show me what goes on in a man's head, and I will tell you what will become of his tuberculosis." We now know that tuberculosis can be cured by drugs. The "cancer personality" theory has been discarded in favour of immunology and genetics, and the idea of using LSD to achieve an "orgasmic" death, popular in the 1970s, is as dead as Timothy Leary.

Is a good death then nothing more than wishful thinking, a figment of our imaginations? The idea that we might gain post-mortem immortality by practising a combination of rituals and prayers, the concept behind the ancient Egyptian books of the dead, surfaced in Christian Europe during the Middle Ages. Erasmus of Rotterdam gave it literary form in *Preparation to Deathe*, published in English in 1538. While Erasmus portrayed dying as the last act in life's drama, it was the seventeenth-century English poet and cleric, John Donne, dean of St. Paul's Cathedral in London, who most memorably transformed his own dying into a public performance.

Donne, best known today for his love sonnets, had suffered the loss of his father, three sisters, and his older brother by 1593, when he was twenty-one, and his wife and a daughter died before him. Through meditation, prayer, and poetry, Donne examined his soul and struggled towards salvation, creating, in the process, some of the most beautiful literature in the English language. Unlike most of his contemporaries, who died of fever or plague, Donne contracted a long, wasting illness when he was fifty-seven. On February 25, 1631, he preached his last sermon: "Death's Duel, or A Consolation to the Soul against the dying Life and living Death of the Body." Donne's friend and biographer, Izak Walton, was in the congregation:

"When to the amazement of some beholders he appeared in the pulpit, many of them thought he presented himself not to preach mortification by a living voice, but mortality by a decaying body and a dying face, many that then saw his tears, and heard his faint and hollow voice, professing that they thought his text prophetically chosen and that Dr. Donne had preached his own Funeral Sermon."

Indeed he had, and the consolation he offered was "not that God will deliver us from dying, but that he will have a care for us in the hour of our death, of what kind soever our passage be. I thank him that prays for me when the bell tolls, but I thank him more that cate-chizes me, or preaches to me, or instructs me how to live." Years before, Donne had told a friend how he wished to die: "I would not that death should take me asleep. I would not have him merely seize me, and only declare me to be dead, but win me, and overcome me. When I must shipwrack, I would do it in a Sea, where mine impo-tence might have some excuse, not in a sullen weedy lake where I would not have so much as exercise for my swimming."

For the actual circumstances of Donne's death we have to rely on Izak Walton's account in his biography. Walton quotes Donne as saying: "I am to be judged by a merciful God who is not willing to see what I have done amiss. I am therefore full of inexpressible joy, and shall die in peace." Since St. Paul's Cathedral intended to erect a monument to Donne's memory, Donne designed it himself. He obtained a plank the size of his body, and a shroud. Removing his clothes, he had the shroud wrapped around him, tied head and foot but turned back to show his face, and stood on an urn while an artist sketched his figure life-size on the plank. He kept the drawing by his bed, and he summoned his closest friends to say good-bye. Having disposed of his possessions and wound up his business affairs, Donne renounced any further contact with worldly matters and lay quietly in bed for ten days.

"In the last hour of his last day," Walton writes, "as his body melted away and vapourised into spirit, his soul having, I verily believe, some Revelation of the Beatifical Vision, he said, 'I were miserable if I might not die,' and after these words closed many periods of his faint breath by saying often, 'Thy Kingdom come, Thy Will be done.' His speech, which had long been his ready and faithful servant, left him not until the last minute of his life. As his soul ascended, and his last breath departed from him, he closed his own eyes, and then disposed his hands and body into such a posture as required not the least alteration by those that came to shroud him."

Izak Walton's account of Donne's death may, like many famous last words, have been entirely fabricated, but coupled with Donne's own sermons and poems, it has left a powerful imprint on our cultural history. *The Hour of Our Death*, a line taken from Donne's last sermon, is the English title of French historian Philippe Ariès's inquiry into the history of death from the Middle Ages to the present, and Ariès, influenced by his study of tombs and funerary statuary, concluded that prior to the twentieth century, when death became taboo, we enjoyed a "tame death" secure in the traditions and rituals of family, community, and church.

Yet the painting, literature, and history of the time Ariès covers seem to contradict his theory. Medieval depictions of the Dance of Death show Death, a grinning skeleton, sneaking up from behind to grab unwary victims by the shoulder, or, shrouded by a ragged cloak, dragging them off by their ankles. Death was depicted as mysterious, unexpected, and violent. Donne's contemporary, Thomas Hobbes, wrote of human life as "solitary, poor, nasty, brutish and short," and when Hobbes was dying in 1679, his last words were: "I am about to take my last voyage, a great leap in the dark."

Diaries, journals, and letters describe how families, fleeing to the country, abandoned their sick during epidemics because the sight of people dying from gangrene, diarrhea, and hemorrhage was too horrible to bear. If, as it is now believed, 90 per cent of the Americas' Aboriginal populations died from infectious diseases following European invasions, what was life like for the survivors? During the Industrial Revolution of the eighteenth and nineteenth centuries, the poor and dispossessed, millions of them children, were worked to death in mines and factories. Rural families who refused to leave their ancestral lands so that sheep might graze them were hunted down and butchered, or died of hunger and cold. What was tame about being murdered in a pogrom, burned at the stake for heresy, or drowned as a witch? John Donne, as a sickly young man, faced death from "spotted fever." Spotted fever may have been measles, chickenpox, smallpox, scarlet fever, or syphilis, and with no remedies except herbs, the sick were often unintentionally killed by doctors who poisoned them with purgatives or bled them to death. Ritual and religion may have been all that was left for the grief-stricken survivors of mass, violent deaths.

Is our contemporary healing journey simply another path in the search for a mystical, elusive state of grace? Larry Librach talks about "the tasks of dying," tasks that should be performed not only by the dying, but by the crews of caregivers ferrying them to the other side.

The dying patient's first task, he says, is to receive and understand the truth, and the doctor's obligation is to tell the truth as the patient wants to hear it. Patients have a right to know the truth because we have a right to refuse or consent to treatment, and we can't exercise that right unless we know what we are being treated for. Unnecessary tests and treatments give patients false hope, cause them pain and fatigue, distract them from important things they want to do, and waste what remains of their precious time. "You can't look in the mirror, see yourself melting away, feeling a hundred years old, and not know you're dying," Larry says. "You look at your relatives and they're averting their eyes. They're telling you something."

I will never forget one visit I made with Larry. It was a large suburban home, new, well kept; an Italian family. We were met at the door by a smiling, fresh-faced young woman in black who showed us into a den or TV room. There, on a couch, curled into a ball, a small, dark-haired woman was moaning and rocking, her face contorted, so possessed by her pain she could not respond to a word or a touch. Maria was dying of colon and liver cancer. Her doctor and her family had told her she had the flu. Librach made out a prescription, and as the smiling, fresh-faced young woman showed us out, we were passed by a smiling older woman in black carrying a frosted chocolate cake. Was it for the wake, I wondered. "Everybody knows," Larry says. "A conspiracy of silence can become a comedy of silence."

In these Fellini-esque movie scenes, the Mount Sinai team tries reality therapy with the family. Larry says: "I'll say to the family, 'If the patient asks me what's wrong, I have to tell her the truth. What if she says, "Take me to the hospital," and the hospital says, "There is nothing more we can do." What is she going to think? Are you depriving her of the ability to manage her own affairs, to say good-bye?'" There is a widespread belief in Ontario, it appears, that the Italian culture, like the Chinese, demands that a patient *not* be told a fatal diagnosis.

Who says? Culture is one of those big, squishy, grab-bag words, and cultural belief can be used as an excuse to dodge a difficult task. Italians, in my experience, are Roman Catholic, and the Roman Catholic rule is not to die ignorant and unabsolved. Is it not dis-criminatory to condone unnecessary suffering for reasons of race and language? There is a difference between culture and folk wisdom. If, in the Old Country, impoverished, uneducated people fell sick in rural communities without doctors, hospitals, or medicine, maybe it was better to pretend. But in Canada, this attitude only deprives the patient of accessible, beneficial medical care.

I am daunted by the tasks of dying Larry Librach describes. Assisted by their caregivers, the dying are expected to accomplish a life review and a search for meaning, confront and understand their suffering, cope with losses, accept love, and live on in someone's grief. Whew. How do people do this? For advice, I turn to three women, a Christian and two Jews.

I had met Susan Locey when she was caring for Barbara, a woman in her seventies who was one of Larry Librach's patients. Before being referred to palliative care, Barbara had been a cantankerous, recalcitrant patient, and Susan, the pastor of Barbara's church, The Christian Community, had acted as her advocate. Librach and I had reason to anticipate an angry, emotional encounter, but when we arrived at Susan's home, Barbara was snoozing in bed and Susan looked serene, almost radiant. The Christian Community, she explained, has a karmic belief that the soul is reincarnated in another human being, while our previous deeds and relationships continue to exist after our death. We are, therefore, eternally accountable.

How many Christian ministers do I know who care for their dying parishioners in their own homes? I had stumbled across a Good Samaritan, and the Christian Community rose in my estimation. After Barbara died, not long after our visit, Susan Locey told me her story.

"Barbara was a difficult person," Susan explained. "She gave me a hard time. She was angry, and she had alienated all her friends." A night owl and heavy smoker, Barbara lived alone – her family was in Germany – and when she became disabled from a series of strokes she rejected all offers of help. Susan was almost the only person Barbara would allow to visit her – "I was fresh blood," Susan laughed – and while Barbara complained of terrible pain all over her body, she was too fearful of being institutionalized to go to the hospital for tests. Her doctor, throwing up his hands, arranged for a homemaker to help her, but Barbara refused to allow the homemaker to vacuum and the homemaker wouldn't take out the garbage. Susan, who began to visit frequently, was shocked to find the apartment a mess and Barbara, now virtually bedridden, improperly bathed.

"I was determined to get her out of that situation," Susan said. "It seemed morally irresponsible to let things go on like that. I got Barbara dressed and drove her to Mount Sinai Hospital." At Mount Sinai, Susan sat with Barbara for seven hours before Barbara was admitted, and Susan had to repeat Barbara's medical history five times to different doctors and nurses. For ten days, Barbara, vomiting constantly, suffered through batteries of tests. Her bones were riddled with cancer, but the doctors were trying, in vain, to find the primary site.

Susan had taken Barbara to Mount Sinai Hospital because of its excellent reputation, but Barbara, who had grown up in Germany during the Third Reich, was terrified to find herself in a Jewish hospital. "They kept doing these tests, every day a different drug, one thing after another," Susan said. "One day Barbara phoned me in a total panic. She was afraid they were killing her. She started apologizing for the Second World War. She was only twelve when the war broke out, but her father was a Nazi supporter and she had grown up with those ideals. Her guilt was a hurdle she had to get over."

Barbara was offered chemotherapy and radiation. She asked, "Is there any hope of a cure?" The answer was no. "Then what's the point?" she said. When Barbara refused further treatment, the hospital arranged to discharge her home within twenty-four hours. Susan was aghast. She had brought Barbara to the hospital because Barbara's home situation was intolerable. "I had never done this before," Susan says, "but I decided that Barbara would come to my house. It was the only light at the end of a dark tunnel." Susan insisted on a hospital bed for Barbara and arranged for a visiting nurse and homemaker. Barbara gave a little speech of thanks to the medical staff and, assuring them she held no grudges, apologized for being so uncooperative.

Her bed was set up in a sunny bedroom overlooking Susan's backyard and, at first, Barbara could eat, sleep through the night, and carry on a conversation. "She was reviewing her life and the memories poured out of her!" Susan recalls. Susan asked Barbara to think about her actions that had caused others to suffer, and invited Barbara's estranged friends in the congregation to make their peace with her.

"Barbara made up a little speech for my daughter filled with life wisdom," Susan says. "She was trying to give back what she was receiving. Her joy in being here was so moving. She was no longer this critical, angry person with a lot of temperament. Her face radiated gratitude and light. She transformed herself."

As Barbara's cancer progressed, however, she developed dementia. She knocked things over, tore off her nightgowns and diapers, rejected her medications, and lay awake all night, calling out for help every few minutes. "I got pushed to my limits," Susan admits. "I begged Barbara please to let me get more sleep. She tried, she really tried, but I had to work out of pure sympathy or it would have driven me crazy. It was part of what she had to do – she was no longer in control of everything. It was like having a baby. You sleep when you can."

Susan became fearful that her own energy would run out. "What will I do if I'm this tired tomorrow?" she asked herself. Barbara rallied, however, when her sister arrived from Germany, a piece of the past finished off, as Susan saw it, and the sister shared Susan's vigil. Barbara's physical distress was relieved when an expert VON nurse, Cindy Rose, took over her care, and Larry Librach prescribed drugs to eliminate her pain and counteract disorientation.

The day before Barbara died, Susan noticed that the tip of Barbara's nose "had become the colour of a dead person." Her breathing was shallow, congested, with a rattling sound. Still, Barbara ate some ice cream, had visitors, and responded to what was said to her. During the night, her breathing became deeper, then slowed. Susan was standing by Barbara's bed when she breathed her last at 5:15 a.m.

"We washed Barbara's body," Susan says. "It wasn't gruesome at all. We changed her bedding, it had become very wet, changed her clothes, said prayers, and called Dr. Librach a few minutes before 7 a.m." The Christian Community had bought a coffin, and Barbara lay in state in Susan's home for three days. "You see how the body changes," Susan says. "At first, Barbara looked twenty years younger. She was a lovely colour, with a mischievous little smile. The second day she looked more earnest, and by the third day she had sunk back into old age." Barbara was cremated, a ceremony filled with laughter and joy.

As Susan Locey tells me this story, her face glowing, eyes intent on mine, she clasps and unclasps her strong hands, trying to express physically an experience beyond words: "It was as if Barbara was struggling in the early stages of labour. I felt like a midwife. Something was coming to birth. She was giving birth to her death, a birth into the spiritual world."

For the dying themselves, however, the picture is not always so spiritually satisfying, no matter how hard everyone tries. Sheila Walker talks enthusiastically about Brenda, near death from ovarian cancer, who has reconciled with her only brother after not speaking to him for years. He visits her every day. When Brenda became too weak to leave her apartment, the Jewish Hospice arranged with her song circle to get together at her place, and Brenda is visited frequently by a music therapist, Mary Rykov, who sings with her, plays the guitar, and gives her therapeutic touch. She has a doctor, David Ouchterlony, from the Mount Sinai palliative care team, a visiting nurse, a homemaker, and cousins who have been coming to see her from all over North America. Brenda, however, is divorced, the mother of a teenaged son, and she is not yet fifty. This ending doesn't strike me as particularly happy, and Brenda is willing to tell me her story.

When I arrive, there are three other women in Brenda's tiny apartment, a friend, a homemaker, and a nurse who is helping Brenda get dressed in her bedroom. "Welcome to Grand Central Station," Brenda jokes as she comes into the living room. Her voice, barely above a whisper, has a sarcastic edge, as if to say, "Who needs this?" and I sense that while she is pleased with the attention, she may find all the company tiring. It is now too much of an effort for her to sing, and her speaking voice is low and raspy. She struggles for breath and I have to lean very close to hear her. Her face is pinched, her body so small and wizened she looks like a sparrow.

"It's wonderful having consistent people who will come to the house to *talk* to you," Brenda says. "Dr. Ouchterlony will spend an hour, no problem. Having someone who will listen to me is comforting, although it's a little late now. In the hospital, you wake up with something that scares you half to death and they say, 'Oh, yeah.' I'd get very angry with my oncologist. I kept asking questions and he got pissed off. He suggested I see a psychiatrist. I nearly kicked him."

Brenda's whisper has a harsh edge: "It took them seven months to diagnose me. I'd had breast cancer, my mother died of breast cancer, I was sick, I was in pain. My GP sent me around to all these specialists for tests, and by then my cancer had spread. I still feel angry. There's no excuse. I think they're incompetent."

Do you feel lonely, even with all these people here, I ask. "*Yes!*"

Brenda rasps. "I'm not getting the holding, the hugs. I need the *touch*. But it's good for my son. My son is unhappy. He would like me to talk to him more, but I just can't do it. The counsellors talk to him. My family is there, but I try to give *them* support by being strong, carrying on." Brenda is tired. Silent, she gazes wistfully around her apartment and out the window. "I have to leave this whole place," she whispers. "It's hard to *leave*." Do you feel you have achieved reconciliation? I ask. Brenda looks me squarely in the eye and answers vehemently, "*No!*"

Cancer patients routinely blame their doctors for failing to diagnose their tumours soon enough. Larry Librach calls this a "retrospective diagnosis" with the benefit of hindsight. Many general practitioners, he says, do batteries of tests and find nothing. Tests are not infallible and cancer can reveal itself very suddenly. Cancer is not the doctor's fault. All the same, I remember Jacqueline, immobile on an air mattress, her body bloated into a brown balloon, who had snapped at Librach, "Is this what you call quality of life, doctor?" Jacqueline was furious. Her doctor had told her the lump in her breast was no problem. Is it a coincidence, I wonder, that the people who exhort the dying to reconcile, heal, and forgive are health care professionals? Are we to forgive abandonment and misdiagnosis? How much of the physical and psychic pain the dying suffer has been caused by the medical profession in the first place?

It is from a self-possessed veteran of the cancer wars that I begin to learn wisdom. Graziella is in her forties, a Jew who came to Toronto from Argentina with her husband and two sons many years earlier. She greets me at the door pushing a pole on wheels. The pole holds her morphine pump and helps support her when she walks. Graziella's body is twisted and bent from bone cancer, but she has soft, pale skin, black hair, and a beautiful smile. Graziella has had metastatic cancer for nearly seven years, and she's done the works: chemotherapy, radiation, a bone marrow transplant, Dr. Cunningham's Healing Journey, relaxation therapy, meditation, herbs, natural food.

"Last summer I stopped," she laughs, "*Enough!* I did all this and it didn't work anyway. I thought, why should I get obsessed? I knew people who did this and they died. I didn't want any pressure. You have to *believe*, and it should be a pleasant feeling, not anxiety. I decided that I will live my life the way I want to."

Graziella is living on borrowed time: six months ago she was given three months to live. "I wasn't surprised," she says. "I have never been okay since my diagnosis. I have to live with cancer, but cancer is not my life. I always thank God for everything extra, deal with it in a positive way. I have never felt angry. I am upset, and sad, but if cancer has to come to this house, it's better that it's me. I am the strongest one. Every morning I feel happy." Morphine keeps her free from the unbearable pain she had suffered before coming into the care of the Jewish Hospice, and she takes chemo to control the spread of her cancer. Since she can no longer drive, and feels self-conscious about her appearance, she has decided to stay at home:

"I don't like to put myself in a situation where I'll be exposed to people who will look at me, where I'll feel upset. I create my own world here. I like to read, search the Internet. My friends come *here*. For a lot of people it's very hard to talk about it. I feel it's up to me to put them at their ease, so I talk about it. If people say, 'I don't know what to say,' I tell them, 'Say what you usually say.' Everybody comes to help and it is up to you if they will want to keep coming back. I am always smiling. I can laugh at the worst moments. Some people die before their deaths, but I have always believed that the day we are born, we die. It's out of my control. The day I die, that's the day I die."

Graziella is blessed with a husband who treats her tenderly and a close, loving family, but she attributes her spiritual strength to Nestor, a shaman, or traditional healer, she visits in Toronto. I am dumbfounded. Graziella seems to me a paragon of rationality, common sense, and self-discipline. Graziella has kept Nestor a secret from the hospice, but she is absolutely serious. "When I first went to see Nestor, he told me my life," she says. "I have experienced some things with him that are very spooky. Nestor has brought me peace."

Could I speak with him? I ask. Certainly, she says, and gives me Nestor's phone number.

VII

NESTOR'S VOICE ON the phone sounds young and nervous, and he's obviously worried that I may be an undercover cop. I am not clear myself about the legality of healers, but Nestor has a proper office in a shabby-chic part of Cabbagetown and he agrees to meet me for an interview. I imagine Nestor as a tall, gaunt figure wearing a cone-shaped hat and a long purple robe covered with silver stars and moons, but when I ring the buzzer and climb the stairs to the second floor, I meet a slim, dark-haired young man wearing a shirt and jacket. Nestor has recently come to Toronto from Argentina, and he is still learning English.

The bare walls of the room are painted a soft ochre, the spare wooden furniture is the colour of ebony or mahogany. A plain, altar-like dresser against one wall holds a plate of yellow fruit, and the fruit, like everything in the room, is artfully arranged. The effect is soothing, understated. When he was fourteen, Nestor says, he was told that he had a spiritual capacity to help people. "I had no clue," he says. "I thought the man was mad." His great-grandmother, however, was a folk healer, and Nestor had been taught to read Tarot cards as a child. He was invited to a temple where initiates learned the rituals of an African religion derived, he says, from the culture of the Yoruba people of southwestern Nigeria. "In the temple, I had a seizure," Nestor says. "I learned that I was able to foresee things."

Nestor is reluctant to reveal too much about his beliefs, but from what he does say I gather that they are similar to those of the ancient Greeks. Spirit is immanent in all things, but particular sacred places, or animals, are endowed with a spiritual dimension conceptualized as gods or goddesses. Nestor mentions, for instance, a tree goddess, Osanha, and explains that a river goddess represents cleansing and metamorphosis. Her colour is yellow. A shaman, he says, learns the secret rituals and offerings sacred to each deity in order to invoke the deity's unique power to intervene. Nestor asks his clients to bring certain fruits, vegetables, or grains as offerings, and he uses the Tarot cards as a tool to shape and organize his thoughts.

Nestor's practice is the reverse of psychotherapy. Once his client has explained the reason for coming, Nestor describes what he visualizes in the cards and in his client's life. "I didn't see death!" he says of his first meeting with Graziella. "I was mute. I was out of words. 'Your life is not short,' I told her. 'You may go through hell. All I can offer is to help you. You have your energy within yourself.'" Rituals and offerings put individuals in communion with a universal life force, and encourage people who are lost and frightened to place their faith in the healer's power.

It is this ability to *trust* Nestor that gives Graziella comfort, and her trust is not misplaced. Six weeks ago, she was in hospital with pneumonia, so near death even she thought, "This is it." Nestor arrived with an offering of boiled corn, performed a ritual by her bedside, then threw the corn into Lake Ontario. "I felt such rage," he says. "I knew she didn't have to die. She allowed me to contribute to her need."

Here I am, a lapsed Protestant Celtic/Norse Canadian talking to a Spanish-speaking Argentinian with a mythic Greek name about African religious beliefs that seem uncannily similar to my own ancestors' worship of the sun, moon, earth, trees, rain, and wind. I like to picture Nestor flinging his boiled corn into Lake Ontario. I'd always thought of the Toronto harbour as an open sewer. Now it has spiritual resonance, and I remember how in 1954 Marilyn Bell, fighting off lamprey eels, emerged from the lake at the end of her marathon swim like a grease-covered Venus. "I am changing people's perceptions of the world," Nestor says.

I find my world After Nestor more interesting than it was Before Nestor, so when Mary Rykov offers an introductory workshop on therapeutic touch, I am less dubious about touchy-feely stuff than I would have been otherwise. I sign up.

The ten or so of us, women of all ages and one man, gather in a meeting room on a Saturday morning. We look sceptical and apprehensive. Mary reassures us that therapeutic touch is easy to learn and respectable. For twenty-five years it has been used by lay therapists and medical professionals around the world to accelerate healing, alleviate pain, and promote relaxation. It should not be confused with faith healing, healing touch, or the laying on of hands. Therapeutic touch doesn't involve touch at all.

"Hold your hands together, keeping them two or three inches apart," Mary instructs. "Can you feel the energy?" Sure enough, after a few seconds I feel heat radiating between my open palms. Therapeutic touch is based on an ancient theory that we are individual energy fields integrated into a cosmic energy system. Illness is an imbalance, or interruption, in our energy field. The healer, acting as a conduit for the cosmic energy, locates the imbalance and clears it away. We will learn by taking turns being healer and healee.

I like the word healee. All the healee has to do is sit, fully clothed, in stocking feet, in a straight-backed chair in the middle of the room. The healer does the work, and it requires intense concentration. We do a yoga breathing exercise, right nostril, left nostril, to clear our heads of "monkey chatter," as Mary calls it, and she asks us to centre ourselves by visualizing an image in nature that gives us a feeling of wholeness and peace.

I close my eyes. I am in my canoe. It's early morning, slanting sun, the lake is calm. I am drifting into the tall, teepee-shaped cleft in the sheer granite cliff that rises out of our lake at its south end. Here the water is deep, black, but it reflects the sunlight, my red canoe, and the soft, multicoloured lichens that cover the walls of the cave like paleolithic paintings. When I look down into the water, the reflection gives me the illusion of looking upwards at the sky. I am perfectly suspended.

I didn't expect to find my centre today, but there it is. I'm grateful, and I feel a shiver run up and down my spine as I watch Mary work. Holding her hands close together, palms out, about three inches away from the volunteer healee's body, she moves them quickly, smoothly, working from the head down to the feet, enfolding the healee in a cocoon of motion. Mary is looking, she tells us, for coldness, blankness, congestion, static, or other signs of imbalance. To "unruffle" the energy field, she uses downward, sweeping motions with her hands and arms, moving from the head to the feet.

Mary has small, delicate hands and their rhythmic, graceful movements remind me of birds in flight. She assesses the effects of her therapy by hovering her hands over the healee once more, then she places them on the healee's feet, her fingers pressing the instep, to ground the energy. Mary explains what she is doing as she works, and the whole exercise doesn't take more than ten or fifteen minutes.

I am mesmerized, and I am completely enchanted as soon as I get to be a practice patient. Most healees, I notice, close their eyes, but I find the unruffling, clumsy as we beginners are, beautiful to watch, and having hands passing over my body like feathers makes the hairs on my skin rise and tingle. I become so relaxed I could fall asleep. Being a healer, however, demands that I be in continuous motion, including bending and kneeling, and my concentration is so complete that I feel an almost physical empathy with my practice patient.

To my surprise, I do notice cold, blankness, and intense heat in her energy field, and I am pleased when I detect a back injury she had never mentioned. When Mary tells us that visualizing the colour yellow will stimulate and energize, I think of Nestor and his golden fruit. Cobalt blue, on the other hand, calms and sedates.

Therapeutic touch originated in Montreal in the 1960s when medical researcher Dr. Bernard Grad began to investigate the powers of a local healer, Hungarian immigrant Dora Kunz. An American nurse, Dolores Kreiger, continued the research with Kunz in the United States and developed the current theory and terminology. A true initiate studies Yogic concepts of *prana* and *chakras*, but anybody can learn the basic techniques from a good teacher without the ideological context. Therapeutic touch does not claim to be a cure, a placebo, or a substitute for medical treatment.

"It is from compassion that it draws its power," says Dolores Kreiger. Molecular biologists, reducing our bodies, including our brains, to a chemical stew, have isolated a substance they call endorphin, our own, homemade morphine. The physical rituals of therapeutic touch, the intense, suspended relationship between healer and healee, may be one way of releasing endorphins that create pleasure and ease pain. It looks weird, but it feels great. How many times in my life do I get a healer's undivided, energetic, compassionate attention for fifteen minutes? All I have to do is receive this gift.

I like the idea of relinquishing control, being passive, being taken care of. What an opportunity! We live in a culture of control freaks. Why do we assume that exercising control over our dying is a good thing? Why not, like Graziella, rest, pamper ourselves, let others do the work and worrying? Traditionally, the dying Chinese relinquished control over decision-making to a chosen relative, usually an elder son or daughter. Many Chinese in North America still do. Why not? A young, healthy person may be much better at asking questions, getting information, organizing the family, and making good choices than someone who is old, sick, and tired. In many families, regardless of their traditions or beliefs, one person volunteers, or is chosen, to undertake this role.

Patients who are passive, even indifferent to their prognosis, run the risk, however, of being condemned for "giving up" or being "in denial." Yet in his study, "Attitudes Towards Living and Dying in Patients on Chronic Hemodialysis," physician Charles Norton observes, "The deathbed does not seem a very opportune place to learn philosophy or to achieve a psychological resolution concerning matters of living or dying." Questioning his dialysis patients, all of them dying of kidney failure, Norton found that half of them gave no indication that they had considered, or even wanted to consider, the implications of dying or the meaning of their lives.

The group as a whole, Norton says, was inclined to think that worrying was useless, and the best thing to do was to keep going as well as they were able, to carry out ordinary tasks and responsibilities, to enjoy life if that was possible and if possible to avoid becoming a burden to others. They appeared to take the world about them at face value, accepting it without being either sceptical or curious. "Indeed," Norton observes, "the great majority of everyday normal people are not particularly inclined to translate the basic assumptions or generalities of their lives into verbal terms. It seems quite clear that a more than ordinary intellectual accomplishment is not a necessary precondition for psychological health or for the attainment of a perfectly workable view on matters of living and dying."

I was glad to find Norton's defence of the unexceptional patient in a book titled *Death Anxiety*. His patients' greatest fear, being a burden to others, showed a practical, unselfish concern for the community rather than a narcissistic search for a private epiphany. Norton's crisp, medical tone was also a welcome antidote to the sentimentality and inspirational rhetoric that so often passes itself off as science in the doom literature. Some of these books are written by bereaved parents or partners. Few are written by the dying.

The best known is Ernest Becker's *The Denial of Death*, a scholarly analysis of twentieth-century psychiatry that won a Pulitzer prize in 1974. Becker, who died that year, argued that we repress the knowledge of our inevitable death to sustain the illusion of a meaningful life. It has become the conventional wisdom to say that we live in a death-denying society.

But what do we see on the television news but war, hunger, accident, catastrophe? Our newspapers feature shootings, beatings, torture, massacres, and corpses, and obituaries take up more and more space. Death is news. Cartoons and children's games are dances of death. "Ring around a rosy" is believed to date back to epidemics of bubonic plague, when people carried "posies," sachets of herbs and spices, to ward off the Black Death. Husha, husha, all fall down. And what do we make of "Rock a Bye Baby"?

In 1955, British anthropologist Geoffrey Gorer published an essay called "The Pornography of Death." Observing the euphemistic evasiveness the British adopted when confronted with a death in the family, Gorer concluded they were as obsessed and titillated by death as the Victorians had been by sex. "While natural death became more and more smothered in prudery," he writes, "violent death has played an ever-growing part in the fantasies offered to mass audiences. The diffusion of the automobile, with its constant and unnoticed toll of fatal accidents, may well have been most influential in bringing the possibility of violent death into the expectations of law-abiding people in time of peace." Gorer anticipated David Cronenberg's movie *Crash* by more than forty years, and 1955 was the year that Hollywood released *Rebel Without a Cause*, a movie in which cars are both deadly and also symbols of death. Its star, James Dean, killed in a car crash that year, became a cult figure.

Perhaps death is invisible because its face is so familiar. I remember the hearselike Lincoln convertible President John F. Kennedy was riding in when he was assassinated in 1963, and the film footage of his skull being blown apart was ritually repeated on television until it left an indelible imprint on the mind's eye. This was followed by the live, on-camera murder of Kennedy's assassin, Lee Harvey Oswald, and the assassinations of the president's brother Robert, and of civil rights leader Martin Luther King in 1968.

Images of the Vietnam War, helicopters hovering like noisy birds of prey, the dead shipped home in body bags, so much garbage, and the naked little girl running screaming towards the camera, fleeing the napalm burning behind her, horrified the world. A helicopter to me is as much an omen of war and death as a raven was to my ancestors, and a green garbage bag reminds me that I too will likely end up in an undertaker's green body bag. Studying New England cemeteries for his book *The Puritan Way of Death*, David Stannard noticed how over generations the leering skulls carved on the early settlers' headstones mutated into sweetly smiling cherubs. What is our ubiquitous Smiley Face, then, but a contemporary, cartoon version of the death's head?

We may not talk about dying, but we read and write about it. There are all kinds of accounts written by surviving parents, partners, children. Simone de Beauvoir wrote about her mother's dying in *A Very Easy Death*, Philip Roth chronicled his father's death in *Patrimony*. You won't find their honest, acutely observed, and beautifully written memoirs in the tai chi, Tibetan, herbal, wellness, self-help, or New Age sections of your bookstore. Nor are you likely to find many memoirs by the dying. The dying, like Keats, are usually too sick, weary, or preoccupied to organize their thoughts into written words. When they do, like Barbara Rosenblum in *Cancer in Two Voices*, they speak of anger and helplessness, pain, sorrow, self-pity, blame, and guilt. This is not a message we, the well, want to hear. I attend conferences on palliative care, and as I sit through presentations by medical researchers, monks, and Aboriginal healers, illustrated, too often, by photographs of flowers, I look around at the beaming, rosy-cheeked faces in the crowd. Where are the dying? Not here.

"Is this a house full of dying people?" my son Aaron asks nervously as we drive past Hospice King. "I don't think so," I say, thinking, gee, I hope not. Hospice King is a plain, two-storey clapboard house on the main street of King City. It looks old and cramped and traffic thunders by day and night. By chance, we have moved to a village which in 1983 opened one of Canada's first community hospices.

Hospice King has an excellent reputation, I hear, but what, exactly, does it do?

When I walk in the door, it's obvious that the clapboard house is only an office. It's crowded, comfortable, and I'm reassured to see a woman my age wearing a sweatsuit, like me. I meet Cecelia, the executive director, Lyn, the volunteer coordinator, and Evelyn, a volunteer who answers the phone. They are casual, friendly, and direct. Why am I here? That's a good question. If someone had told me two years ago that I'd be volunteering to visit the sick, I would have hooted in derision. Me, in a little pink smock carrying my basket of fruit? *Me?* In fact, if someone had suggested in July 1995 that a volunteer might visit my father and me, I would have said, "No! No smarmy do-goodies in this house, please!"

Where did I pick up this prejudice? Who knows. It's as old as I am. There was nothing smarmy about the hospice volunteers I met in my therapeutic touch workshops. They were professional women, smart, funny, unpretentious. There's nothing unctuous about Hospice King either, and nobody's wearing a smock.

Why *am* I here? Because the oncologist's promise to my father – you can die at home – was never fulfilled. Hospice King is committed to supporting people with life-threatening illnesses within the comfort of their homes and families. I believe in that. I believe that it's cruel and cowardly to abandon the sick, and the dying are sick people who are getting sicker. I believe that all the sick have a right to expert, appropriate medical care, including nursing, for free. I know from experience that family members need instruction, reassurance, and companionship. I hope that if I can *be there* for someone else, someone will be there for me. I like the nautical term *standing watch*.

This is often what volunteers do. They sit with the patient, or in the house, while family members shop or sleep. They may sit in silence, watch television with the patient, play cards, or chat. Hospice King, like most hospices, does not normally provide the constant, daily attendance June Callwood describes in her classic 1986 book,

Twelve Weeks in Spring. Visits usually last about two hours, once or twice a week, and volunteers are part of a kaleidoscope of caregivers that includes family doctors, visiting nurses, and home care workers. Volunteers cannot give medication, but they need to be knowledgeable about standards of care and alert to symptoms of suffering so they can report neglect or distress. They are not expected to do housework, but they can make light meals, run errands, help sort out bureaucratic problems, and provide a sympathetic ear.

I know how to do these things. Listening is part of what I do for a living, and in hospice my lack of conventional religious belief is an asset. Hospice King is looking for open, broadminded people in the community who make no assumptions and have no agendas. It's called unconditional acceptance, not love. It's important to have a high tolerance for individual lifestyles, especially those that differ from your own, sensitivity towards family dynamics, and a sense of humour. Volunteers are not social workers, but patients often confide in them simply because they are *not* powerful authority figures. The qualifications are summed up by the word TOUCHSTONE:

> **T**alent conveyed to
> **O**thers with
> **U**nderstanding and
> **C**aring, along with
> **H**umour and
> **S**ensitivity, and to be
> **T**ouched and aware of
> **O**ther people's
> **N**eeds with
> **E**ase and enthusiasm.

I'm happy with this. No sanctimony, no teary-eyed hand-wringing. Hospice King was organized by a group of local people, many of them neighbours, who found themselves, as I had been, trying to care for a dying relative at home with no professional or community support. "We were scared," says Barbara Marshall Houlding, whose first husband, Bill, died of cancer at home in 1980. "I needed help: someone to advise, to say, 'Good job, hang in there,' and someone who would bring the world into the home."

The volunteer hospice idea came from Jane Reid, whose mother had died with good hospice care in the United States, and the King Township group included Sally Blaney, a nurse with excellent contacts in the Ontario health care system. The group consulted the few experts around at the time, and, after educating themselves by reading whatever hospice literature they could find, particularly Sandol Stoddard's *The Hospice Movement*, they created a volunteer training manual. With the support of various churches and foundations – the hospice began operating out of the Anglican church – Jane Reid and Barbara Marshall Houlding went to England to visit hospices there.

Hospice King's philosophy is not to criticize the professionals, but to provide, where needed, an additional free community service. I am impressed, however, by Hospice King's professionalism. The volunteer reports to Lyn after every visit, and she keeps a comprehensive case file. This information and the identities of hospice patients must be kept confidential. A hospice nurse interviews patients before taking them on, and the hospice both screens and educates its volunteers. After an intensive personal interview, I must take a three-hour-a-week palliative care training course that lasts for nine weeks. This course, sponsored by York Region, is followed by three hours of in-house training at the hospice. My first class is at 6:30 p.m. on April 3, 1997.

There must be sixty or seventy of us, almost all women, seated at round tables in a stuffy, uncomfortable church basement. Most of the older women, like me, intend to volunteer at hospices in the region, the rest are professional nurses and home care workers. With hospitals laying off staff to cut costs, nurses are being hired by private agencies, and I notice during the next three or four weeks that a lot of them split at the half-time coffee break. I can't really blame them.

They are either going on or coming off a long shift, and they are here to get a certificate that might lead to a raise or a better job.

I almost walk out myself during our session on "Psychosocial and Spiritual Issues" when a funeral director pitches the psychosocial and spiritual benefits of viewing an embalmed corpse in an open casket. Years ago, I had viewed my father-in-law's embalmed corpse in an open casket. Once is enough. The previous week, our panel discussion on cultural beliefs had concluded that culture is what an individual says it is. Good idea, I'd thought, and embalming, viewing, and burying the dead are not my culture.

I get restless because the lectures, most of them packed with information, rarely allow opportunities for questions or discussion. I have another bad session when a sprightly young music therapist illustrates how she serenades the dying with songs from *The Sound of Music*, then leads us all in a rousing chorus of "This Land is Your Land." If she comes near me when I'm dying, I will kill her.

Respect. That's what hospice is all about. Whoever you are, respect the mortally sick, their weakness, sadness, loneliness, dependency, fear. Reserve judgement on their values and opinions, however much you may disagree. Do what they ask you to do, make breakfast, brush their teeth, get them to the toilet, without argument, advice, or repugnance. Don't pray or preach. You don't have to be a bossy, arrogant know-it-all. There is no need for you to talk. If you don't know what to say, say nothing. The dying can hear, and they can talk. If the task of the dying is to review their lives, the task of the volunteer is to provide an attentive audience. Attentive listening requires sensitivity to nuance, emotion, facial expression, and body language. *Listen. Shut up and listen.*

But what if the dying ask questions? Do you think there is life after death? What will happen at the moment of death? We are told to be honest and truthful, to be ourselves, yet, at the same time, we must not impose our own values or beliefs on others. We are there to comfort, not argue, discourage, or frighten. This requires tact and tongue-biting, but evasive replies – "You'll be okay" or "Let's not be gloomy" or "Isn't it a lovely day?" – trivialize the question and stop the conversation cold. What if there are no answers? Say simply, "I don't know." Respond with a question. What do you think? Why? What have the doctors told you? Answering a question with a question is a Socratic technique, and any psychiatrist, Christian catechist, or atheist journalist will tell you that the person asking the question will probably answer it.

After enduring twenty-seven hard hours in a church basement on this course, I have learned patience. I have been taught that the dying often speak to ghostly, invisible people, dead or mythic, and that the physical incapacity and maelstrom of emotions I felt as my father lay dying is a common, predictable phenomenon called anticipatory grief. It is perfectly normal for the grieving to be unable to eat, to suffer from depression, insomnia, panic attacks, blurred vision, and forgetfulness, to feel guilt, helplessness, and abandonment and to be angry at everybody, including the dying person. Crying is only one, visible, socially accepted aspect of grieving. The dying grieve their own impending deaths, and these emotions may contribute more to their suffering than their illness.

I am wiser now, and after a session with Hospice King nurse Sheila Darnowsky, I hope I know the proper way to assist a patient out of bed and into a wheelchair, how to change a bed with the patient in it, and how to evacuate a bedridden patient in case of fire. I have a certificate, a name tag, and surgical gloves to wear when dealing with bodily fluids. I do not have a smock. I am a hospice volunteer, and I have a patient.

VIII

NORMA LIVES IN A town about a fifteen-minute drive from my home. She is a widow in her late seventies, and she lives with her daughter, Kathy, son-in-law, Ian, and two teenage grandchildren, Alison and John. Norma, I am told, is an independent, strong-minded person. She expects high standards of care, and when it doesn't measure up, she says so. I admire that. Norma doesn't enjoy dealing with a succession of strange caregivers, but Sue, the volunteer I am replacing part-time, is moving to another town. I'm the strange caregiver. My visits, once every week or two, will primarily involve driving Norma, with her wheelchair, to the library or the bank.

August 12, 1997: My first visit. I am nervous. What if she doesn't like me? What if I do something stupid or say something tactless? Sue meets me at Norma's house. Norma's small bedroom is full of antique dressers and easy chairs, every surface covered with family photographs and memorabilia, the quintessence of her life. Norma is sitting on the edge of her bed, dressed in a flowered skirt and blouse, smoking a cigarette. She looks up, and her smile illuminates her face. She is a pretty woman, her curly hair more brown than grey, her dark eyes large and wide-set.

Sue is supposed to be my mentor during this visit, but after about twenty minutes Sue looks at her watch and says she has to help her husband move a barn. Off she goes. We're on our own. Norma can walk down the stairs unaided if she takes her time, and she climbs into the front seat of my Toyota 4Runner. It's the wheelchair that gives me trouble. It's bulky, clumsy, and its little front wheels wiggle off in all directions. The wretched thing weighs a ton, and it's all I can do to heave it into the back of the truck. Once we get to the bank, I have to lug it out, unfold all its collapsed parts, and get Norma into it without letting it roll out from under her. The parking lot is full of potholes, and when the wheelchair's front wheels snag, I'm fearful that I'm going to pitch Norma out face first. Norma, fortunately, is amused by my ineptitude. We both laugh when a strange woman comes over and offers to help me wheel my mother into the bank.

Curiously enough, Norma does look a little like my mother, and she is at least as tall as I am. We are both plain-spoken, and we find the same things funny. We both love to read, and Norma, like my mother, enjoys murder mysteries. When she tells me that her first hospice volunteer drove her nuts by constantly stroking her hand, I can honestly agree that it would drive me nuts too. I am dubious about the hand-holding aspect of hospice. Sure, if touch is welcomed and the best way to communicate, but if I were lying helpless in bed and some stranger grabbed and held my hand, I'd be frightened and annoyed. I remember as a little kid being tossed up in the air like a rubber ball, terrified I was going to be crushed against the ceiling. I'm one of those people who needs a lot of space, and so, I think, is Norma.

She misses the big apartment she and her husband, Carl, used to have in Hamilton. Three years ago, Norma was diagnosed with a cancerous tumour that encroached on her heart. Their family doctor gave her four months to live. Then Carl fell sick. He was operated on, and sent home in agony. Norma says that Carl was told nothing about his illness, and when she insisted he be taken back to the hospital, their doctor asked her, in a voice that all could hear: "Do you want your husband to die in the hospital or at home where he belongs?" The doctor walked out and never returned. Carl, she says, had not been told his illness was terminal.

In this crisis, Carl went to live with his daughter from a previous marriage, and Norma came to stay with Kathy, her daughter from a previous marriage. Carl was dead in four months. "My daughter certainly didn't expect to have me around this long!" Norma laughs. Her illness now appears to be something of a mystery, and since Hospice King volunteers are not supposed to pry into medical details, I don't ask. Norma wouldn't be caught dead in one of the support groups for exceptional patients Bernie Siegel describes in *Love, Medicine and Miracles*, but she is an exceptional patient. And she beats the pants off me at Scrabble.

As the weeks pass we settle into a routine. I become more dexterous with the wheelchair, and I like the way people scurry out of our path. Sometimes, if Norma is feeling too tired to go out, we sit and talk. She is astute and observant, vigilant about managing her own affairs, up-to-the-minute on politics and international issues, a Blue Jays fan, like me, and a good storyteller. I look forward to my visits. Norma makes her own tea, but I get her a bit of breakfast, and before I leave I prepare a sandwich or snack for her to eat later. Some days I go to the drugstore to pick up her prescriptions.

Volunteers do, within reason, whatever patients or their families need us to do. They set the agenda, not us, and we're there because we want to be, not because we're paid. Pat, a hospice volunteer who has visited Norma weekly for three years, plays Scrabble with her, and I make sure there is always a bag of books near her bedside table. Norma is very appreciative of hospice. Our tasks are homely, but Hospice King was founded on the homely perception that it's not necessarily the big, existential issues that preoccupy people when they near death. They worry about the myriad mutual obligations that sickness entails. It's hard having to be *helped*, and families need a break from constant care and anxiety. As Lyn Strathy puts it: "Hospice King is just folks helping folks."

Besides her family, including her son Don and his family in New Brunswick, Norma has a lot of people in her life. A homemaker comes in two days a week to change her bed, do her laundry, clean, make meals, and keep her company. Hospice volunteers visit another two days a week, and on the fifth day a community nurse comes in to check her over. On top of Norma's caregiver pyramid is her doctor, who visits from time to time, and her case manager, who coordinates all these services through the region's Community Care Access Centre. It takes a lot of Norma's energy to establish a meaningful personal relationship with each of these individuals. It's irritating to have to give her medical history to the umpteenth strange nurse who breezes in with a cheery, "Hi, how are you?" and can't be bothered to read her chart. The nursing agency now tries to send the same nurse every week.

October 4: I find Norma in bed, hooked up to her oxygen tank, struggling to breathe. She has a terrible cough. She has been sick for a week and is getting worse. She is in distress but she doesn't want to go to the hospital. Her doctor has prescribed antibiotics over the phone but they don't seem to be working. She is in pain and feeling nauseous. She takes Tylenol 3 for pain, but she's afraid to take too much in case she develops a tolerance. I try to explain that she doesn't have to worry, and there are lots of painkillers stronger than Tylenol. This seems to reassure her.

Norma has lost all confidence in her doctor. She wants a new one. Kathy strongly agrees, and she has already been asking around. However, the local family physician most highly recommended refused to take Norma on for fear of antagonizing his colleague. "To hell with the patient," Norma snorts. She certainly has a right to a second opinion, but this is a small community with few physicians to choose from. Do I know of a clever doctor? she asks.

This raises a difficult problem of diplomacy. I do know clever doctors, but it's not my role as a hospice volunteer to make decisions about medical care. At the same time, my Hospice King literature says: "Care givers should be willing to get personally involved. Are you willing/able to intercede? BE KNOWLEDGEABLE about good care and ENSURE that the dying person receives it." Damn right. I am not satisfied with Norma's care. Neither is Pat, my volunteer colleague, and Pat is a nurse.

I report Norma's request to Hospice King. Can we find her a doctor expert in palliative care? The only ones I know about don't live in her area. It appears, however, that Norma's request has to go through her case manager. Lyn will give her a call.

The days stretch into weeks, and Norma struggles on, thinner, weaker, and more distressed. I am beside myself with frustration. Her doctor has no intention of relinquishing his patient, and he claims to be a specialist in palliative care. Norma is reluctant to ask him for a referral. What if he slams out the door, leaving her with no doctor at all? He visits more often, but tells her, "You're not ready for morphine." He gives her a prescription for nausea the pharmacist rejects because it is improperly filled out. He doesn't address any of her other symptoms. Typically, Norma's nurse, a meek, gentle soul, is taking blame from the doctor for Norma's suffering. The nurse is upset. I feel responsible. I have caused a fuss. What else could I do? My responsibility is to my patient and her family. Volunteers, I realize, may be at the bottom of the health care hierarchy, but at least we can advocate for the patient without fearing for our jobs. Everyone is anxious, especially Norma's family. Kathy has taken time off work. She is taking charge.

In the midst of the crisis, I receive a newsletter from Palliative Care Services of York Region with an article praising the region's pain and symptom management team. What luck, a consultant! A clever doctor has been under our noses all along! I tell Hospice King. I give the newsletter, with the phone number, to Norma. Why not call York Region?

Kathy does, in the nick of time. Norma's doctor has prescribed morphine, without a laxative, and she has suffered agonies of constipation. I give her a patients' booklet, *How to Manage your Pain*, that I picked up at a conference. Then I am told that York Region's pain and symptom management team does not include a doctor in Norma's area. Why advertise it, then, I'd like to know. The good news is that a young doctor setting up in practice five minutes away will take her on, and he is willing to learn.

November 11: "I'm still here!" Norma grins at me as I come in the door. She looks frail, but cheerful and out of pain. The new doctor seems to have everything under control. He visits and phones. *She likes him!*

What a relief. It has been a stormy passage for all of us. When I had gone to Ottawa for a few days in October, I'd feared to hear on my return that Norma had died. I was anxious too that, as a clumsy rookie, I had butted in where I didn't belong and made a mess. But I had tried to practise hospice principles, Hospice King had taken action, and Norma had accomplished her goal. She is *alive*.

"I'll see you in two weeks," I say as I wave good-bye. "I may not be here in two weeks," she replies, but there is a twinkle in her eye.

November 25: Norma is flat on her back in bed. She is black and blue, her face and arms covered with bruises. One foot is swollen purple. Spidery black surgical stitches close a gash on her forehead and another on her arm. She looks like Frankenstein's monster. She smiles a little sheepishly. A few nights ago, when her family was out, she fainted in the hall and fell down the stairs. She lay unconscious in a pool of blood until they returned three hours later. She was rushed to Emergency by ambulance and, after a wait of several hours, stitched up. No bones were broken. When the hospital refused to admit her unless she agreed to a brain scan, she insisted on returning home. "I'm *with it*," she told them. Good for her.

Norma seems invigorated by her experience. She is reading, smoking, and talkative. A week later, her stitches are out and her bruises are fading. By Christmas, she's her old self and we are talking about rearranging the furniture in her room. Sue, my predecessor, had suggested this to her earlier, so I volunteer our services.

It would be great to position Norma's bed so she can see out the window. She hasn't been outside for three months. I go to the bank and library for her by myself. We have virtually exhausted the murder mystery resources of the local library and I will have to travel farther afield.

January 6, 1998: Moving day. Norma and I have made a map of where she wants her furniture repositioned. She sits in the next room while Sue and I dust and scrub and vacuum and shove furniture around. Three hours later, Norma can lie in her bed and look out the window. *She likes it!*

A hospice volunteer, I am finding, has to be flexible and adaptable. Our role is ambiguous. We may not be health care professionals, but we have specialized training many professionals lack. Our visits are precisely scheduled and reported on, yet we relate to patients and families as neighbours. We are informal, but we need to be observant. After Norma fell down the stairs, Pat spent her entire visit gently soaking dried blood out of Norma's hair. Norma greatly admires Pat's attentiveness to detail. Hospice tries to improve quality of life, and to avoid enforcing punitive rules and regulations. I don't smoke, but since smoking is one of the few of life's pleasures Norma has left, her smoking is okay with me. The damage has been done, the doctor says, why quit now? When Norma is short of breath, she uses oxygen. It calms her and helps her breathe. Oxygen is highly flammable, and in spite of Norma's precautions, there is a risk that she'll blow herself up with a lighted cigarette. If Norma and her family are willing to live with this risk, however, so is Hospice King.

As a volunteer, I have difficulty with the words "patient" or "client." I like the word friend better, and I have become very fond of this generous, resourceful woman. Over the months, Norma has talked to me about her children, her husbands, the places she's lived, her work as an executive secretary, and her ancestors, one of whom was a colonel in the British Army. Her family story is not that different from my own. We are clannish, proud, and prickly with strangers, devoted to our own. Norma may sometimes feel like a fifth wheel in her daughter's busy, hard-working household, but she has the rare and precious opportunity to get to know and love her grandchildren, and they her. Norma tells me how Alison always comes up to say good-night, and when she had seemed near death, Alison had held her hand and told her how much she loved her. Norma is only a few years younger than my mother would be if she were alive, and by getting Norma's perspective on life, I understand my mother better and appreciate her more. This is Norma's gift to me.

For Christmas, I had brought Norma a potted amaryllis. In mid-winter, an amaryllis bulb produces thick stalks of lush, trumpet-shaped flowers in brilliant shades of reds and pinks. To me it is a symbol of life. I'd bought an identical amaryllis for myself, and put the pot in my sunroom. By February, Norma's amaryllis is three feet tall and each of its sturdy stalks leans over from the weight of six or eight huge blossoms. Mine is a scrawny thing with four puny flowers. They say that hospice care can enable people to live longer, and I'm beginning to think Norma will outlive me after all.

IX

WHEN I WAS TRAVELLING with Larry Librach early in 1997, he was still shaken by the death of a five-year-old patient, Samantha Posen Young, the previous December. Samantha's death had been so difficult for everyone involved that it was spoken about with shudders. I am surprised, then, that in the spring of 1998, Samantha's mother, Robyn, is the guest speaker at the annual meeting of the Palliative Care Council of Toronto. Robyn has to be a brave woman to speak in public about her daughter's dying, and I am glad that a mother is being given a chance to tell her story to a room full of health care professionals. I find it curious too, given the circumstances, that Robyn would be speaking in praise of palliative care.

Robyn, her long blonde curls set off by a dark suit, looks young enough to be Samantha's teenage sister, but her manner is forceful and mature. Choking back tears, she speaks in a voice harsh with an electrifying edge of rage. The trauma, for Robyn, was not Samantha's dying, terrible as that had been, but the ten months of surgery, radiation, and medication Samantha had endured in a futile attempt to save her life. "My baby girl was tortured by treatment," Robyn tells us, and as she itemizes Sam's wounds – lost hair, deafness, blurred vision, loss of feeling in her arms and legs – Robyn tears matching pieces from a life-size paper doll pinned to the wall behind her. The mangled doll represents Samantha.

I am shocked by Robyn's use of the word "torture." Torture is not how we, in Canada, usually describe treatment we believe to be benevolent and life-saving. Don't physicians believe "First, do no harm"? Isn't torture something that happened long ago or at least faraway, in Nazi Germany, Chile, Argentina, Rwanda, Uganda, Iran, Yugoslavia, countries run by dictators and war criminals? Yet Samantha's suffering did sound cruel and unnecessary to me, and I had no reason to doubt Robyn's credibility. She was intelligent and articulate, a special-education teacher and a doctor's daughter. When I ask her to go over Samantha's story with me, she is happy to agree.

I arrive at Robyn's comfortable suburban home to be greeted by a small white poodle she and her husband, Michael Young, had bought for Samantha, and by Robyn, carrying Jaimie, their five-month-old daughter. I notice bright abstract paintings on the walls, and a fading colour snapshot of a blonde little girl in a blue party dress is taped to the fridge door. Samantha is still part of this household, and her artwork, now yellowing with age, is pinned to the kitchen notice board.

"Samantha was the centre of my life," Robyn says. "She was my best friend, my voice, my heart, my soul, my breath." Robyn's marriage to Samantha's father had ended bitterly not long after Samantha was born, and as a single mother, Robyn became fiercely attentive and protective of her only child. She worked hard to give Samantha a safe, loving childhood, and by January 1996, Samantha was a bright, happy four-year-old enjoying her first year in kindergarten. Samantha looked liked her mother, and the bond between them was profound. Robyn and Michael had recently married, and Michael adored Samantha.

On a Tuesday towards the end of January, Samantha was kicked in the face in a tobogganing accident. She was bruised under one eye, and during the next few days she began to walk erratically, her head tilted to one side. By Sunday, her face was gaunt. Fearing concussion,

Robyn and Michael took Samantha to a pediatrician. He found nothing wrong.

"He told us we were crazy," an emotional Robyn recalls. "He said, 'You're paranoid. Even I can't walk a straight line. You're wasting my time.'"

Angry, and not reassured, they took Samantha to a neurologist. He ordered a CT scan for Tuesday. Later that day, he called to say the scan showed "a little brain tumour." Samantha had to go into hospital that night.

"I didn't even know children got brain tumours," says Robyn. "Surprise! I was okay though. I thought that since it was a little tumour, she'd be fine."

Arriving at the hospital with Samantha, Robyn was greeted by a neurologist who spoke almost no English. This upset her, especially since she had to sign forms consenting to Samantha's treatment and surgery.

"The decision-making was left to me," says Robyn. "I was fighting for this little girl's life, fighting for her survival. There were no resources. They gave me a little book to read, but it didn't say what the choices were." Robyn was in no psychological state to comprehend unfamiliar medical literature. "No one came to sit with me and explain any of it," she says.

Robyn didn't get a firm diagnosis until Thursday, when an MRI scan revealed that Samantha had a brain stem glioma. Surgery was scheduled for Friday, and the surgeon assured Robyn he could probably get most of the tumour out. "I was told that after the surgery Sam would be fine, a normal child," Robyn says. "We trusted the doctors. We bowed to them. This thing had smacked us right in the face." During the six-hour operation, Robyn and Michael sat together in an isolated room, crying and praying. "I'm not religious," says Robyn, "but I'm spiritual. When we thought of Samantha having her head opened up, we wanted to die."

Robyn wept with gratitude when the surgeon reported that he had removed a benign tumour, and if any cells remained in Samantha's brain, they would likely disappear. Samantha could expect to lead a normal life, he said, and she could leave the hospital as soon as she was able to walk. Robyn moved into the hospital, sleeping in Samantha's room. Samantha was bright, cheerful and alert, completely herself. She was able to talk and move her hands, and although she couldn't yet walk, she was trying so hard that she was discharged the next week. Robyn was told that some active cells remained in Samantha's brain. Active meant malignant.

"I freaked out," Robyn says. "I asked questions. Is she still going to walk? What will we do? I asked the surgeon, 'Is she going to die?' He stood there laughing, 'No, she's not going to die. She's going to be fine.'"

A month later, Samantha was still unable to walk. The symptoms of brain cancer had not disappeared. "She started going downhill," says Robyn. "I spoke to the surgeon. 'Oh, it's just a little bit of water on the brain,'" he said. "'No big deal. These things fade away.' When I called the hospital, they told me repeatedly, *repeatedly*, that Samantha would be a normal child."

In March 1996, six weeks after surgery, an MRI revealed that the tumour had grown back. It was four times its original size.

A day or so later, Samantha was becoming clumsy and losing sensation on her right side. Robyn and Michael rushed her back to the hospital. The surgeon had gone on vacation, and no decision on treatment would be made until he returned in two weeks.

Haunting the hospital's gloomy corridors, Robyn entered a twilight zone of silence, evasion, and obfuscation. "No one would tell me anything," she says. "The residents would say, 'This is not a good situation,' but we were totally in the dark. They talked around everything. They never talk about *cancer*. It's a secret on the ward. How could I make rational decisions if I didn't know the facts?"

One day, by accident, Robyn learned the truth. She was sitting by Samantha's bed when a doctor abruptly entered the room. Glancing at Samantha's closed eyes, he asked, "Is she breathing?" Startled, Robyn replied that Samantha was sleeping. Why wouldn't she be breathing? "I froze," Robyn says. "I'd figured it out. The doctor *knew* that Samantha was going to die! I fell to the floor. I was hysterical."

Demanding confirmation, Robyn confronted Samantha's physiotherapist. "I need someone to *tell me*," she cried. The physiotherapist wept and admitted yes, Samantha would die. Robyn requested an interview with the oncologists. "I told them that I knew, and I wanted to know what our choices were. I can't live in a fantasyland."

The oncologists told her that Samantha's tumour was "very active," in other words, malignant, and growing rapidly. The treatment option presented was radiation, with the probability of learning disabilities if Samantha recovered. Her chances of survival were 5 per cent. Robyn and Michael opted for radiation. "If you have a chance, you'll try and take it," Robyn says.

Before radiation began, Samantha became semi-conscious. Her brain was filling with fluid, and she underwent emergency surgery to install a drainage tube. After ten radiation treatments, at the maximum adult dose, she was swollen, and vomiting and choking on her food. She had lost sensation in her right hand. The tumour was still growing. Robyn had vivid dreams that Samantha was dying: "I was in a room. I ran to a door where there was a black shape, like a spirit. The door opened and I saw a bright light. I thought, 'Sam is in there. I have to fight to get her out. Let me get her!' I woke up screaming and crying, 'She's going to die! I know she is!'"

Radiation wasn't working, and the radiologist recommended that it be stopped. Robyn agreed. "'Thank you,' I told him. 'Leave her alone.'" Palliative care, called "home care," was discussed, but, at the surgeon's insistence, Robyn and Michael agreed that Samantha would complete her full course of thirty radiation treatments. "We went along," Robyn says, "We were scared to stop." Six weeks after Samantha's radiation ended, the tumour was still growing. Chemotherapy was proposed. Robyn refused to consent.

When Samantha went home, she was bald, bloated, and virtually paralyzed. She had difficulty swallowing, urinating and defecating. She was on a dozen medications to control pain, nausea, swelling, and infection. The most important was a corticosteroid to reduce the fluid buildup in her brain. The steroid had been prescribed early in Samantha's treatment, and as her condition deteriorated, the dose was increased. The steroid was keeping her alive.

Robyn had been told that steroids caused some weight gain and growth of facial hair. She was not prepared for what happened. Samantha became obese. Her hair darkened, her skin turned swarthy, her cheeks puffed up like red rubber balls.

"She looked like a monster," Robyn says. "When I took her out in the stroller, people actually pointed and stared. It was degrading." Samantha stopped looking in the mirror, but she was cheerful and never complained. She tired easily, her speech was slowing down, and her resistance to infection was low. She suffered from pain, nausea, constipation, viruses, urinary infections, and other side effects of cancer, radiation, and medication. Robyn and Michael, who were keeping a twenty-four-hour watch, repeatedly rushed Samantha to the hospital for tests and emergency care. They had both taken leaves of absence from their jobs, but for all their love and dedication, they seemed to be losing their fight to keep Samantha alive.

The surgeon offered a possible explanation for Samantha's deterioration: the shunt draining fluid from her tumour had become blocked. He scheduled corrective surgery for June 25. It was Samantha's fifth birthday. Robyn broke the bad news to Samantha in the hospital. Robyn says: "Samantha ripped the identification bracelet off her wrist. 'Get me *out of here!*' she screamed. 'No more doctors! No more hospital! *Get me out!*'" Robyn, stunned, collected her daughter's things and bundled her into a wheelchair. Robyn realized that there had been choices all along, and that, in desperation, Samantha was making her own decision. Pushing Samantha past the nursing station, Robyn called out, "We're leaving!"

The nurses panicked. Samantha could not be discharged without her doctor's permission. Robyn persuaded the nurses to issue Samantha a pass for the weekend, and on Monday, she brought

Samantha back for a shunt scan. The shunt was working perfectly. Surgery was unnecessary.

"Samantha was right," Robyn weeps. "No more doctors. No more hospital. Let her be. We had been through such a nightmare, we felt like we had been sucked through a black hole."

Samantha was discharged. She would die at home. A sympathetic nurse put Robyn in touch with the palliative care team at Mount Sinai Hospital, and Larry Librach began to spend hours talking with Samantha, Robyn, and her family. He showed Robyn the location of Samantha's brain tumour on an X-ray and carefully explained its fatal consequences. Robyn was grateful. "We should have known the truth from the beginning," she says. "We were owed the right to make the right decisions." Visits from a nurse and social worker were arranged, but Robyn preferred to look after Samantha herself.

"Samantha and I wanted that," Robyn explains. "We were like one person. Michael and I wanted to be left alone. We were feeling such fear, such stress, we didn't want people hounding us. We didn't want to have to take care of *them*. We shut out family members. We shut out friends. They understood."

Robyn made Samantha's life the purpose of her own: "Samantha was so happy to be out of the hospital. We took her to Disney World through the Children's Wish program. We bought the dog. We went to the cottage, went fishing. We drew pictures, played on the computer. I took her to the mall and bought her a new toy every day. We lived *every single second*."

Samantha knew she was going to die.

"She spoke about 'the other side,'" Robyn remembers. "She asked questions. 'Mummy, when I die will you come and visit me?' 'Do animals go to a different heaven?' 'Can I be buried with Sailor Moon?' When she saw Casper the Ghost, she asked, 'How do you become a ghost?'"

Robyn found it difficult to answer Samantha's questions. How do you talk to a five-year-old about dying? She had lost her family's

Jewish faith, and she couldn't find any books to guide her. Parents who talked about their dead children depressed her. "There was no one to help us explain to Sam what was going on," Robyn says. "Nobody understood. We were *alone*."

By October, nine months after her diagnosis, Samantha was very tired. She was losing her hearing and her ability to speak. She had difficulty swallowing. Robyn tried herbal remedies, therapeutic touch, crystals, and prayer, but the tumour was filling Samantha's brain. On October 29, 1996, Samantha made a drawing. It was a round circle like a Smiley Face, except the mouth, wide open, turned down at the corners and two red lines bled from the eyes. Samantha explained it to her mother: "It's a boy with no hair. He's crying. They're red [the tears] because he has a fever. He's sad because he has to have an operation and he doesn't want to. His hair came off. His mouth is open because he's screaming."

Now Robyn fully understood the agony Samantha was enduring. She could bear it no longer. "My only blessing," she says, "was for my precious daughter to die peacefully and quickly." In consultation with Dr. Librach, Robyn and Michael decided to stop the steroid. As fluid from Samantha's tumour filled her brain, she would become unconscious and die.

Robyn, her family, and a nurse gathered around Samantha's bed on the evening of December 4. "We read to her. We played her favourite movie," Robyn says. "I was crying so hard, Sam grabbed a Kleenex and gave it to me. She pulled at my finger and kissed it. She was kissing me good-bye. I begged her to let me give her an injection for the pain. 'Okay, mummy,' she replied."

The nurse gave Samantha an injection of morphine. The family said their good-byes and waited. Samantha appeared to fall into a coma, but Robyn noticed that she could hear everything. As Robyn sat at the bedside, she had a vision of spirits whirling through the room in a wave of light. One seemed to take the shape of Michael's late father, a man she had never met.

"I felt he had come to get Sam," Robyn says. "I knew she was in good hands. It put me at such peace. She would be out of her pain, we would be out of our pain watching her tortured."

Then Samantha went into convulsions. Blood spurted from her mouth and nose, but her heart kept beating. The convulsions went on for hours. "Blood poured out of her body," says Robyn. "There was blood all over the room."

Larry Librach, called at home, arrived at the house at 3:00 a.m. to find the family in terror, the nurse sobbing in a corner, and Samantha still semi-aware. He sedated Samantha, settled the nurse, who should have been monitoring Samantha's sedation and staunching her blood with towels, and, after two hours, had managed to calm the family. Samantha slipped into a coma and died in the early morning of December 5, 1996. "Even after she was dead," says Robyn, "blood was still pouring out of her nostrils."

"It was horrible," says Librach. "I still have nightmares about it. I will never get over it."

Only after Samantha's death did Robyn learn that internal hemorrhaging can be an invisible side effect of corticosteroids.

"It was a side effect of a drug that could have been avoided," says Librach. "Samantha was incurable right from the word go. There was not a chance in hell she would get better. The oncologist was very clear about it." Yet Robyn and Michael, isolated, intimidated, and emotionally distraught, clung to every hope, however faint, that Samantha might recover.

"Conventional medicine is a yellow brick road," Robyn says. "But there's a turn in the road. We made the turn to the red brick road too late." Robyn believes that if Samantha had not been treated following the recurrence of her tumour, she would have died peacefully in her sleep.

"She would have been a whole person instead of a mangled person, a medicated creature, a specimen to be worked on. She was tortured by treatment. They might as well have punched her and beat her.

They beat the daylights out of her. They had no right to do that. They robbed us of life, of time, they robbed us, they robbed her. It's very wrong."

After Samantha's funeral, Robyn and Michael went back to work, trying to emerge from the cocoon of caring and suffering that had enveloped them for nearly a year. Yet Robyn found life hollow. In April she went to see Mount Sinai's family and bereavement counsellor, Michele Chaban.

When Robyn told Chaban the harrowing story of Samantha's death, Chaban helped her see her own positive role in the drama: "It was a very powerful experience for Robyn, trying to save her child. It was futile, and she suffered a great deal. I see that as heroic. There is a lot of wisdom and spirituality in Samantha's story. I think the experience deepened the family. The question is: How do you live with that depth of experience?"

Once Robyn and Michael had defined the underlying issues that had made them so angry with the hospital, they took their grievances to the chief of neurology. He was respectful, and they came away feeling that they had been heard.

"I encouraged Robyn and Michael to act as parents of a child who had died," says Michele Chaban. "They needed to honour Sam's experience. Sam changed the world. The spirit of who she was should continue to be at the centre of the family."

Nearly two years later, Sam's drawing of a rainbow, yellowing with age, is pinned to the wall in Robyn's kitchen. Robyn has two albums of photos of Samantha, many taken when Samantha was grotesquely deformed. As Michele Chaban says: "It wasn't that Sam stopped being beautiful. The family loved her. That love can't be touched."

In the front hall, near the door, hangs a beautiful watercolour, one of many Robyn has painted since Sam died. The background is gold, with darker, mysterious shapes in the centre. A figure in black clothes stands in the foreground, holding a child's hand. They have their backs to us, and smiling figures dance in the yellow sky above them.

Robyn says that it's called *Samantha's Dream*. As she was dying,

Samantha dreamed that her grandfather, an Orthodox Jew, was taking her to heaven. Robyn's painting shows the two of them setting out along a path towards a tunnel that looks like a setting sun. Around these figures, Robyn has drawn Samantha's favourite things: roses, tulips, and daisies, a unicorn flying over a rainbow, children laughing, a swing, and an angel sitting on a cloud. Robyn, without a conventional idea of Heaven, is creating her own. She has also written children's stories based on her memories, and when Sir Paul McCartney's wife Linda died of cancer in April 1998, Robyn sent a copy of Samantha's "screaming face" to the *Toronto Star*, which published it together with Robyn's words: "There is often a belief held by medical doctors, parents, and others that even a child who has terminal cancer needs radiation, chemotherapy, and/or other treatments. This belief is not so. Death, though excruciatingly painful for those left living, can be a blessing. We need to be educated on the realities of cancers. Palliative care, we found, was a wonderful refuge."

The quiet cadence of this letter hints at Robyn's tearful passage, but when she speaks about Samantha's death, as she often does, her fists clench and her eyes blaze with fury. "Yes, I am angry," she says bluntly. "I always will be."

A year later, I have the opportunity to meet Dr. Marcia Levetown, a specialist in pediatric palliative care with the University of Texas Medical Branch at Galveston, Texas, and an outspoken critic of extremism in pediatric medicine. "We are willing to throw anything and everything at children without proof that it works," she says. "Our threshold for continued medical intervention in the face of a poor prognosis is much higher for children and it's wrong. It's magical thinking on the part of the medical profession to believe that we have the technology and the technology is going to make everything better. We can't look at these therapies critically because we want to believe they're 'life-saving.' If technology is available, and there is any hope of prolonging life, we're going to use it, especially on a kid."

Levetown, who began her career as a specialist in pediatric critical care, gives numerous examples of children who, she feels, suffered "avoidable harm" from treatments that held little promise of benefit. "The prognosis for brain tumours is dismal," she says. "Kids do horribly. Yet still we continue. I had a kid who'd had five relapses, yet they were still doing surgery, radiation, and chemotherapy. The radiation had caused the child to have a purple head, blisters, and his ears were cracked and weeping. His dad said to the doctors, 'Please stop doing this.' The oncologist said, 'But I'm killing the tumour.' And the radiotherapist said, 'It's only skin.' Most doctors don't recognize that what they're doing is inhumane. They stop seeing these children as people. We don't think of children having spiritual or existential lives so we need to make them survive because all there is about this child is biologic life and future potential. Parents are often guilty of the same thinking."

We also expect children to endure pain, says Levetown. "Infants are routinely circumcised without analgesia. Infants undergo insertion of chest tubes without analgesia in some institutions. Children routinely have their veins punctured in clinics and hospitals without the presence of parents, psychological preparation, or the use of local anaesthetics. Parents report screaming children being restrained and told to 'toughen up.' Finally, children in most institutions have inadequate treatment of pain related to surgery and cancer."

Recent research disputes the long-held assumption that infants do not feel pain, and that children cry more from fear than pain. Crying, too, was considered a sign of weakness. Children being stuck with needles were admonished to "stop being a baby," or "take it like a man," and a child who blubbered openly felt ashamed. Adults assumed that children forgot their pain. New studies, however, indicate that a twenty-four-week-old fetus can feel pain, infants exposed to long periods of pain may suffer psychological damage, and young adults who have survived childhood cancer can vividly recount their experiences. I clearly remember the pain of having my tonsils out at age five, surgery once routine but now considered unnecessary and potentially dangerous.

"Kids will continue to undergo painful invasive procedures, even though they know they're not helping," says Levetown. "They are trying not to alienate their doctors and parents. Kids want to please. They will sublimate their own needs for the adults who love them. But kids feel powerless. That's why they draw superheroes. They are putting the power they wish they had on paper." Children will also try to protect their parents from grief and suffering.

"Even when severe pain is acknowledged," Levetown says, "practitioners who have the power to ameliorate a child's suffering often do not." Physicians may see pain as an inevitable by-product of treatment, or something too subjective to assess accurately. They may fear that children will become addicted, or that painkillers will kill their patients, although, in the hands of a knowledgeable physician, these risks are minimal. "It is very difficult," says Levetown, "for medical caregivers to acknowledge that they have inflicted unnecessary pain on infants and children throughout their careers. This acknowledgement is a necessary step to embark on change. But it's a message that's very hard to accept and I don't know how to overcome that."

Levetown believes that children as young as three should be involved in decisions about their medical care. "It's an abandonment of children not to speak with them," she says. "At least Robyn listened to Samantha. This is not often the case." If children are too young or sick to say much, they can draw pictures or show their feelings through play therapy. They may express their powerlessness by drawing bold lines and brilliant colours, or if they are dying, they may leave themselves out of a family portrait. An eight-year-old, bald from chemotherapy, poses for a photograph holding two crossed sticks, a skull and crossbones. Robyn noticed that when Samantha drew pictures of rainbows, she placed herself over the rainbow.

Consent, in Canada, is more a question of mental competence than age, and when it comes to making decisions on behalf of children, Levetown points out, they tend to be made in the interests of the decision-makers. As we spoke in April 1999, the example of a

Saskatchewan boy, thirteen-year-old Tyrell Dueck, was causing an uproar across the country. In November 1998, oncologists at the provincial Cancer Centre in Saskatoon had diagnosed an osteogenic sarcoma in Tyrell's right knee. They proposed chemotherapy, followed almost certainly by amputation. Tyrell's parents, fundamentalist Christians, refused. They would place their trust in God and explore alternative medicines.

The Saskatoon Cancer Centre, believing that Tyrell had a good chance of survival with treatment, applied for a court order giving the minister of social services guardianship over the teenager for purposes of consenting to medical treatment. The order was granted in December, and the Duecks agreed to take him to the centre. After two rounds of chemotherapy, the oncologists told the Duecks that if Tyrell's leg were amputated immediately, he would have a 65 per cent chance of surviving. Without amputation, his chances were virtually zero.

On March 1, 1999, Tyrell told his oncologist he didn't want his leg amputated and he didn't want more chemotherapy. The Saskatoon Cancer Centre, which hadn't thought to include Tyrell in its decision-making process, applied to the court again, this time to determine whether Tyrell was a "mature minor" capable of refusing treatment. A court-appointed psychologist, who interviewed Tyrell alone, concluded that his father, Tim, was controlling him and that the Duecks' religious beliefs were keeping Tyrell from the only treatment that could save his life. On March 18, Madam Justice Alison Rothery ruled that Tyrell Dueck was not a mature minor and could not refuse medical treatment. Tyrell would have to return to the hospital to have his leg amputated, and he would receive treatment alone, without the presence or influence of his parents.

The Duecks complied, but Rothery's ruling ignited an emotional debate over medical ethics. "What are they going to do, force him down in order to deliver an anaesthetic and amputate his leg?" asked University of Saskatchewan law professor Ron Fritz. But a *Globe and Mail* editorial intoned: "It takes a village to raise a child. In the case of Tyrell Dueck, the village unhappily finds itself forced by its knowledge and moral duty to intervene profoundly in the care of a child, against the child's will and that of his parents."

Tyrell did have a village, Martensville, and the religious community to which he and his family belonged, yet Judge Rothery had not been persuaded by testimony from a psychiatrist who said that within the context of the Duecks' faith, Tyrell knew his own mind. "Tyrell holds views consistent with those of his parents," said the Duecks' lawyer, Owen Griffiths. "They include a belief that God has or can heal him."

"We need so much wisdom, compassion, and sensitivity beyond belief in dealing with this situation," said medical ethicist Dr. Margaret Somerville of McGill University. "It's a very important question to ask – whether someone would drag this kid into surgery kicking and screaming. Probably the doctor wouldn't do it."

She was right. On March 19, after Tyrell had undergone further tests, the Saskatoon Cancer Centre announced that the cancer had spread to his lungs. Intervention appeared to be futile. Tyrell was discharged from hospital and returned to the medical custody of his parents. The Duecks flew to Mexico for a four-week stay at American Biologics, a treatment centre that prescribes vitamins, apricot pits, and shark cartilage. Front-page news for weeks, Tyrell's case ignited a public debate over patients' rights, the value of alternative therapies, and freedom of religious belief. That Tyrell might have a right to palliative care, medical treatment at home in Saskatchewan that respected him, his parents, and their spiritual beliefs, was not part of this public debate.

"Some kids are chronically dying and we keep dragging them out of the grave," says Marcia Levetown. "Physicians walk away thinking they've done a great job saving this kid's life, but don't acknowledge the suffering they've left behind. Are we really helping these kids?" Among Levetown's palliative patients are drowned children who have been resuscitated and maintained in a permanent vegetative state, and children who are kept alive by ventilators, IV lines, feeding tubes, and cardiac bypass machines long after their spirit and personhood have vanished and their vital organs have failed.

"We've become a culture of feeding tubes," she says, "and the feeding tube has more rights than the child. The child's interests should be *paramount*. I say to my colleagues, 'Did you stop and think when you surgically implanted these pieces of plastic in this kid? Why don't we wait and understand what the family's values are? What the child's long-term outcome is going to be? We should review the child's progress every day and see if he or she is benefitting from an intervention before making it permanent.' There is no ethical or legal reason that we *have* to give nutrition through a tube to a permanently unconscious child who can't suck or swallow. It's natural for them not to get nutrition. That's *natural*."

Disconnecting children from life support is part of Levetown's job as director of the pediatric hospice program at Galveston's Children's Hospital. Mothers who have accepted that their children are not benefitting from medical therapy are often made to feel that they do not love their children, she says. Making the decision to disconnect life support is an appalling responsibility: "Asking people to take their child off a ventilator makes them feel they've killed their child. Prolonged resuscitation efforts in a child with a cardiac arrest predictably lead to this terrible situation. It is unfair to the parents and the child."

When consulted to assist parents to make decisions, Levetown asks them: What does your child want? Why are we doing this treatment? What are the burdens? The benefits? What is your goal? What do you mean by "doing everything"? What is "everything"? Loving parents in your situation have made the decision to stop attempts to prolong life, she tells them. "If you choose this path, no one will accuse you of loving your child any less; in fact, some may even say this is the most loving choice you could make. Whatever you choose, we will support you."

Levetown's Butterfly Program provides what she calls "essential care," intensive comfort measures for the child and emotional support for the family, social work, nursing, spiritual care and hours of her own expertise and undivided attention. Once a decision is made to disconnect life support, the child and family members move into the hospital's Butterfly Room, a fifth-floor suite overlooking the Gulf of Mexico. They have all day to hold the child, cry, say good-bye, and perform whatever rituals they feel appropriate. "There is only one rule," says Levetown. "The ventilator comes off when the sun goes down."

Levetown says that efforts to relieve symptoms can be more "intensive" care than efforts to cure: "There is *never* a reason to say: 'There is nothing more that we can do.' This is the most dreaded sentence of all. Above all, it is patently untrue. Despite our inability to cure or prolong life at all times, we *always* have something to offer, even if it is only ourselves."

Tyrell Dueck died in hospital in Saskatoon on June 30, 1999.

$$\overline{\underline{X}}$$

I SEE JASON GHELANI'S big, beaming smile for the first time in April 1998. Jason has been dead for eighteen months, and he is grinning at me from a colour snapshot enlarged on an overhead projector. Dr. Brian Berger, the family physician who cared for Jason for the last six months of his life, is telling a story he calls "Jason's Journey" to a room full of palliative care professionals at a Toronto conference.

It's unusual for Canadian doctors to talk in public about their patients, even the dead. In England, on the other hand, Dame Cicely Saunders talks about her patients to the point where she has immortalized David Tasma, the young Jewish Holocaust survivor, dying in a London hospital, who gave her the inspiration to found her hospice. Why, during my volunteer training, was I forced to sit through a soppy video drama, *The Last Snowfall*, when I could have seen *The Last Days of Living*, an excellent documentary about dying, featuring real people, made in 1980 by the National Film Board at Montreal's Royal Victoria Hospital's Palliative Care Unit? If telling our stories is something we're supposed to do when we die, why keep the good ones secret? All you need is consent.

Berger has been encouraged by Jason's parents, and speaking in his lilting South African accent, he tells us that for him, Jason's dying had been an emotional, enlightening experience. "It taught me a lot," he says, "about courage and strength and how families can cope." I try to imagine how I would have coped if my son had died of a malignant brain tumour at age ten. This must be an unusual family.

Berger briefly outlines the story. In 1988, when Jason was two-and-a-half years old, surgeons removed a massive tumour from his brain. The surgery, followed by radiation and chemotherapy, was successful, but six years later a new cancerous tumour developed. It was inoperable. In March 1996, doctors gave Jason four to six months to live. Jason's parents, Berger says, made the "very, very tough" decision to refuse further hospitalization and to devote themselves to Jason's comfort and happiness during the brief time he had left. They took the family, including Jason's older brother and sister, on long car trips to Jason's favourite places, borrowed a summer cottage, played games and records Jason enjoyed, read to him, talked to him, bought him toys, and gave him a fluffy miniature poodle he named Cody.

As Dr. Berger speaks, a succession of colourful photos of Jason flicks up on the screen. I see a happy boy holding a stuffed toy, a goofy hat sometimes hiding his baldness – his first treatments had left him permanently bald – an ear-to-ear smile lighting up his face. How could a dying child be so cheerful? "Jason had accepted his illness as part of his personality," Berger explains. "It was a norm for him." But as Jason becomes more emaciated, and his skin turns from cocoa brown to pale grey – his hair had once been a mop of black curls – I notice that his smile seems pinched, his eyes apprehensive.

Dr. Berger tells how Jason's bed had been moved into the family room, which opened off the kitchen, so he could join in meals and be part of the daily routine. After Jason suffered painful seizures and became semi-comatose, family members crawled into his bed to hug, talk, and comfort him. Classical music played constantly. "They did not create Jason as the focus of their lives," Berger says. "Jason was continuously part of the family. He wasn't isolated." At the same time, his parents reassured their older children, both in their early teens, that they too were loved and appreciated.

Jason, in a coma, died at daybreak on November 8, 1996. When Dr. Berger arrived, he found the night nurse and the family gathered closely around the deathbed. "His mother was cuddled up next to the body. I came up and kissed Jason and certified the death. I felt privileged to be part of the setting. It was a wonderful experience we all shared together."

A good death achieved, with wisdom and fortitude, by a typical Ontario family. An inspiration for us all. Jason's mother had taken the photographs, hundreds of them, of her dying son. Berger praises her as a strong, loving mother who, through sheer force of character, kept the family going. She sounds to me like a remarkable person, and I ask Dr. Berger if I could speak to her.

Karen Ghelani lives not far from me, in Richmond Hill, Ontario. She grew up in Regina, Saskatchewan; her husband, Subhash, was among the thousands of East Asians expelled from Uganda by Idi Amin in 1972. Their daughter, Shalimar, was seven years old when Jason was born; their son Devon was four.

When I phone Karen, I ask her why she had taken so many photographs of Jason. "It was one way of reminding myself how sick he was," she says. "It was a way of keeping him alive, I guess. I was preparing myself, mentally." I had anticipated a decisive, take-charge sort of woman, but Karen's low, soft voice sounds sad and reflective. She will be glad to tell me her own version of Jason's story, she says, but she wants to wait until after the summer. It will be emotionally difficult for her to look through her photo albums and diaries again. She needs time.

Jason's story, I realize, is not going to be as simple or as happy as it seems. When I meet Karen in October, I find her gentle, thoughtful, and, almost two years after Jason's death, inconsolable. She sobs brokenheartedly as she speaks, and as I listen, blinking back tears, I begin to understand why.

Jason had been a healthy, easygoing baby. A few weeks before Christmas 1988, when he was two, he seemed to come down with the flu. His pediatrician diagnosed a common viral infection, but Jason became more and more lethargic. Karen noticed that he was walking off-balance and staring fixedly at objects for a long time. "We kept dragging him back to the doctor," she says. "We had this awful sick feeling in our stomachs." When they had a hard time rousing Jason on Christmas Day, they took him to The Hospital for Sick Children in downtown Toronto. Says Karen: "The neurologist put a stethoscope on Jason's head and rushed him off for a CT scan. The tumour was *huge*."

Jason was scheduled for surgery the next day. The surgeon described the tumour and explained the operation to the Ghelanis, but Karen didn't hear much. "I was in shock," she says. "I felt I was in a shell. I could hear people talking, but I couldn't take it in. I had never experienced shock like that before, but I have many times since."

Karen spent the night of December 26 curled up on a couch in the ghostly hospital rotunda. "It was a long surgery," she says. "I didn't think Jason would make it through the night." She had another shock when she saw Jason in the intensive care unit the next morning, tubes and wires coming out of his small body. He was in an induced coma, wearing an oxygen mask, his eyes fixed, dilated and brimming with tears.

"The surgeon told us Jason's tumour was very 'angry,'" Karen says. He had removed only part of it. The remainder would not likely respond to chemotherapy or radiation, and removing it surgically could induce a fatal hemorrhage. Karen and Subhash took turns keeping a twenty-four-hour vigil by Jason's bed. "A nurse told us, 'You're not going to have your little boy back again,'" Karen says. "One day I came into his room and his crib was gone! It was so symbolic. I fainted. *He was gone.*"

Jason had only been taken for tests, and although Karen and Subhash were grieving his coming loss, they prayed for his life. "Even though he was unconscious," Karen says, "we read to him, played his musical toys, talked to him. We were trying to make sure there wasn't an empty space around him, that he felt familiarity." They literally lived in the hospital, their routine driven by medical decisions, their closest companions the shell-shocked parents of other sick children. "You fall off the world," Karen says. "Time ceases." When a biopsy showed no evidence of malignant cells, the surgeon decided to risk a second operation to remove the entire tumour. The operation lasted for hours. "It was *awful*," Karen says. "I had this cold, cold feeling. I walked. I paced. I had to keep moving to stay warm."

The operation was a success. "The surgeon told us it was the biggest benign tumour he'd ever seen," Karen says. "He'd got it all." Ten days later they were told that Jason's tumour was, in fact, malignant and cancerous cells remained in his brain. "The surgeon told us he would not have operated had he known it was malignant," Karen says. "It was a saving grace that he thought it benign." The doctors told Karen that as a result of his surgery, Jason had suffered severe trauma to his brain and nervous system. "They gave no hint of hope," Karen says. "They were frightening."

Jason was scheduled for radiation and chemotherapy. "The oncologist told us that radiation would jeopardize Jason's intellectual potential," Karen says, "but you don't care. You want your child to be alive. If the cancer came back, he would die. You have no choice."

Karen, however, was not prepared for the agony of Jason's treatments: "The IV needles used to sedate him were painful. After chemo, he'd be screaming in pain from nerve damage. These needles, these invasive treatments, are so alien. Your instinct is to protect your child." The Ghelanis took Jason home at Easter 1989. His tumour had disappeared, but he had no immune system. He couldn't run, and walked with effort. His speech was delayed. But Jason was an affectionate, lovable child. His grin charmed everyone. "Jason was always so upbeat," Karen says. "He would make you laugh. He never saw himself as being different."

Jason's family didn't see him as different either, and it was a shock when a psychologist informed Karen, when Jason was old enough for school, that he was mentally retarded. "Cancer can be beaten," she sighs, "but there is no cure for retardation." A special class for Jason was found in a public school, and Karen, a psychologist and social worker before she became a full-time homemaker, decided to take a graduate degree in education. "I wanted to learn how to teach Jason, and children like Jason," she says. "I asked Jason if he thought it was okay for me to go back to school and he said *yes!* He inspired *me*. He still does."

Fevers and infections required Jason to be frequently hospitalized, and in spite of taking hormones, his growth was stunted. "There was always a hope that he'd catch up," Karen says. "Then you have to realize, 'This is the way it is.' It was an ongoing grieving process."

Jason's greatest need, she says, was to have his family around him, and he was happiest when all five of them were squished into a single room in a resort hotel. The Ghelanis took as many trips together as they could afford and by 1995, when Jason was nine, they had evolved into a comfortable, secure, close-knit family. Jason would always have the cognitive ability of a four- or five-year-old, but his cancer had been cured.

In May 1995, Jason was hit by a swing on the school playground. He seemed dazed, and an MRI scan at the hospital revealed a tiny tumour, half a centimetre in diameter, on the side of his brain where he'd had surgery. It was an adult tumour, a malignant gliobastoma, caused by Jason's radiation. The oncologist felt that further treatment would be futile, but she left the decision up to Karen and Subhash.

"I couldn't let it go," Karen says. "I could not live with the guilt of not trying. We had to fight. Jason had the strength." When a six-month round of radiation, followed by aggressive chemotherapy, failed to halt the tumour's growth, Karen and Subhash decided that a stem cell transplant, a drastic treatment generally used for leukemia patients, was Jason's last hope. The Memorial Sloan-Kettering Cancer Institute in New York was willing to fund the transplant as an experiment, but Jason's oncologist, vehemently opposed, tried to talk them out of it.

"We were prepared to take Jason to the States," Karen says. "Sloan-Kettering were saying, 'Go for it!' It was a battle. The oncologist was pessimistic. The doctors were within their rights to have refused, but they left it up to us. The hospital agreed, reluctantly."

Karen and Subhash felt they had made the right choice. They were buying time for Jason, and if he died, they would never have to fear that they might have done more to save his life. But they were unprepared for the toxic chemotherapy that preceded his transplant.

"Now, I'm not comfortable with what we put him through," Karen sighs. "It was brutal, *brutal*. They were horrendous drugs. It looked like Jason's skin was burnt off. We were doing terrible things to our child. But we thought he could get through that, and he did." On March 20, 1996, a day they will never forget, Karen and Subhash were told that Jason's transplant had failed. His tumour was growing. It was untreatable, and Jason would die within six months. If they wished, they could take him home.

"I thought, 'How are we going to get home?'" Karen says. "'How are we going to tell the kids that Jason is going to die?' We put Jason in the back of the car, and on the way home, we decided, 'We are not going to that hospital again.' We would use the time left to provide what Jason wanted, and the best quality time for him was not being in the hospital. So we came home."

Karen had spoken to nurse Maria Martin, head of the hospital's palliative care team, and Martin arranged for the VON to provide home nursing for Jason. When Jason's pediatrician felt he couldn't cope, a nurse recommended Brian Berger, an expert in palliative care. "He wanted to come in early," Karen says, "and I'm glad he did." Among the many difficult issues Berger discussed with the Ghelanis was the need for an order not to resuscitate.

During the spring and summer, Jason was well enough to travel. The family took off in the car to Regina, Florida, Muskoka, and, several times, to Jason's favourite place, Lake Placid, New York. "We couldn't save him," Karen says, "but we could control what we gave him. He depended on us so much. It gave us a purpose." For Karen, however, the strain of giving Jason a happy family life was enormous:

"How do you wake up in the morning and know your son is going to die and find the strength to provide normalcy? Jason *hated* it when we cried. He'd get very concerned. He didn't need that concern. I never talked to him about the fact that he was dying. I have no guilt about that. It would have added a burden. He had no knowledge of death, no fear. He had an inner peace." Jason, Karen says, was her support to get through the day. "If I faltered, he kept us going. That was our momentum, his calmness, his tranquility, his innocence. He had quality of love. He was very secure."

Karen and Subhash set up a double bed for Jason in the family room so he could be close to the stereo, television set, and the kitchen table. Jason couldn't eat much – a feeding tube had been inserted in his stomach – but they got him up to the table for family meals, and on warm days wheeled him outside under the trees. Karen often slept beside him at night. On August 15, Jason suffered a seizure and lapsed into a coma. Karen describes the following ten weeks as one big nightmare.

"Dr. Berger had explained that Jason was living with his cancer. 'You have him here today. He's not dying until he's dying.' That helped energize us. We needed to make sure Jason lived today, and not concentrate on our fear. But living in the present is exhausting. I thought about soldiers in the Second World War facing death every day. How did they do it? That's what I felt, battleworn, in pain. I was numb. And it gets worse."

Dr. Berger and the VON nurses were such a constant, compassionate presence in the house they became like members of the family, but Karen, much as she liked and trusted Dr. Berger, almost dreaded his visits: What does he know? Is today going to be the day? On November 7, the nurse alerted Karen that Jason's blood pressure was erratic. "The nurse knew," Karen says. "She kept upping the morphine. I could see the pain on Jason's face. She kept upping and upping the morphine. I got the kids up about 6:00 a.m. the next morning so they could spend time with him. 'Tell him anything,' I said, 'just be with him.' We all crawled into bed with him. I held him in my arms. His breathing was erratic. 'This is not the way it's supposed to be,' I thought. 'It's supposed to be peaceful.' Jason seemed to be hanging on. I felt my mother's presence. 'Grandma is there,' I told him. 'Go to the light. Don't worry about your mother. Go in peace.' I felt that his body was very hard. He'd gone, he'd left. All I was holding was a hard shell."

That night, Karen dreamed that Jason's body was rising through the air. She tried to hold it down, but it kept rising until it disappeared into a portal of white, pulsating light. "I had such a sense of peace," Karen says. "It was existential peace, a state of grace. Only later, when I saw a white dove, I realized that was what the white light was, a dove." The feeling passed, and Karen still felt Jason's presence:

"Jason loved blowing bubbles. The day he died, a bubble escaped from the dishwasher. It started rising and floating towards the family room. The bubble seemed deliberate, as if it had a goal, a personality. Jason's Tickle Me Elmo doll was sitting on the mantelpiece of the fireplace. The bubble floated up to Tickle Me Elmo and burst. How much meaning do you put in things like that?"

Karen finds it comforting to talk about Jason, although the images of his suffering are as painful and intense as when she was lying with him in his bed. "The pain comes in waves," Karen says. "It's more manageable, but still as strong. My emotions are as strong. Some days, life has no sense. It's such a vacuum. People talk about 'healing.' What does that mean? How can you heal? The images are in your mind. The grief will walk with you. The wound will always be there. You can feel the wound. I will never forget."

One of Karen's worries had been the psychological impact of Jason's long illness on her two healthy children, Devon and Shalimar. Had they felt neglected? Unloved? When I speak to Devon, a tall, reserved high-school student, he chooses his words thoughtfully. "I was just six the first time Jason got sick," he says, "and I didn't understand what was going on. The second time, I was thirteen and I knew he was terminally ill. The most difficult thing was finding out he wasn't going to make it. My parents decided the family would stick together. I agreed. Making Jason happy, making memories, gave us a framework. I was happy with that."

Devon hung out a lot with his friends. He felt "different" having a dying brother, and he didn't talk to them about Jason. His friends cheered him up. "I sort of dealt with it on my own," he says, "but my parents were here for me all the time." Devon also learned from Jason's disabilities. "If I see other people like Jason now, I would not make fun of them. I am wiser." After Jason fell into a coma, Devon found it hard to spend time with him. "I knew it was good to be with him, he knew I was there, but sometimes I wanted to run away. I kept telling myself, '*You have to go through with this.*'" Jason's death had been expected, Devon says. "I remember lying in the bed and feeling down. It hurt a lot, but I just got through it." I ask if there was anything positive for him in Jason's death. Devon is silent for a long time. His face is utterly sad. "I can't think of anything," he says, shaking his head. "There was nothing positive."

Shalimar is three years older than Devon, and she was very close to Jason. She read to him, helped him with school work, played with him, and watched television cartoons with him. "He was dying, and I didn't know what they could do," she says. "I felt resentful that this was happening. I wouldn't see my parents, they were busy, and I couldn't see Jason in the isolation unit. I was losing my brother. I'd never lost anybody before. Sometimes I got mad. I separated myself from my family. School was somewhere I could get away. I had to be independent."

Shalimar thought the family trips were okay, but when Jason fell into a coma she found his lack of response to her stories and songs hard to deal with. "There was no interaction," she says. "I didn't know what to do. I dealt with it on my own. I kept to myself." When Jason died, she says, "I was scared." Shalimar has ambivalent feelings about having lived eight years with Jason's illness. "There are a lot of good memories. I'm glad I spent as much time with Jason as I did. I should have spent more. I should have helped my parents more.

There were more things I could have done for them, and they for me. It has made me more independent, a lot stronger. Now I feel that if other people are going through this, maybe I can help out."

I was puzzled that in his telling of Jason's story, Brian Berger had made almost no mention of Jason's father, Subhash. Yet when I speak to Subhash, I discover that he had been intimately involved in his youngest son's care and in all the decisions about Jason's treatment. At the same time, Subhash had to manage his business and support his family both emotionally and financially. When Jason was in the hospital, Subhash would go to his office from 7:00 a.m. to 3:30 p.m., pick up Devon and Shalimar at school, and meet Karen at the hospital. After the family had dinner together in the cafeteria, Karen, who had been with Jason all day, would take the kids home, and Subhash would spend the night in the hospital.

"I was running on adrenalin," says Subhash. "Tiredness and stress did not come into the picture. Nothing else mattered." Subhash, whose background is in biochemistry, realized the seriousness of Jason's tumour from the beginning, and the more he read about brain tumours, the more apprehensive he became. "When your child is sick, you have fear," he says. "Life cannot be normal. There is insecurity about the diagnosis and prognosis, fearfulness and concern about the other children. You live a guarded life."

Although his own research confirmed the doctors' opinion that Jason's tumour was incurable, Subhash insisted on the experimental stem cell transplant. "We were fighting to grab anything that would come. Jason was a very strong boy, a determined boy, a stubborn boy. It was fortunate that he did not know what was happening to him. He did not understand. It was not a painful procedure for him, but for the family it was torture."

Subhash responded to the news that Jason was dying with a feeling of release. "The fear of death was gone from me," he says. "I thought, 'Yes, it is going to happen now.' There was no more fear. What we had feared was facing us. Now that I see it, I am not scared."

Subhash bears no resentment towards the doctors. "They did

their best," he says. He has no regrets about Jason's treatments: "There was nothing more we could do." Had palliative care been offered as an option at Jason's first or second diagnosis, Subhash and Karen would have refused it. "It would have frightened us," Karen says. "I had to accept the possibility of Jason's death before I could go on." They look on Jason's last eight years as bonus years.

With Jason at home, Subhash felt much more in control. "The decisions were ours," he says. "We are a strong family." The toughest decision was disconnecting Jason's feeding tube as he neared death. The fluid was filling his body, and Subhash is grateful for the counselling provided by Dr. Berger and the nurses. "They were great," he says. "The nurses were guarding us. It was a relief." As Jason's nursing care grew from four hours a day to eight, then to twenty-four, the Ghelani family grew to include Jason's teachers, who came by to see him, and volunteers from Hospice Thornhill who kept Jason company. The kids found having all these new people in the house weird, but nice.

During the last weeks of Jason's life, Karen and Subhash were getting by on very little sleep. "There is no choice," Subhash says. "We can fall flat on our faces afterwards." Since Jason's death, Subhash has had time to grieve his losses. "My belief is wiped out. I don't believe in God any more. I lost a part of my body, like a heart. I cannot talk to people about it. They don't understand. It is a tragedy. I can never overcome this loss."

Subhash confesses that he and Karen have not been able to bring themselves to watch the videos they made of Jason. "On the video, we can see him," Subhash says, weeping, "but we can't touch him." Karen too finds that words of comfort, however well meant, ring hollow. "No death is a good death," she says. "People tell me that Jason has enriched our lives. Yes, we *are* enriched, but we are not the same." Karen pauses, her face flushes. She clenches her fists and cries: "*I don't want to be enriched! I'd rather have my son here!*"

XI

THE SORCERERS WEAR new disguises, but medicine still reflects our cultural, ethical, and spiritual beliefs. Sometimes, however, cultural beliefs clash with medical science. If that happens, what takes precedence? When, after months of prayer and meditation, Lesley and François Paulette of Fort Fitzgerald, Alberta, decided to decline a liver transplant for their infant son, K'aila, they had to defend their choice in court.

François is Dene. Lesley, ancestrally part Mohawk, defines herself culturally as Mohawk. They live an Indian lifestyle in a remote cabin overlooking the Slave River. K'aila, whose name means "willow tip," was born at home in June 1989. He was a little jaundiced, but otherwise a lively, thriving baby. Lesley, however, had a nagging feeling that something was wrong, and when K'aila was still yellowish at three months, she took him to an expert pediatrician in Edmonton, Dr. Adrian Jones. After an extensive series of tests, K'aila was diagnosed with biliary atresia, an incurable, untreatable liver disease. Dr. Jones urged Lesley to have K'aila assessed for a liver transplant and placed on the active waiting list at the liver transplant centre in London, Ontario. Jones considered liver transplants standard and accepted treatment for end-stage liver disease, and he assured the Paulettes that while finding a suitable donor was an obstacle, the survival rate was 80 to 85 per cent.

"My husband and I had an immediate feeling of misgiving and uneasiness," Lesley said later in a speech, "A Choice for K'aila," published in the journal *Humane Medicine* in January 1993. "We had a general and overwhelming sense that it would be an unnatural thing to do. As Native American people, whose cultural and spiritual traditions are steeped in a reverence for the wisdom inherent in the Creator's natural order, we felt we might be committing a grave error if we tried to recreate our son's body. It seemed obvious that, while trying to play at being God, we would run the risk of violating K'aila's spiritual as well as physical identity. I found it deeply disturbing to consider taking out part of K'aila's body, given to him by the Creator, and discarding it in favour of a part of someone else's body, associated with a different spirit. Such a radical intervention in his life, which not only would defy the physical laws of nature but also might disrupt his spiritual path, seemed utterly perverse."

Lesley and François found Dr. Jones unsympathetic to their point of view, and he urged them to agree to a transplant. "We have a responsibility as a society to bring these children up," Jones said later in a television documentary, "A Choice for K'aila," on the CBC series *Man Alive*. "You don't own your children."

Anguished by the certainty of K'aila's death if they refused a transplant, Lesley and François searched for more medical information. Lesley, her hair in a long braid, may have looked like an unsophisticated northern Indian, but she was a registered midwife with a B.A. in psychology from Toronto's York University, and she had been born and raised in Westmount, Montreal, the daughter of an English professor at McGill University, Archie Malloch, and his wife, Barbara. The Mallochs agreed entirely with Lesley's misgivings. Lesley phoned the London transplant centre and spoke with the director, Dr. Calvin Stiller, and Archie researched articles on liver transplants at Montreal's Osler Library. The literature revealed that at American transplant centres, the survival rate was only 70 per cent, and these figures were for one year. After five years, the survival rate was closer to 60 per cent.

If K'aila survived, Lesley discovered, his transplant was only the beginning of a lifetime of chronic illness and drug dependency. "I came to realize that rejection is an ongoing phenomenon," Lesley says. "Without the cyclosporin and the steroids, the body's immune system kicks in again, even years after the operation, and fights to get rid of the graft organ. Immunosuppressive therapy leaves the body vulnerable to a host of viral infections. Chickenpox in a normal child is relatively benign, but it can be fatal to a child on immunosuppressants. The drugs themselves have side effects, including damage to the kidneys, cholesterol buildup, hormonal changes, and neurologic disturbances. The chance of cancer developing increases tenfold. I could not bring myself to coerce K'aila to live. I would be doing violence to him."

What would K'aila want? "It's tough to make a decision on behalf of a baby who is not able to decide for himself," Lesley says. "Either way, the decision is irrevocable. Saying 'no' to the transplant meant that K'aila would die a baby. Saying 'yes' meant that he would live with the consequences, happy or otherwise, of an irreversible decision someone else had made for him. I felt the burden of responsibility for making that decision because of all the people who knew K'aila, I knew him best. I tried as often as I could just to be quiet and to listen to him tell me what he wanted. It was in quiet moments with K'aila that I felt most lucid."

When K'aila was hospitalized for treatment, Lesley slept in his room. One night when K'aila was restless, struggling with the IV line in his foot, Lesley took him out of his crib and brought him to bed with her on her narrow cot: "As he snuggled into my arms and began to nurse, he relaxed and fell asleep. I watched him sleeping peacefully, and it became clear to me what I had to do for him. I imagined him like a butterfly, so beautiful, indeed exquisite, and yet so fragile. With my palm open wide, he had alighted on my hand and now rested there for a few moments, his wings shimmering in the light. I longed for him to stay forever, but I knew that at any time he might flutter his wings and be gone. The only way I could hang on to him would be to close my hand around him, to entrap him in my grasp. I knew that in doing so I would run the real risk of harming him; I might open my fingers again to find his wings broken and crippled, his colours faded and smudged. I knew in that moment that I must keep my palm open and let him take flight when the time came."

Lesley and François felt at peace with their mutual decision to let K'aila live out the remainder of his natural life span, but when Dr. Jones, who considered a transplant essential, insisted that they give a definite yes or no, the Paulettes grew fearful that if they refused treatment they might be charged with neglect. Native children are routinely apprehended by provincial authorities and taken to foster homes, and the Paulettes daily scanned the sky for a helicopter carrying a social worker and an RCMP officer. Says Lesley's mother, Barbara: "I have never known such a period of *dread*."

Lesley and François decided to seek refuge with Indian friends in northern Saskatchewan. They made an appointment with Dr. Jones to give him their answer. They packed their truck, closed up their cabin, and with K'aila and his older brother, Thaidene, drove to Edmonton. They told Dr. Jones they would not agree to a transplant, jumped in their truck, and dashed for the Poundmaker Indian Reserve across the Saskatchewan border.

"I identified with other mother animals who become powerful defenders when their young are threatened," Lesley says. "I felt a tremendous love for my son and, along with it, great pain and sadness when I envisioned that he would be with us for only a short time. Like our ancient warrior grandmothers, we are empowered by a fierce love to become brave-hearted women. I knew in my heart that, if need be, I would fight with everything I had to protect K'aila."

Archie Malloch was alarmed when Lesley phoned from Poundmaker to ask if he knew of a pediatric specialist in Saskatoon. Archie, a volunteer at the Royal Victoria Hospital's Palliative Care

Unit, called its director, Dr. Balfour Mount. Mount referred him to Dr. Richard Hamilton at Montreal's Children's Hospital, and Hamilton recommended Dr. Garth Bruce at Saskatoon's University Hospital. Bruce, easy with the Paulettes' decision, took K'aila on as a palliative patient.

Within weeks, a field worker from Saskatchewan's ministry of social services tracked the Paulettes down to Poundmaker First Nation. Dr. Jones had indeed reported them to Alberta's social services department, and the transfer of K'aila's medical records to Saskatoon had apparently tipped off the authorities as to the Paulettes' whereabouts. Alberta wanted K'aila apprehended and taken into custody immediately, but Saskatchewan insisted on obtaining a court order. The application, claiming that the Paulettes were in breach of the Family Services Act by refusing to provide proper medical care or surgical treatment, sought temporary custody of K'aila for one year to authorize surgery.

From Montreal, Archie Malloch contacted a law professor at the University of Saskatchewan. He recommended a family law specialist in Saskatoon, Henry Kloppenburg. Kloppenburg boned up on liver transplant research, and when the government's custody application was heard in provincial court on April 20, 1990, he intensively cross-examined the government's only medical witness, Dr. Jones. François and Lesley were knowledgeable and eloquent in their own defence, and their evidence was supported by three pediatricians, including K'aila's doctor, Garth Bruce.

"We consciously fought the case on the grounds of the rights of any parent to make the decision we made, given the very uncertain outcomes of organ transplantation," Lesley says. "We chose not to argue the validity of our cultural and spiritual beliefs, or our political and legal rights, as set out under Treaty, to make such a decision for our son without interference from outside institutions. We felt that a Canadian court was not an appropriate place, also not a safe place, to argue those things, especially when K'aila's life hung in the balance. We only hoped we could argue on grounds which the court could understand and give informed consideration."

The judge dismissed the Saskatchewan government's application for custody with these words: "The parents have made a thoughtful and carefully considered decision which is totally within the bounds of current medical practice. A transplant operation of this nature is a difficult, complex, non-commonplace major surgical procedure. The decision of whether to partake in this procedure is not truly a medical question. There is also an emotional, social and psychological component both for the child and parents. The parents have given a much more profound consideration to these other components." The government did not appeal the judge's decision.

Fearful that K'aila might still be apprehended by Alberta authorities if they returned home – the Saskatchewan provincial court had no jurisdiction in Alberta – the Paulettes remained at Poundmaker First Nation. The Saskatchewan department of social services, so intent on K'aila's welfare before the court's decision, took no further interest in the Paulettes.

"In all the time that we were providing care for our son in the last weeks of his life, under the duress of being away from home, with no employment, they never once called to see how we were getting along or if we could use any help," Lesley says. The Paulettes relied on family, friends, and the reserve's social worker.

"In the weeks that followed," Lesley says, "K'aila's body grew weaker and more frail, yet his spirit seemed to grow immense. He had a powerful way about him that touched everyone who met him. Sick as he was, he loved to eat, to 'dance,' and to spend time in the company of good friends. He taught us by example to enjoy each day as it came, and when we became downhearted he uplifted us with his courage and quiet will. In his own way, he reassured us and let us know that everything would be all right."

K'aila died suddenly and quietly at home on May 27, 1990, less than a month before his first birthday. "As he was taken gently from us," Lesley says, "we held him in our arms and talked and sang to him. His brother and many of his friends came and said good-bye. In those moments, I felt the presence of the same power and energy I had felt at his birth. I felt immensely grateful that he had made it through this life whole and that his transition to the next life would be tranquil. In the moment that he left, my heart broke wide open and I experienced a love and a sense of inner peace that I had never known before."

XII

Have you built your ship of death, O have you?
O build your ship of death, for you will need it.

D. H. LAWRENCE WROTE three versions of a lyric, meditative poem called "The Ship of Death" after seeing in a museum a model ship retrieved from an Egyptian tomb. The Egyptians believed that the soul, like the sun, travelled by boat to the underworld, and model ships, or drawings of ships, were included in their grave furnishings. For Lawrence, dying of tuberculosis, the ship of death, an alternative to Charon's crowded ferry, was a metaphor for his own soul's imminent departure:

A little ship, with oars and food
and little dishes, and all accoutrements
fitting and ready for the departing soul.
Now launch the small ship, now as the body dies
and life departs, launch out, the fragile soul
in the fragile ship of courage, the ark of faith

with its store of food and little cooking pans
and change of clothes,
upon the flood's black waste
upon the waters of the end
upon the sea of death, where we still sail
darkly, for we cannot steer, and have no port.

In another version, Lawrence depicts his soul at the oars, rowing across a shadowy, twilight sea towards dark oblivion, exactly as my father used to row across our lake to the far shore. Harry had built his ship of death, many ships, real ships, model ships, enough for us all. He was always happier repairing or recanvassing an old canoe than he was paddling it, although he could paddle well, but I understand now the significance of the rituals. I have read *Treasure Island*, his favourite book. "Fifteen men on the dead man's chest, yo-ho-ho and a bottle of rum!" Blind Pew, Black Dog, the black spot, Long John Silver, bloodshed, murder, corpses, Skeleton Island, a ship-of-death story by a dying writer.

Had Harry met death as a boy and, like Jim Hawkins, escaped? He didn't fish, and he wouldn't go near a gun. I once saw him club a porcupine to death with an axe, and he silenced a nest of raucous young crows by chopping down the tree, but as a kid I was much more bloody-minded: "We deaded 'em, Daddy!" I rejoiced over the crows' corpses. "We deaded 'em!" I loved the satisfying *snap* of the mousetrap. I still do.

Where did psychologists get the peculiar idea that young children have no comprehension of death? I have been on intimate terms with dead birds, bugs, fish, frogs, and crayfish since I could walk. I knew they were dead. My favourite book as a child was Felix Salten's *Bambi*, and I wept over the death of Bambi's mother. In 1947, when I was five, we closed up our cottage on Labour Day and took the early CNR Campers' Special back to Winnipeg. The late train, crammed with families returning home from lakes along the railway's main line, crashed head-on into an eastbound locomotive at Dugald,

Manitoba. The Special's old, gas-lit wooden coaches exploded into flames. Passengers trapped in the wreckage, some of them our friends, were burned alive, their ashes eventually identified by watches and jewellery.

A black steam engine is a death symbol to me. So is a black telephone ringing in the night, my grandmother calling from Vancouver, terrified that we had been killed. Long before Vietnam, when I was ten or so, army helicopters *whack whack*ed over our lake for days, searching for a little girl, a few years younger than I, who was lost in the bush. I was frightened, especially after she was found dead. There were bears and wolves in the bush too. A few years later, our cottage was struck by lightning. The colour of light in this near-death experience was electric-pink.

Michele Chaban uses the phrase "history of harm" to describe our personal psychic baggage of painful, frightening, or traumatic memories. In *The Broken Connection*, psychiatrist Robert J. Lifton calls this kind of memory "an indelible image, an image of ultimate horror." When it comes to experiences of death and dying, some people have a history of much greater harm than others. Lifton interviewed American veterans of the Vietnam War and Japanese survivors of the atom bomb dropped on Hiroshima in 1945. Michele Chaban and Sheila Walker of the Jewish Hospice have studied dying Holocaust survivors in Toronto.

Puzzled that, in hospitals, these elderly, respectable citizens were uncommunicative, suspicious, and secretive to the point of deceit, Chaban and Walker began to perceive the similarities between a modern hospital and a concentration camp. The hospital admission process could be seen as a form of interrogation by uniformed strangers in an alien, antiseptic environment. Patients are issued identity bracelets. Their clothes are taken away, and they are given cheap, identical gowns to wear. They may be subjected to painful surgery and injected with unfamiliar drugs. Hospitals have bright lights and noisy intercoms; ambulances have sirens. Patients must do as they're told. They can't leave.

Dying in a hospital can trigger survival behaviour in a Holocaust survivor incomprehensible to anyone ignorant of the patient's personal history. But since we all suffer harm to some extent, can't the history-of-harm theory be more broadly applied? My father was barely in his hospital room before orderlies whisked away his clothes, which I had washed, to rewash, label, and stow in his closet. Over his indignant objections, they insisted on raising the steel bars on the sides of his bed as if locking him in jail. Whenever I closed the door to his room to give us some privacy, it was opened immediately. Was all this necessary?

The concentration camp – the Indian reserve is an early model – was invented in the nineteenth century at the same time that Canada was building monumental hospitals, prisons, and lunatic asylums. The similarities are obvious, once you look for them. When I visited the remains of the Nazi concentration camp at Auschwitz in 1962, I was sickened by the barbed wire fences and glass cases full of human hair, but the real horror was that Auschwitz, with its chimneys, cobblestone yard, and rows of neat red-brick buildings, looked like a quaint, old-fashioned European factory. The ovens in the crematorium buildings might have baked loaves of bread.

I wonder if Hannah Arendt's phrase "the banality of evil" might be more easily understood as the familiarity of evil. Auschwitz, where hundreds of thousands of Jews, Communists, homosexuals, and other enemies of the Reich were exterminated, was disguised as a factory because the victims were told they would be put to work. The sign over the gate reads, in German, "Work will make you free." The workers' showers turned out to be gas chambers, and if artist Robert Pope was an accurate observer, those gas chambers bear an eerie resemblance to the radiation therapy rooms in modern hospitals.

When he died in a London hospital soon after the Second World War, Holocaust survivor David Tasma left Cicely Saunders five hundred pounds "to be a window in your home." It was Tasma's suffering in Poland during the war as much as his pain from cancer that inspired Dame Cicely to found St. Christopher's Hospice. At the same time, another Holocaust survivor, psychiatrist Viktor Frankl, published a short memoir, *Man's Search for Meaning: From Death-Camp to Existentialism*, that had a profound impact on the way suffering was perceived. Frankl, imprisoned in a Nazi slave-labour camp, writes sparely but graphically about the hunger, cold, disease, and humiliations he and his fellow prisoners were forced to bear, their suffering so extreme he concluded that the meaning of life lies in suffering itself:

"When a man finds that it is his destiny to suffer," Frankl says, "he will have to accept suffering as his task, his single and unique task. His unique opportunity lies in the way in which he bears his burden." The camp inmates, Frankl says, gave up asking about the meaning of life, "a naive query" that presupposed their lives had some value and purpose. "For us," he says, "the meaning of life embraced the wider cycles of life and death, of suffering and dying. Without suffering and death, human life cannot be complete."

Frankl's perception that suffering and dying could be honourable as well as inevitable, a philosophy derived from the Greek stoics and the Old Testament Book of Job, enabled him to keep intact his sense of human worth. *Man's Search for Meaning* inspired post-war generations of psychiatrists, psychologists, and sociologists to investigate death and dying in all its manifestations, including within hospitals, and provided a philosophical, not religious, justification for treating the dying with respect.

Did it take the deliberate, systematic, and brutal murder of six million Jews and other innocent civilians before and during the Second World War to alert us to our inhumanity? We are still struggling to come to terms with the Holocaust, including this country's history of anti-Semitism, but what about the rest of the uncountable millions who have been deliberately, systematically, and brutally murdered within living memory? The history of the twentieth century is a history of harm, and therapists argue that even *hearing* about a catastrophe can be traumatic. Our continuing obsessive interest in two terrible world wars, long after all, or almost all, the participants are dead, suggests the compulsive replaying of a hurtful event characteristic of the "stuck" behaviour psychiatrists call post-traumatic stress syndrome.

Thousands of veterans of both wars suffered from "shell shock," a euphemism for any one of a myriad of psychiatric problems. Thousands more came home haunted by unforgettable images that aroused both pity and guilt. American author Paul Fussell, who served in the United States Army during the Second World War, describes his first encounter with death in his memoir, *Doing Battle*. On November 10, 1944, Fussell, a raw young recruit, spent the night with his company in pitch darkness in a forest overlooking the French city of St. Dié:

> At dawn, I awoke, and what I now saw all around me were numerous objects I'd miraculously not tripped over in the dark. These were dozens of dead German boys in greenish gray uniforms, killed a day or two before by the company we were replacing. If darkness had mercifully hidden them from us, dawn disclosed them with staring open eyes and greenish white faces and hands like marble, still clutching their rifles and machine pistols in their seventeen-year-old hands. Michelangelo could have made something beautiful out of these forms, and I was astonished to find that in a way I couldn't understand, at first they struck me as awful but beautiful. But after a moment, no feeling but horror. My boyish illusions, largely intact until that moment of awakening, fell away all at once, and suddenly I knew that I was not and would never be in a world that was reasonable or just. To transform silly conscripts into cold marble after passing them through unbearable humiliation and fear seemed to do them an interesting injustice. I decided to ponder these things.

Thirty years later, Fussell, an English scholar, published *The Great War and Modern Memory*, an analysis of how the letters, memoirs, and poems written by British servicemen created a common memory, or myth. This literature, with its angry, cynical tone and charnel house imagery, made Tennyson's "The Charge of the Light Brigade" as obsolete as the cavalry itself.

Like Britain, Canada sent artists to the front during the First World War. Most stuck to painting ruins of churches and fields of crosses, but F. H. Varley painted the dead. The first human corpses I laid eyes on were two large oils by Varley on display at the National Gallery in Ottawa during an exhibition of works by the Group of Seven in the 1960s. Expecting the usual colourful scenes of Algoma and Quebec, I was stopped dead in my tracks by *The Sunken Road*, a subtle, delicate landscape of mangled soldiers sprawled in a mass of rubble, their bodies blending with the earth. In the second, a gravedigger stands in a sea of muck behind a farmer's cart piled high with bits and pieces of khaki-clad human flesh. Varley called it, *For What?* To his wife, Maud, he wrote:

"You must see the barren deserts war has made of once fertile country, see the turned-up graves, see the dead on the field, freakishly mutilated, headless, legless, stomachless, a perfect body and a passive face and a broken empty skull, see your own countrymen, unidentified, thrown into a cart, their coats over them, boys digging a grave in a land of yellowy green slimy mud and green pools of water under a weeping sky."

The modern image of ultimate horror is the mushroom cloud of the atom bomb. We have lived with The Bomb for fifty-five years, and in spite of the collapse of the Soviet Union and the end of the old Cold War, the threat of nuclear extinction has not diminished. Progress towards disarmament has been made among the super-powers, but all kinds of unstable little countries have, or may have, The Bomb. We live in the Valley of the Shadow of Death, but as Robert J. Lifton argues, no one seems to know, or care. He interprets our blithe indifference as a common response to terror. We "domesticate the ultimate," he says. Act as if nothing is wrong, pretend it's not there, keep busy, don't worry, be happy, have a good day. He calls it "nuclear numbing," a frenetic, escapist response to a threat we can neither face nor escape. As atomic scientist Robert Oppenheimer watched the first fiery cloud mushroom over the Nevada desert, he understood its meaning: "Behold, I am become Death, destroyer of worlds."

XIII

I HAVE BEEN RUMMAGING through the scraps of my cultural inheritance much as I used to play with my mother's sewing basket, making patterns of images as I once did with bits of cloth. I have read *The Iliad*, *The Odyssey*, Virgil's *Aeneid* and Dante's *Inferno*, and I have realized that the Roman Virgil drew his Stygian imagery from Greek poetry, myth, and drama, and Dante, centuries later, drew on Virgil. Their accounts of Hades, Tartarus, Hell, differ in detail – Virgil's, with its swamps and monsters, is by far the most frightful – but they are so vividly imagined and share so much in common they create a cumulative myth that lies at the root of all western culture. In his notes to "The Waste Land," a modern poem about death I know well, T. S. Eliot acknowledges, among other literary and mythic influences, the *Inferno* and Frazer's *The Golden Bough*.

I am reading too about ancient Norse and Celtic spiritual beliefs. It appears to be myth that the Norse sent their dead chieftains out to sea in fiery ships. But in "The Ship of the Dead," her essay in *The Journey to the Other World*, English archaeologist and anthropologist Hilda Ellis Davidson quotes an eyewitness account of the cremation of a Scandinavian ship on the Volga River northeast of the Black Sea in 920 A.D. Ibn Fadlan, an Arab diplomat, was visiting the king of the Bulgars when he encountered a party of Scandinavian merchant-warriors who had come there to trade. During Fadlan's stay, a Norse chieftain died. His ship was pulled out of the water onto a wooden platform or pyre, and his body laid out amidships on a silk-covered couch under a canopy. Two horses, two cows, a dog, a rooster, and a hen were slaughtered and their bodies placed in the ship. According to Fadlan, the Scandinavians travelled with slave girls as concubines, and one of the warrior's slaves volunteered to be killed to provide a wife for him in Paradise. She was stabbed and strangled at the same time, a ritual, Davidson says, associated with the cult of Odin, and the sacrifice was presided over by an old woman called the Angel of Death. The ship was set alight, and it burned to cinders within an hour.

According to Fadlan's account, the dead man was equipped for a journey to a green and beautiful world where he and his ancestors enjoyed all the physical comforts of an earthly existence. The slave went willingly to her death, convinced that she would enjoy a wife's status in Paradise.

The most astonishing thing about this story is that the Scandinavians were trading with Arabs on the Volga River. The Rus, as they were called, appear to have made their way south from the Baltic Sea along the rivers, carrying furs and fair-skinned slaves to trade for silver, jewellery, spices, and silk. More than a thousand years ago, my ancestors, depicted in English and Wagnerian stereotype as fat, hairy barbarians swathed in animal skins with funny-looking horned helmets, were in contact with all the ancient civilizations of Europe and the Mediterranean basin, and, through them, with Africa, Arabia, India, and the Far East. Their wealth may well have come more from trade than plunder, and since cultural baggage is light and portable, they would have taken home as well stories, legends, and religious beliefs.

They buried their dead in boats, the humble in scows and dugout canoes, the poor with a few ship's boards thrown over them, the prototype of the coffin. Kings and chieftains were buried in sea-going ships that were dragged ashore, lowered into pits, then covered with mounds of earth. Excavation of a royal Bronze Age ship buried at Sutton Hoo on the east coast of England uncovered, in addition to the corpse's bronze and gilt armour, a purse containing forty gold coins. The ship had forty oars, and the coins may have been payment to the forty ghostly oarsmen who would row the king on his last voyage.

Now that I have read Ronnie Terpening's *Charon and the Crossing: Ancient, Medieval and Renaissance Transformations of a Myth*, I understand why the old geezer popped into my head as my dying father's tour guide. Charon is ubiquitous in myth and literature, and he has been hiding in my memory since I learned smatterings of Greek mythology in school. My image of Charon is not the grey ferryman of the livid marsh with red wheels of flame about his eyes, who chides Dante's horde of damned souls weeping and wailing on Acheron's dismal shore, nor Virgil's filthy ferryman with his scraggy beard, leaky boat, and rough manners, but the jocular ship's purser Charon of Aristophanes' comedy *The Frogs*. Hurry in, Charon says. Step in. Who's for the rest from every pain and ill? Who's for Lethe's plain? Who else for the boat? Be quick. *The Frogs* was first performed in 405 B.C., but Charon sounds like a Canadian train conductor. " 'Board!"

In *The Frogs*, Charon ferries his passengers across a marshy lake full of singing frogs who chorus *brekekekex, ko-ax, ko-ax, brekekekex, ko-ax, ko-ax* in time to the oars. An underworld with frogs chorusing in praise of Dionysius sounds like a wonderful place to me, and the dead who had been wise, good, and brave in life rest in the pleasant meadows of the Elysian Fields. Ronnie Terpening traces Charon back another three thousand years to Egypt, where the dead were ferried across the Nile River from their towns and cities on the east bank to tombs and burial ground in the arid, rocky west. The image of Charon standing in the stern of his boat, an oar or pole in his hand, is derived from the dhows the Egyptians used to ply the Nile. The Norse ship funerals imitate the Egyptian practice of placing the body amidships, under a canopy, with jars of food and drink for the journey.

In her investigation of Bronze Age Scandinavian rock carvings on the shores of the Baltic Sea, Hilda Ellis Davidson has studied images of ships dating back to 1600 B.C. These carvings may commemorate battles, voyages, or religious ceremonies, but the singular thing about them is the ships' shape. At a time when fishermen in the Irish Sea, if they dared put out to sea at all, were puddling about in coracles, stubby little boats made of wickerwork covered with animal hides, the Scandinavian carvings show a crescent moon with bow and stern riding high out of the water. These carvings, prototypes of the Norse dragon boat with its billowing sail and carved animal-head prow, look like the ships the Greeks might have sailed to besiege Troy.

Contact between Scandinavia and the people of the Mediterranean may have predated the tenth-century encounter on the Volga by more than two thousand years. At Simrishamn on the southern tip of Norway, a Bronze Age stone tomb, unearthed in the eighteenth century, was carved with elegant, stylized images that have been found nowhere else in northern Europe. The images – double-bladed axes, a cauldron, rows of female figures – do, however, resemble the more detailed and realistic iconography on a sarcophagus found in Crete dating back to 1600 B.C. Before they suddenly and mysteriously disappeared about 1300 B.C., the Minoans, their island strategically placed between Egypt, Greece, and the Near East, were, for centuries, famous seafarers and traders. In *The Ancient Celts*, British archaeologist Barry Cunliffe speculates that between 2000 and 1300 B.C. there may have been a thriving trade in gold, wine, oil, furs, tin, cloth, and precious stones between Crete and the British Isles.

One carving on the tomb at Simrishamn depicted a crescent moon-shaped ship, and Cunliffe is among the archaeologists who wonder if Bronze Age Mediterranean ships, sailing west through the Gates of Hercules, never to return, may have created the myth of the Hesperides, nymphs, who, with their dragon, guarded a garden of golden apples on a mythical western Island of the Blessed.

Scholars have speculated that the golden apples were Spanish oranges, and that Hades was Spain's Atlantic port, Cadiz. As exploration advanced, Hesperus eventually became the dead King Arthur's English island, Avalon.

Frescoes recovered from the ruins of Minoan cities on Crete show buxom, bare-breasted women with long curly hair, images archaeologists interpret to be priestesses in temples dedicated to a fertility goddess. The figurine of the goddess, wearing a long, layered skirt, her bare breasts bulging forward from a tight jacket, is sometimes rendered with snakes, birds, and animals. In *The Woman's Dictionary of Symbols and Sacred Objects*, Barbara Walker argues that the double-bladed axe, or labrys, was a ceremonial sceptre associated with the goddess's shrines. The labyrinth, or house of the double-axe, was home to the legendary Minotaur, a blood-thirsty half-bull, half-man that Walker believes represents the sacrifice of bulls at the ritual marriage between the king, Minos, and the goddess.

Hilda Davidson notes that at some sites in Norway, women, with female companions, were buried in boats. Since this was a sign of high social status, Davidson believes that they may have been priestesses at a shrine sacred to a goddess, and she interprets Lewis Carroll's *Alice in Wonderland* as a rare example of a woman's descent, down a rabbit hole, into the underworld. Alice has been part of my mystical life since I could read, and in Terpening's introduction to *Charon and the Crossing*, I find a brief, puzzling reference to a similar story told in Mesopotamia more than three thousand years ago, a descent to the underworld by a Sumerian goddess, Ishtar. I have a hunch that Ishtar may be the guide I have been looking for. I will seek her out, and since this is Canada, not Mesopotamia, I will scout the landscape for the best place to make my own final descent.

XIV

HOW WE DIE IN Canada is largely a function of where we die. Some hospitals have hospice or palliative beds and wards, many do not. Some regions have teams of pain- and symptom-management consultants, others don't. A directory published by the Ottawa-based Canadian Palliative Care Association lists nearly six hundred hospice and palliative programs across Canada, but the list includes regional health centres, long-term care institutions and private nursing agencies that may or may not have palliative specialists. A lot of agencies talk about "comfort care" or "support care." I have learned to be wary of the word "comfortable," and these ill-defined phrases may cloak minimal, non-medical care.

Not every hospice is listed in the directory, and while a committee sponsored by the CPCA has been working for years to achieve a consensus, I am shocked to discover that Canada has no nationally accepted standards of practice for hospice or palliative care. Unless they are affiliated with a hospital or accredited health care centre, community hospices are independent charitable corporations that raise their own money, sometimes with government assistance, and run their own shows. They are not medically licensed, inspected, or accredited. There is no universal format for care, and they are not accountable to anyone beyond their own governing boards. Every hospice is different, and their programs change.

Community hospices arose in response to the medical establishment's failure to care adequately for the mortally ill, and since they reflect their communities, hospices tend to be jealous of their independence and individuality. Canadians generally think that hospice is a good thing, but fragmentation has left everyone baffled about what a hospice actually does. Doctors may be leery about referring patients to a service whose reputation depends solely on self-reporting and word-of-mouth, and knowing somebody who knows somebody who knows is how people tend to find out about hospice and palliative care.

Unlike Great Britain, where hospice was successfully championed by many prominent, influential physicians, hospice in North America developed as a volunteer, consumer-driven service largely organized and dominated by women. Hospice, a philosophy and practice, was labelled a "movement," a counterculture word that conjures up images of hippies, feminists, and civil rights demonstrators. In Toronto, June Callwood, writer, social activist, hospice volunteer, and founder of Casey House, partly fits this image, but it certainly doesn't apply to the hundreds of nuns, nurses, doctors, social workers, clergy, and homemakers who have organized home care for the dying as an act of community compassion.

Hospice is not alternative medicine. It places more emphasis on medical care and nursing, and less on complementary therapies such as meditation, diet, and journalling than cancer-patient support centres. Oncologists, however, readily refer cancer patients to support groups, and not to hospice. I can understand how doctors might see hospice as an expression of patient power and a rival model of care, but why are they so reluctant to refer patients to fellow physicians who specialize in caring for the dying? The unwillingness of doctors to refer patients to hospice and palliative care is, by far, the biggest single reason that care for the dying remains a largely unknown "underground" medical service.

Michele Chaban believes that responsibility for marginalizing palliative care within mainstream medicine rests with the doctor most praised for bringing dying out of the closet, Elisabeth Kübler-Ross. For seven years, Chaban studied Kübler-Ross's life and work for her Ph.D in thanatology from the University of Wales, and she discovered an untold story.

Chaban knew when she began her research in 1990 that Dr. Kübler-Ross wasn't the pioneer she had portrayed herself to be in her famous 1969 book, *On Death and Dying*. Cicely Saunders had been writing and speaking about the needs of the dying since 1957, and in working out her five-stage theory – denial, anger, bargaining, depression, acceptance – Kübler-Ross had access to the work of many others, including two ground-breaking books, *Awareness of Dying* and *Time for Dying* published in 1965 and 1968 respectively by sociologists and co-authors Barney G. Glaser and Anselm Strauss. Glaser and Strauss had described patients' responses to the news that they were dying as "depression," a reaction that was followed by a struggle between "denial" and "acceptance." Acceptance, they observed, tended to be interpreted as a death "acceptable" to the family and medical staff.

Chaban, unimpressed by *On Death and Dying* when she had first read it, read it again with a critical eye. She noticed, tucked away at the end of the book, a diagram depicting ten, not five, stages of dying, including shock, partial denial, preparatory grief, hope, and decathexis or "letting go." The diagram contradicted Kübler-Ross's own five-stage theory, and suggested to Chaban that Kübler-Ross had borrowed it from someone else. Kübler-Ross had never published her own research or revealed the scientific method she used to develop her theory, and she had closed her research centre and retired to Arizona. Chaban's letters to her requesting an interview went unanswered, then an assistant responded to say Elisabeth's poor health – she had suffered several strokes – made an interview impossible. Kübler-Ross's practice of omitting dates and names, or using only first names, initials, and pseudonyms in her published accounts of her work, made it impossible for Chaban to verify her sources or corroborate her research.

In 1993, facing a dead end, Chaban was making conversation with a group of American chaplains at a conference when one of them casually asked what she was working on. She spoke of her difficulties with Kübler-Ross's theory. "Oh, it's not her theory," someone said. "She got it from Carl Nighswonger, the chaplain who ran the death and dying seminars." Incredulous, Chaban listened as they told how Nighswonger, a professor in the University of Chicago Divinity School as well as a Billings Hospital chaplain, had organized the seminars and interviewed patients jointly with Kübler-Ross. The immediate goal of the seminars was to teach chaplains how to prepare patients to receive the news they were dying, and it was Nighswonger who had proposed a staging theory as a way of inter-preting how patients reacted to discussing death. Nighswonger, who continued the seminars after Kübler-Ross abruptly left the hospital in 1970, died suddenly in 1971.

Chaban confirmed the story by contacting chaplains who had taken part in the seminars at Billings Hospital, and when she read Nighswonger's own theory of stages – he called them "dramas" – she saw a striking similarity to the ten-stage diagram in *On Death and Dying*. The seminars had been started before Kübler-Ross had arrived at the hospital, and she was a relatively junior member of the team. In *On Death and Dying*, Kübler-Ross took personal credit for what had been a collaborative effort.

Then Chaban discovered that as early as 1980, George Fitchett, a professor in the department of religion, health, and human values at Chicago's Rush University, had published an article pleading "It's Time to Bury the Stage Theory of Death and Dying." Stating that "not one distinguished investigator in the field agrees with Kübler-Ross's findings," Fitchett traced staging theories – shock, false hope, despair, rebellion, bitterness, acceptance – to psychologists working with patients in rehabilitation in the 1950s. He speculated that the ideas of rehabilitation psychologist Dr. Beatrix Cobb had been introduced into the death and dying seminars by Carl Nighswonger. Fitchett wrote to Kübler-Ross, then in California, asking her if she had been influenced by Cobb. Kübler-Ross replied that she knew nothing of Cobb, and that she had developed the stages from her earlier work with the parents of multiple-handicapped, retarded, and blind children.

In *On Death and Dying* Kübler-Ross describes walking hundreds of miles through hospital corridors seeking, in vain, a dying patient. "I set out to ask physicians for permission to interview a terminally ill patient of theirs," she writes. "The reactions were varied, from stunned looks of disbelief to rather abrupt changes of topic of conversation; the end result being that I did not get one single chance even to get near such a patient." Kübler-Ross portrays these doctors as arrogant, deceitful, and heartless, but Michele Chaban has a different view.

At the time, Kübler-Ross was a tiny, middle-aged Swiss immigrant who spoke with a thick German accent. She had no specialized education in psychiatry, and no reputation for scientific research. Reputable psychiatrists don't scrounge for patients, and hospital physicians didn't refer patients to her because the dying weren't crazy. Her habit of stalking the corridors at night earned her the epithet Angel of Death. Some called her the vulture.

Physicians avoided Nighswonger and Kübler-Ross's death and dying seminars, but by 1968 they were attracting standing-room-only crowds of student nurses, theologians, and psychologists, who watched from an adjoining room through a one-way window. Not all of the patients interviewed, recruited by chaplains from a pool of "potentially terminal" prospects, understood that they were dying. Kübler-Ross was a skilful interviewer, and if an unsuspecting patient chattered on about cheerful things, she quietly dropped the word "death" into the conversation or asked, "Do you ever think about dying?" If the patient seemed frightened or upset, she changed the subject, only to return to it a few minutes later. Her grim game of cat-and-mouse made the tension almost unbearable for the hidden spectators, who knew the truth.

At the time, one member of the divinity school, Dr. Nathan Scott, condemned young seminarians who "pounce on the anguish and suffering of helpless people." Today Scott says of the interview method: "I found it unspeakably coarse, too ugly for words." Since the seminars were educational – the patients were told they were "teachers" – issues about privacy and exploitation didn't surface until Kübler-Ross invited *Life* magazine to do a photo story. The heartbreaking pictures of a dying young leukemia patient, Eva, smiling, while nurses, observing behind the one-way window, wept, created a public sensation. Kübler-Ross, encouraged that *Life* had broken the silence around a taboo topic, began, without hospital authorization, to arrange interview sessions with dying patients in front of television crews. When the interviews were broadcast, some of their relatives, who had not known the truth, became distraught, and the hospital was held responsible for breaching confidentiality.

The chaplains, who depended on relationships of mutual trust, refused to refer any more patients to Kübler-Ross. With the hospital furious at her, and her application for tenure rejected, Kübler-Ross had no choice but to resign. But *On Death and Dying* had made her a celebrity. She lectured widely and started a popular private practice, but, as the years passed, her therapeutic cocktail of mysticism, rage, group therapy, emotional bonding, and unconditional love did not enhance her reputation as a medical doctor. To their dismay, doctors and nurses who tried to move their patients through Kübler-Ross's five stages discovered that her theory didn't work. Patients who failed, or rebelled, died with feelings of anger and guilt, or retreated into silence.

Michele Chaban's theory of the history of harm includes the influence of Elisabeth Kübler-Ross. "The only attitudes towards dying Kübler-Ross's work tells us about are her own," Chaban says. Chaban believes that Kübler-Ross isolated the dying from their doctors, distorted and medicalized the complex, individual process of dying, and convinced a gullible public that she had vanquished Death. Only recently have researchers in palliative care woken up to the fact that modern medical practice has to be based on hard evidence, not emotion or anecdote, and that as long as palliative care is perceived as squishy science it will lack credibility. The medical term for death, however, is "bad outcome." The problem for palliative medicine is that since death is its only outcome, success has to be measured by standards other than mortality rates.

The difficulty I face trying to explore the options of where to die in Canada is that I have nothing but rumour and opinion to guide me. I decide to incorporate a hospice visit into my travels, wherever I may go. My first opportunity is during a trip to Ottawa in late October 1997. Linda Lysne of the Canadian Palliative Care Association recommends a visit to the Hospice of All Saints at 18 Blackburn Avenue. All Saints is noted for its day hospice program, and Diana Fowler LeBlanc, wife of Canada's governor general at the time, Romeo LeBlanc, is its honorary patron. I am a little dubious about the saints, but a humble hospice with vice-regal patronage is worth looking into.

Hospice of All Saints invites me to visit its day hospice on Thursday, but my first stop is ApoptoGen Inc., a research program affiliated with the Children's Hospital of Eastern Ontario on the outskirts of Ottawa. Here, scientists George Robertson, Robert Korneluk, and Alex Mackenzie have discovered a way to prevent brain-cell death in rats who have undergone the experimental equivalent of a stroke by treating them with a neuronal apoptosis inhibitory protein. The implications for human stroke victims are positive, but my interest is in apoptosis itself.

Greek for "falling leaf," apoptosis (a-pop-to-sis) means cell suicide. Scientists have been aware for years that cells reproduce and die, but, Alex Mackenzie says, "we'd always assumed that the cells had died by necrosis, a violent death. The realization in the last decade is that cells can methodically settle their affairs, parcel themselves up, and slip off this mortal coil. The unobtrusiveness of the process is what has kept the blinders on us for so long. We are seeing for the first time the centrality and ubiquitousness of programmed cell death."

Mackenzie and his partners call it a Darwinian model. "Those cells which make the most fortuitous and appropriate connections will receive the feedback to go on and live, and those that don't will die a programmed death. It's a microcosm of natural selection ensuring a functioning organ. Dying is intrinsic to birth. It's essential."

Each human cell is composed of a genetic centre and eighty thousand proteins, the cell's worker bees. Mackenzie imagines the human body as a battlefield, with our proteins exchanging continuous barrages of conflicting life and death signals. "Cells that deviate too far from the norm will trigger apoptosis," he says. "It's a morality play." Malignant tumours are caused by cells that have lost their ability to commit suicide, and while there is evidence that estrogen and growth hormones can slow the aging process, Mackenzie questions the ethics of creating a dismal society like the immortal Struldbrugs Swift describes in *Gulliver's Travels*. Freud's theory of the death wish appears not to have been so theoretical after all, and our unconscious mind may merely be our body talking to our brain. If the mind can influence the body, as the inner healers contend, why shouldn't the reverse be true?

Hospice of All Saints occupies the former manse of Ottawa's All Saints Anglican church, a handsome red-brick house in the fashionable Sandy Hill district. Its only drawback as a hospice is that its steep front steps are hard to climb. In winter, patients, driven here by volunteers, have to use an electric lift in the garage. The door from the lift opens into a warm, cosy kitchen where chef Deborah Hebert is brewing coffee and setting out freshly baked cookies and muffins.

The hospice is already crowded when I arrive shortly after 10:00 a.m., and as I look around at all the beaming faces and listen to the laughter, I feel at a loss. Who is dying here? I can't tell the patients from the volunteers from the nurses. Everybody is wearing woolly, comfortable everyday clothes. No pyjamas or housecoats. No IV poles. No smocks. No name tags. No uniforms. No oxygen tanks. No beds. Charlotte, a huge, fluffy golden retriever, pads up to sniff my ankles. I might have stumbled into a neighbourhood brunch.

This is exactly the effect Barbara O'Connor, the hospice's executive director, strives to achieve. Day hospice at All Saints is not a drop-in centre, a support group, or a therapy session. Open two days a week, Tuesdays and Thursdays, from about 10:00 a.m. until 2:30 p.m., the hospice provides its guests, a word that seems more apt than patients, with an opportunity to get out of the house, enjoy company, paint, play cards, have a manicure or a whirlpool bath, and consult the staff nurse about medical or emotional troubles. In turn, the hospice is able to monitor patients who live alone or in difficult circumstances. Family members may drive patients, but they are not allowed to stay. Day hospice is their chance to go shopping, see friends, clean the house, grab some sleep. Each day hospice can accommodate up to fifteen patients, and, like any good hostess, Barbara O'Connor tries to get a compatible mix. Once admitted to the program, patients are expected to attend hospice every week.

Most of them, it seems, would come every day if they could. So would I. Sitting in comfortable sofas and armchairs in front of a crackling fire in the living room, men and women of all ages gossip, catch up on the news, or sit, eyes closed, and listen. Volunteers pass coffee and snacks or we help ourselves from the trolley. A tall woman in red walks through the room quietly playing a small harp she holds cradled against her chest, pausing occasionally to play for individual patients. This is Ruth Charles, a social worker and harp therapist. I find it a bit macabre to have a harp at a hospice, but the harp's plaintive, soothing chords are beautiful.

At 11:00 a.m., the group disperses for cards, drawing, foot massage, or rest and meditation. The group includes one volunteer for every two patients, but apart from the occasional summer outing on the Ottawa River, no events are organized. Activities reflect what the patients feel like doing. If they feel like doing nothing, that's fine too. Nobody is drawing today, and I'm not a card player, so I join the

Fresh Air Club on the back porch. Hospice of All Saints has nothing against smoking, as long as you smoke outside. It is bitterly cold, but Susan Smith, the nurse coordinator on duty, hands out tuques, mitts, quilts, and afghans. Sitting on lawn chairs, bundled up like refugees from some quixotic country, we huddle around the faint fire of glowing cigarettes.

I have never smoked, hard as I tried as a teenager, and it grieves me to know that these women are likely dying of cancer because they do. They're not feeling sorry for themselves. They smoke aggressively, defiantly, and they appreciate day hospice for allowing them to do this *together*. The conversation, in brief, goes something like this:

Jane: "Cancer is a very isolationist disease."

Bea: "You lose some of your friends. They don't know what to say, feel embarrassed. I didn't want a support group. Support group and treatment I don't need to hear. Here, you can go up to new people. Nobody sits around bemoaning the fact that they're sick. If you've got real problems, see a staff person. Don't dwell on it. Forget the outside world."

Zoe: "I love the camaraderie. I've been coming over a year. At first it was very overwhelming, so many giving people in one place at one time! In the outside world, you'd bump into one once in a while."

Bea: "I'm not in remission, but I'm not as sick as a lot of people here. I wonder, am I taking someone else's place? But I can make them laugh, and I need their support."

Zoe, smiling, with a nod towards Bea: "She's *so* obnoxious, very outspoken."

Bea: "I call a spade a shovel. Zoe was so down the first day she came I said, 'Get a life.'"

Zoe: "She has a head on her shoulders. I used to be very independent, very strong. I thought, 'What's happened to me? It's time to revert back to living. Start thinking about yourself.' Being sick is like becoming a weak female. Everybody has to help you. You leave yourself open to *predators*. Things changed drastically after I started coming here and I'm a hell of a lot better off."

Danielle: "Zoe, you listen, you *see*. It's very important that we listen and hear what people are saying."

Bea: "I listen better since I became ill."

Danielle: "We are all vulnerable."

Zoe: "My home has been invaded by my daughter's boyfriend and I'm not dying until things are back on track. Don't think about pain, puking all the time, there are other things to think of. People ask, are you afraid of dying? No, I'm not. It's either utopia or nothing. I've made my will, planned my memorial service, written my obituary."

Justine: "If you're a single, senior woman nobody pays any attention to you. I had my knee replaced twice. The second time, the doctor says to me, 'Maybe you should start slowing down.' He refers me to a specialist in ortho-oncology. Uh-oh, I think. The specialist does not tell me I have cancer, but I know. He refers me to a doctor near my home. I go in to see what's up. 'I assume you've been told you have bone cancer,' he says. 'No, I haven't.' You play the game, the patient game."

Bea, inhaling: "I want to go to Australia, but I can't smoke on the flight. I'm quitting soon."

I enjoy the company of these wry, entertaining, hospitable women so much I forget that I'm cold and breathing second-hand smoke. We speak English, but Danielle and Justine are francophone. Hospice of All Saints was founded by the church in 1987 to care for dying parishioners, but in 1992 it incorporated as a non-denominational service available to anyone in the Ottawa-Carleton region with a terminal or life-threatening illness. The hospice serves forty to forty-five home-based patients at any one time, plus another twenty to thirty families in bereavement follow-up. It pays full market rent for the manse.

At 12:30 p.m. we shed scarves, mitts, and matches to come in for Happy Hour. Wine, imagine! The house is filled with delicious aromas. Deborah Hebert is a cordon bleu cook, and the dining room table is set for lunch. In the centre, a lighted candle surrounded by clay figures with joined hands represents the hospice's motto, A Circle of Caring. Beside the candle is a colour photograph of a hospice patient who had died that morning. He wasn't well known – he'd come only two or three times – but it isn't unusual for a patient to go home from day hospice and die. The mood becomes more sombre.

Lunch is a savoury soup, a salad, and a light dessert. Conversation is lively, but by 2:30 p.m. we are all tired. The volunteers, mostly men, arrive to take the patients home. As they go down the lift, they glance back, already looking forward to next Thursday. I'm sorry I won't be here.

The day hospice is free for the thirty or so patients who attend once a week, but it costs the hospice $40 per patient per day, a total of $64,000 a year. Nearly half is the nurse coordinator's salary, and Susan Smith has worked hard today. Bringing together fifteen physically and emotionally fragile people for hours of intensive interaction requires planning, concentration, a calm demeanour, and constant, unobtrusive vigilance. Susan helps create a mood of good cheer – patients say her smile alone cheers them up – but she tries as well to have a serious conversation, however brief, with each patient during the course of the day. Special attention is paid to newcomers – Bea took me under her wing – and to people who seem depressed or upset. I am impressed by the attention to detail – fine china, wine served in glasses, not plastic, the aroma of woodsmoke from the fire – and the pervasive, reassuring feeling of *control*.

This feeling of control is strongest when Barbara O'Connor comes downstairs from her office to say hello. A small, shy, plainly dressed woman with an open, Irish face, Barbara has run Hospice of All Saints since the beginning, and she is fondly reputed to run it with a will of steel. A nurse with twenty years' experience in palliative care and case management, O'Connor insists on professional standards, and out of the hospice's total annual expenses of $258,000, $185,000 is spent on staff salaries.

"We *need* standards," Barbara says. "People come to me and want to start a hospice. Anybody who has a good feeling can call themselves a hospice. Hospice isn't hand-holding. If you insist on the principles of palliative care, they get defensive. I get so frustrated. Without standards, it's very injurious." All Saints originally intended to build a free-standing hospice, but abandoned the plan as financially unfeasible. As it is, to operate its day hospice, home support program, bereavement follow-up, and caregiver support group, the hospice works hard to raise enough money to meet expenses. Most of the revenue comes from private citizens and memorial donations, foundations, and fundraising events – the hospice employs a full-time resource development officer, Megan Doyle – and only $57,000 from government. This suits Barbara O'Connor. A hospice too dependent on government funding runs the risk of being swallowed by the health care system that failed the dying in the first place.

O'Connor's hospice philosophy and practice is based on integrated, intensive, hands-on care. Not only is the patient served by a multidisciplinary team, but the hospice itself is run by an interdisciplinary advisory team that includes, beyond Barbara, medical and spiritual consultants, the bereavement coordinator, and the two nurse coordinators, Susan Smith and Diana Conner. Each week the team monitors the status of the forty to forty-five patients on the hospice caseload.

"There is a lot of inadequate physician support for patients in the community," Barbara says. "We are an advocacy organization. If our patients are not getting the right care, we go to their doctor, to their case manager, and advocate for them. If the doctor is removing himself, we find another doctor *immediately*." O'Connor doesn't hesitate to criticize professional caregivers if she believes they are doing a bad job. When one hospice patient, a child, was in pain, Barbara called the child's doctor. Nothing happened. She insisted on a patient conference. The child's VON nurse became upset. "I got into trouble with the VON," Barbara says calmly. "I had my knuckles rapped, but I would not change my behaviour in any way."

Hospice volunteers report in after every visit and attend monthly volunteer meetings. They go through a twenty-hour, ten-week training course which, because the group is small, allows for more questions, reading, and discussion than the lectures I attended. As a student nurse, O'Connor chose to specialize in care for the dying after Elisabeth Kübler-Ross spoke to her class. "I was inspired by her compassion," Barbara says, but she uses Cicely Saunders and Derek Doyle, founder of St. Columba's Hospice in Edinburgh, Scotland, as her models.

Anyone can refer a patient to Hospice of All Saints, including patients themselves, but they must be assessed by the home care nurse coordinator and, if accepted, sign an advance directive refusing resuscitation. The directive offers a choice between two levels of care: home care with no transfer to hospital, or transfer to an acute care hospital if symptoms so indicate. Patients can, and do, move back and forth from home to hospital.

Hospice of All Saints has a good relationship with the Ottawa Civic Hospital, and it has on its board Dr. John Seely, a former dean of medicine at the University of Ottawa and a senior physician with the university's Institute of Palliative Care. In addition to undertaking public education and medical research, the institute's physicians serve the Elizabeth Bruyère Pavilion, an in-patient palliative care unit run by the Sisters of Charity. This forty-five-bed facility is intended for the terminally ill who cannot be cared for at home, or whose symptoms are so severe they need institutional care. Dr. Seely is also instrumental in setting up a pain and symptom management consulting team for eastern Ontario.

Ottawa looks to be a good place to die, but for all its vice-regal patronage, excellent medical connections, innovative programs, and enthusiastic citizen support, Hospice of All Saints struggles to survive. "We don't get the referrals," Barbara sighs. "We don't have the resources to educate the public, so we don't meet the need that's there. We're just scratching the surface." O'Connor, like many others in hospice and palliative care, believes that hospice should be part of an integrated continuum of treatment and care introduced as soon as a patient is diagnosed with a potentially incurable disease. Hope for the best, but prepare for the worst: if the patient recovers, great, but if hospice is available, it can be used as soon as it's needed. No one would ever have to hear again the dreaded words, "There is nothing more we can do."

XV

I DIDN'T EXPECT my journey to the underworld to take me to Rideau Hall, the governor general's residence in Ottawa, but here I am on a dark October afternoon the day after my visit to Hospice of All Saints. Diana Fowler LeBlanc, unstuffy and approachable, is willing to tell me the story behind her personal commitment to hospice and palliative care. Wives of governors general are usually expected to be seen and not heard, but Diana, as I'll call her – this is a family story and she avoids "Her Excellency" whenever possible – has made short radio broadcasts, spoken at conferences and visited the dying in hospices across the country. Tall, straightforward, and articulate, Diana has a degree in social work from McGill University. With her long neck and flyaway hair, she reminds me of Alice in Wonderland in her elongated phase, and the aides-de-camp padding about in gold braid would be at home at the court of the Queen of Hearts.

Diana's story is about Mary, her nanny, who remained in the Fowlers' Montreal home as a companion to Diana's widowed mother after the five Fowler children were grown. "Mary, a young woman who had recently arrived from Scotland, came to our family when I was born," Diana says. "She stayed to raise all of us. She was always there for us, never sick, never complaining, never judgemental or critical. She saw us through bruised knees, bad dreams, broken hearts, failed exams, good and bad marriages, childbirth, all those transitions which are painful and difficult to achieve without help. She provided that help. Meem, as we called her, was the rock in our family. I knew her far better than I knew my mother."

In November 1994, when she was eighty-one, Mary, her abdomen swollen, and vomiting continuously, was rushed to the Royal Victoria Hospital. Surgeons removed a malignant tumour, but cancer had spread throughout Mary's body. She was transferred to the intensive care unit, and the Fowler children, told she was dying, rushed to her bedside to say good-bye. Diana was angered and upset by what she saw. "Mary had a catheter, a colostomy bag, an IV, nasal tubes, tubes everywhere. Once, when a tube came out, she was told she had to learn to get it back in. She was confused and humiliated. The surgeon had zero compassion. He talked about her above her head. She was very frightened."

Differing opinions about Mary's care caused friction within the Fowler family. Diana found the ICU intolerable, and her sister Robin from Vancouver, knowledgeable about hospice, was adamant about referring Mary to the Royal Vic's palliative care unit. The sisters sought out Balfour Mount, toured the facility and registered Mary. Once Mary's pain and nausea were under control and her tubes unhooked, however, Mary made up her own mind.

"She wanted to go to Victoria to be with her brother and his family," Diana says, "and she was determined to be there before Christmas."

On December 17, Diana accompanied Mary on the long flight from Montreal to Vancouver. Mary beamed in triumph as the plane descended over the Pacific Ocean. She had nearly made it! Robin took over on the short relay flight to Victoria, and stayed to help Mary find a place to live. They chose a retirement home that provided some nursing care, congenial company, and freedom to come and go. Robin registered Mary with Victoria Hospice, a home care and in-patient hospice based at the Royal Jubilee Hospital, and the hospice referred Mary to a Scottish physician she loved. Mary's nephew and his wife took charge of her care.

"Mary went shopping, choosing her own curtains, sheets, and towels in colours she wanted," Diana says. "She went to restaurants and movies, cooked some of her own meals, went for drives. She was free and enjoying every moment. It was marvellous for us to see her so happy and finally mistress of her own existence. She went through her papers, made her will, and began to express things she had felt but could never articulate." One day, Robin found Mary undressing in front of the window. "I've been undressing in the closet for eighty-two years," Mary said. "I'll undress where I want to." When Romeo LeBlanc was installed as governor general in February 1995, Mary phoned Diana to say how proud she was of "my children." Says Diana: "Palliative care gave Mary hope. She experienced a spiritual, physical, and mental liberation."

On February 24, Mary began to suffer pain and confusion. She was taken to the Royal Jubilee Hospital and transferred to the hospice pavilion. Robin, her favourite child, kept vigil with Mary's relatives as her condition deteriorated. Robin memorializes Mary's dying, and living, in a lament, "Meem."

Your breath on my face. You are leaving. Unlike the dark breath I have seen in death before, yours is sweet and cool as it labours. You offer it to me as if to transfer your very essence. I breathe it in to calm my pain, drawing this strength deep into my own being where I can keep it forever. You are leaving. It is so. I cannot hold you, cannot keep this saint who nourished me so long. I cannot cry out to the white coats and have them reverse this departure. You have reached an end.

My heart races to match the thready beat under my fingers. Your heart pushes little into these cool arms. This thread hangs on for hours so we might be together, like this, as you go. We, your earthly charges. I stroke your head, your arm, offering my presence in this family ritual of comfort that never included you. Hours ago, you asked for my touch to distract you from this strange new pain that descended. Your need for comfort, hope. You, who ask for nothing. "Here's my guardian angel, she'll make me better." And now I am unsure where you are. I trust that my touch takes you to a better place, quietly assuring that I am with you always. I force a steady voice as I speak softly, telling you we are here. We, your charges. My being fights words that allow you to leave. I long for you to stay, to continue this freedom we have lived for weeks. Two months of power removed. Of time alone, and together. Having broken away, fearless. An ending consciously realized, actualized, more vital than ever imagined. Such joy I saw in your eyes, heard in your voice. We escaped.

And now you are leaving. I'll be back. My soul silently screams and cries, begging you not to leave, clutching at this centre of my emotional universe. Your hand reaches to my face that your vision has lost. You grasp my cheeks, my hair. Trying to make sense of this enormous change, this final experience. I see the transfer takes time. A process. You pull at the air with furrowed brow. Your world is no longer there. You are leaving.

And your breath rages on with deep, regular strokes. So much work for this body. I continue to breathe in parts of you not yet absorbed. A gift. In random moments, you emerge to speak, a soft, toothless voice, barely discernible. "She's gone back to the Old Country, to Scotland." I am comforted, as you want me to be. My heart races on. I wonder how long your breath can hold on to this body, this life, this little girl who sits in agony beside you.

"Weren't we having an old-fashioned kind of chat?" Careful nurses drift in to offer relief from pain, to allay the anxiety that they know to be a part of this journey. They read your brow, your movements, your thoughts, and know well of this tortuous path. For six hours you have worked since that moment when I saw you grow clammy and distant, when I ran to the nurses, in denial, demanding that they lower the doses of the drugs that were clearly too high, insisting that they be reduced so that you were not threatened by their force. They met me with kindness, with words that challenged my refusal to see that . . . you are leaving.

I briefly emerge from this trance, this dance where time disappears, where life and death blend, where enormous questions find the simplest of answers. I become acutely aware of my own cramped body as I lean into yours, your cool arm, watching your pale face. I must stretch these limbs to gather strength to remain by you. Rising briefly from the dance, lifting my fatigue, my despair, my disbelief, I stand slowly, always holding your familiar smooth hand. Panic darts across my mind with the thought of this long moment of labour ending. In this instant, you sense my movement away. As if a signal. Your breath immediately responds, changing to the shallowest gasps that stop short in your throat. No longer labouring, this new effortless salute continues only for seconds. My heart races. My own breath stops.

You are gone.

The dying too, lament. During a visit to the Elizabeth Bruyère pavilion earlier this week, I met Dr. John Scott, director of the Ottawa Institute of Palliative Care. Scott, a Presbyterian minister as well as a pioneer palliative physician, has listened to many laments, and he ponders the phenomenon in an article, "Lamentation and Euthanasia," published in *Humane Medicine* in 1992:

> The lament is both a literary motif and a psychologic
> pattern, both an individual and communal response to pain

and death. Lamentation is seen in all cultures of the ancient and modern world and across all socioeconomic groups. The lament I hear on my patients' lips is a cry of the spirit, a passionate expression of total pain. Depending on cultural restrictions, it issues forth with tears and moans and intense, urgent emotion.

The lament begins as a repetitive description of the sources of suffering, a listing of complaints lamenting the past – unfulfilled dreams and relationships, regrets and guilt – the present – physical pain, loss of function and role – and the future – impending death, family's future distress. It is a cry of fear and anger and despair. The cry may be addressed to God or family or doctor, but often it is a diffuse moan. This is the verbal overflow of an inner struggle, an agonizing process of finding meaning in the midst of suffering. The lament is a plea that begs for help, for relationship, for deliverance. It is a cry that begs us to come closer.

Commonly the lament includes a cry for death, which is phrased in a variety of ways – "I would be better off dead," "I wish I were dead," "I can't go on," "Let me die," "Help me to die." In western cultures, the social demand to control emotion often leads to hidden forms of nonverbal or symbolic lament such as withdrawal, increased physical pain or vomiting, dreams, exaggerated anger or grief. Whether hidden or expressed, the lament contains a cry for death in a complex mix of horror and longing.

Yet the lament is not a cry of depression and suicidal ideation. Suicide is rare among cancer patients even when strength and means for it are available. Despite its frequent repetition of the word or symbol for death, the lament is a cry for life. Its emotional content demands and invites human relationships. When death forms a central part of a lament, ("I want to die,"), the health care system is in danger of misinterpreting this cry. When a patient cries out for an end to suffering, that person is not requesting a euthanasia consent form. The cry does not declare a consumer's choice and demand a bureaucratic and clinical response. In fact, the lament invites us to affirm life.

What about *our* lament? As healers in the presence of suffering we, too, lament. When we hear our patient's lament we may experience false guilt and view the suffering as our responsibility to resolve through clinical action. When drugs or surgery cannot relieve the complaint, we may contemplate death as a treatment. Instead, we must learn to listen to lament, resonate with its pain but not feel driven to frantic action.

Yes, we struggle. As we watch suffering and listen to lamentation, we may be tempted to cry out for death on our patient's behalf. We should not suppress the urge to share our patient's lament and shout our own. Yes, cry out, even cry out for death, but reject the temptation to kill. Hear the cry for life at the heart of the lament. Do not respond presumptuously to the pain by silencing the one who issues the cry.

In the face of suffering we must learn to listen and wait. As we wait, paradoxically we become a new source of hope and life for the one who suffers, both through our professional skill in comforting and in our personal commitment to share the lament. In the face of imminent, irreversible death, our vocation is to wait, not only for death, but until the lament of life has come to completion.

How many of us love to quote, or misquote, Dylan Thomas's famous lines, "Do not go gently into that good night, rage, rage against the dying of the light," yet, as Scott suggests, we tend to react to this display of raw emotion with anger, fear, and disapproval. Few of us want to have anything to do with someone else's suffering, and if we regard lamentation as cowardly, manipulative, disruptive, an intolerable burden on the listeners, the impulse to silence it may be irresistible.

Scott gives us permission to lament, and I find this comforting. If I were facing imminent death, I'd find keening and raging more appropriate than brooding over my past, performing a list of tasks, or composing myself, like John Donne, into a corpse-to-be. Sure, my lamenting would be hard on those around me, but hell, they get to hang around later, for a while. I'll load lamentation into my little ship of death, and before I die, since I'm unlikely to die in Ottawa, I'll look for a music therapist who plays the harp.

XVI

IT'S 10:00 A.M. on a Saturday morning in mid-January 1998, and I'm in an almost deserted parking lot on the outskirts of Victoria, British Columbia. Ten or twelve people stand around, bundled up against the chill, and as I get out of the car, a big woman layered in sweaters comes up to me, arms outstretched. "Hospice Hug!" she cries, and crushes me in an embrace. I hear the cry, "Hospice Hug," as other newcomers arrive, and after several more breathtaking bear hugs, I realize that this is the standard greeting for Victoria Hospice's Walking Group for the Bereaved.

My hosts this morning are the group's coordinators, John and Claire Tomczak. This is the second marriage for both, and their romance blossomed when they took part in an earlier walking group for the bereaved. Today's group includes three or four more volunteers; the others are recent widows, widowers, or adult orphans grieving the deaths of their parents, all of them people Victoria Hospice feels could benefit from fresh air, friendship, and exercise following a death.

This morning we will walk for about an hour through a park – the location varies every week – then drive to the nearby home of a volunteer for coffee, conversation, and a snack. John emphasizes that the walking group is *not* a support group. There is no professional counsellor in the crowd, and while individuals may share their personal stories of loss as they walk, they are not to bring them to the group during coffee hour. Men in particular tend to feel uncomfortable blabbing in public about their private lives, and widowers often lose the informal social networks their wives had created. When John Tomczak's first wife, Colette, died, he discovered that all the friends he thought were his, were hers. It's always good to get out of the house and *do something*, and in Victoria, walking, like gardening, is a healthy, enjoyable, year-round activity.

Once we set off, the walk turns out to be more of a stroll. We can go only as fast as our slowest member, and the purpose of the walk is to give people a chance to get to know each other. "The program is very simple," John says, "just friends out for a walk on a Saturday morning in beautiful surroundings. The idea that nobody will offer advice or ask questions works wonders. I was in walking group number four, and I am still playing bridge with those I met nine years ago."

The concept was brought to Victoria Hospice in 1986 by Beth McLean, who had started the first walking group in the community in 1980. The hospice organizes three groups a year, and each group walks together every Saturday for eight weeks. The volunteers then withdraw, encouraging the group to choose a leader and continue on its own. Many do, and new groups may bump into hospice veterans who have been walking together weekly for years. If a group disintegrates – its purpose, after all, is to give its members the security and strength to carry on with their own lives – walkers left stranded may join another group.

Friendships are encouraged, and marriages are not uncommon, but John and Claire are alert to the possibility that a freewheeling mixed group of emotionally vulnerable people could be exploited. An elderly man once marched into the hospice's Saturday night drop-in crowd and announced in a ringing voice, "Well, I'm here to find my new wife!" He may have meant it as a joke. However, a seventy-five-year-old retired executive in Ontario has told me with pride that six weeks after his wife's death, before he had buried her ashes, he had introduced himself to a fifty-five-year-old widow in a hardware store. He married her within six months.

We walk through a Japanese garden, the azaleas and rhododendrons bloomless but beautiful in their winter foliage. The sea air is bracing, the company cheerful. "In the world, it's so confrontational, so competitive," a young widower tells me. "Here, it's warm and accepting." John Tomczak had had to call this man repeatedly to persuade him to join the walking group, but now, as well as the walking group, he belongs to a group that goes out for dinner together on Friday nights. "I'm a changed man," he smiles.

"I find it hard to mention hospice to my friends," a widow confesses. "I feel like the death's head at the feast. Friends have died on acute care wards. It's a terrible experience, but people are putting blocks up in their minds about hospice. They are not hearing it."

This is only the group's third walk, and people are still shy with each other. The walk was stimulating, but when we join up for coffee and cake, the atmosphere feels strained. There is a wide discrepancy in ages, from college kids to octogenarians, and I wonder if some of the people here might prefer a Coke, beer, or a glass of wine. Two young women would like to talk about the deaths they have recently experienced, but given the mandate of the group, they have been discouraged. I sense that it's hard for them to find anything else to talk about to people who are so much older, and to whom they would naturally look for parental, or grandparental, wisdom and solace. People preoccupied with a death find it hard to talk about anything else, and if the group can't acknowledge the elephant sitting on the table, what is the polite thing to say?

Victoria Hospice offers more traditional bereavement alternatives to the walking group – potluck suppers, card games, barbecues, drop-ins, home visits by volunteers, and personal professional counselling. I love to walk, but I wonder if I would fit in to a Victoria

Hospice Walking Group. I walk fast. I am impatient with small talk, and to tell the truth, I hate being hugged by strangers. What's wrong with a big, friendly, welcoming hug? Am I antisocial? Snooty, snobby, standoffish?

I brood about this fault until, when I'm thinking about something else, a word from the movie *Rob Roy* floats into my consciousness. *Backstabbing*. Rob Roy had a reputation as a backstabber, and in the Scottish Highlands, backstabbing meant embracing your enemy in a big, friendly, welcoming hug as you drove your dagger between his ribs. It occurs to me that I may be alive today because my Highland ancestors hated hugs. I am carrying my own history of harm around with me, in my gut.

On Monday morning, I visit Victoria Hospice in the Richmond Pavilion at the Royal Jubilee Hospital. Founded in 1980 as a pilot project by the British Columbia government and the Victoria Association for Care for the Dying, Victoria Hospice has a reputation for excellence and innovation. Public education is a big part of its mandate – it has a speakers' bureau – and the hospice's nurse educator, Fern Anderson, will be my guide.

The hospice's seventeen in-patient beds are on the third floor of the Richmond Pavilion, an attractive old Art Deco building across a quadrangle from the hospital itself. A cancer clinic is next door. A convenience certainly, but I will have to ask how many dying cancer patients ever make that short trip down the hall.

The lobby of the pavilion is shabby and cluttered. Why must hospitals leave buckets and mops, commodes, garbage bags, and trolleys piled with towels sitting around in the corridors? Why do they leave the doors to their storerooms open? Why must the walls be painted blech blue, antacid pink, or bile green? Don't they understand how depressing this all is? Maybe that's why – they don't want people to hang around.

I take the elevator to the third floor. The door opens, and lo!

Sunlight! Big windows. Pale, off-white walls trimmed in dark teal green. To my left, a small, pale quilt with an appliqué of two intertwined Celtic circles, the hospice's Circle of Care logo, hangs on the wall. To my right, an open, carpeted lounge with sofas and chairs, an upright piano, card table, books, magazines, and children's toys includes a kitchen area equipped with a fridge, microwave, and coffeemaker. A tray of muffins sits on the counter.

People are cautiously inching up and down the hall with walkers and wheelchairs. They must be patients, but they're dressed in sweatsuits, slacks, sweaters, blouses, street clothes, *their* clothes. Alert, athletic women in cotton drawstring pants, baggy shirts, and Reeboks stride swiftly ahead with a sense of purpose. They must be nurses. *Nurses without uniforms.* Where am I? A sports club? Spa? The only discordant note is the volunteer who's making coffee, a man wearing a turquoise blue smock.

Fern Anderson, forthcoming and informative, takes me on a tour. Seven of the hospice beds are acute care. These patients are actively, imminently, dying. The other ten are long-term care beds for people who cannot get proper care in remote communities up Island or in their own homes, if they have homes. One resident is a homeless young woman with multiple incurable illnesses including psychiatric problems and AIDS. Long-term care facilities in Victoria's Capital Region refuse to admit people with AIDS. Victoria Hospice does admit them.

As well as offices for the executive director, three staff doctors, volunteers, counsellors, including a Spiritual Care counsellor, and a conference room, the hospice has a small, quiet solarium, private consulting rooms, a vented smoking room, and a meditation room that can be used as a chapel. Victoria Hospice isn't about to deprive smokers of one of life's last pleasures, and an old man is in there now, furiously puffing away. He has just been admitted, and he's agitated. The meditation room is empty. I can understand why. One entire wall is covered by a painting of roiling yellowish clouds in a thunderous blue-black sky. It was a gift.

With an annual budget of $3.7 million, Victoria Hospice has to raise more than $1 million a year to supplement the $2.5 million it receives from the provincial government. Sandra Richardson, the hospice's manager of fundraising and community relations, has come up with ingenious ways to do this – auctions and golf tournaments, a Swimathon that brings in $100,000 a year, planned giving, appeals for memorial donations and bequests – but donors like to *see* where their money is going.

Last year, she was able to raise $350,000 in three months to build a rooftop garden for the hospice pavilion – "Everybody wants to buy a bench for the garden," she says – but almost all the hospice's budget is spent on staff salaries and benefits and physicians' fees. Some families like to memorialize the deceased by donating a lamp, a chair, a stained-glass window with a plate attached, "In memory of . . . ," but gifts create clutter and the visible presence of too many ghosts has a gloomy effect on the living. The stained glass makes me think of churches and funerals, but one colourful glass panel over the window at the end of the hall shows a small white boat with a billowing sail surging through a bright blue sea against a backdrop of snowcapped mountains. A rainbow, improbable against the blue sky, reminds me of the rainbow in Varley's *The Sunken Road*.

Two-thirds of the six hundred people who die every year in the care of Victoria Hospice do not die here. They die at home. Facilitating a death at home is the hospice's primary goal, and beds in this unit tend to be used in emergencies or to give patients a temporary residence while their families get some respite from care. After eighteen years at the Royal Jubilee Hospital, the hospice floor is still called Death Row, but in fact patients are encouraged to leave if they're feeling well and able to manage at home. Today, a man carrying a small black dog has come to take his wife home in a wheelchair. She grins from ear to ear. He wheels her into the elevator, still smiling, the dog cradled in her arms.

"We're not a dumping ground," mutters Dr. Jim Wilde, a grizzled hospice physician whose uniform is a brown tweed jacket. Dr. Wilde and hospice medical director Dr. Michael Downing have to be vigilant that terminal patients from acute care wards are not kited over to the hospice floor without the patients' consent. One surgical patient, wheeled in, took one look at the stained glass and candles, and said, *Where the hell am I?* Heaven may look like Victoria Hospice, but nobody had told him he was going there.

Victoria Hospice serves 20 per cent of the people who die in the Capital Region district of Victoria every year, including two-thirds of the cancer patients and more than half the AIDS patients. It is spectacularly successful by Canadian hospice standards, serving two to four times the estimated average number of hospice patients, but where are the other 80 per cent? Who knows? Most of Victoria Hospice's referrals come from provincial home care nurses, with whom the hospice has a strong working relationship, but while the nurses consider a third of their patients to be palliative, not all access hospice.

Part of the reason is the patients themselves. They may be cautious about an organization that has a "churchy" connotation – the word hospice is still associated with religious orders – or suspicious of a medical service that seems peripheral to their hospital or cancer clinic. They might be too proud and independent to ask for outside help, or may not see themselves as needing it. We associate counselling with antisocial behaviour and psychological problems, social work with single mothers, street punks, poverty, and welfare. Who needs this? It's not uncommon for the dying to understand intellectually that their time remaining will be short, but not to believe it: "Sure, hospice is a great thing, but it's not for me."

Patients can't register with Victoria Hospice unless their family doctors agree that hospice services are appropriate and desirable, although the hospice will help find cooperative physicians. Family doctors may think that hospice is hogwash. They may have told their patients nothing about their prognosis, given them false hope, or scared them half to death with horror stories about drug overdoses, addiction, and euthanasia. The University of British Columbia medical school is only now beginning to teach classes in pain management, and ignorance and misconceptions are as widespread here as they are elsewhere in Canada. Doctors are notoriously inept at breaking bad news, if they break it at all.

This task often falls to Dr. Debra Braithwaite, Victoria Hospice's house-call physician. Braithwaite, a lanky young blonde with a striking resemblance to actress Goldie Hawn, is known in the community as Dr. Deb, or, as she laughs, Dr. Death. She doesn't mind. "I *can* give people difficult news," she says confidently. "I have an ability to break bad news well. It's a talent, an art, a formula. You set aside time, set up a comfortable environment. Your body language is important. Your hand is not on the doorknob. Speak in a slow, stylized way, very clearly, in short chunks, using language that is not medicalized. Ask questions: 'Do you want to continue?' Then sit in the full force of their reactions, the full force of the other person's grief." As she speaks, Dr. Deb leans forward intently, gesturing expressively, her eyes on mine. The doctor's task, she says, is to weather the full range of the patient's emotions, draw threads of meaning together, and offer reassurance that they won't be abandoned.

"You listen to people tell their story, the story of their illness," she says. "They tell what has happened to them, how they learned they had a terminal disease. You *hear* that. Okay, it *is* disastrous. Some people want part of the news, others want all of the news, but they all want the recognition that this is *the* sacred moment for them. Everything will be measured by this moment, everything before and after. I need to create a sense of importance and sacredness for that patient. It's destructive to treat a death sentence casually, not as the important moment it is. People become despairing and desperate. If you can't deliver bad news, you can't make plans to deliver care. We start a plan, set dates for the next visits. It can be empowering."

Empowering a patient and family to manage a death at home is the essence of Victoria Hospice's philosophy and practice. It's not for the faint of heart. On registration, patients receive a thick blue binder divided into sections with coloured tabs. It looks like a cookbook, or a university course manual, and essentially it is. Victoria Hospice's *Palliative Care at Home* manual is a comprehensive guide to the services available, and by checking off appropriate boxes, patients can draw up their own individualized plan of care. First, however, the patient or proxy must sign a consent-for-service form which states: "I understand that my care will be palliative only, i.e., it is comfort-oriented and will not involve life-prolonging procedures."

No cardiopulmonary resuscitation. No intensive care unit. No respirator. No feeding tube. No monitors. As Jim Wilde puts it, "We don't weigh people." No oxygen unless the patient is already on oxygen and feels better for it. According to *Medical Care of the Dying*, a handy little pocketbook published by the Victoria Hospice Society, oxygen is rarely helpful especially if the patient is restless or confused. No repeat blood transfusions unless the patient is up and about and the previous transfusion was clearly beneficial. IV lines are problematic. "We take out more IVs than we start," says Fern Anderson. "If the patient is already swollen from excess fluid, extra fluid will aggravate the problem. It's a myth that dehydration is painful. It's not. A dry mouth can be treated with moist swabs or atomizers full of water."

It is not easy to kick away a life support apparatus we have come to take for granted, especially if we have been hooked up to needles, tubes, and electrodes during years of treatment. Even when the patient signs a consent form, anxious relatives may perceive non-intervention as neglect. Therefore, the manual spells out the patient's rights to:

- Receive correct information
- Know if one is dying
- Consent to appropriate treatment
- Receive appropriate treatment
- Not receive useless treatment
- Stop treatment which has become useless
- Refuse investigation

- Refuse treatment
- Change one's mind
- A second opinion
- Stop investigation or treatment before completion
- Confidentiality as desired
- Receive effective palliation of symptoms
- Receive consistent, compassionate care

The manual is blunt about the practicalities of dying. Have you considered your present finances and the cost of care? Estate and funeral planning? Organ donation? It puts into stark print sensitive issues that otherwise might never be discussed. Would a family conference help? Do you want your family present when you die? Patients check off the issues that concern them and, if it works, the process initiates productive discussion and organization among the team of caregivers.

The manual is a map. It includes medication charts for the doctors and nurses to fill out, blank pages in which to keep a daily journal, and a weekly calendar for planning visits. It is a public document, in the sense that it is only effective if all the caregivers read it, but it can also be a map of the soul. Included is a three-page self-assessment worksheet designed to encourage the dying to explore their thoughts and feelings. "You may want to do the worksheet alone or with others," the instructions advise. "You may want to keep it in the binder or take it out. You may not want to even look at it. It's intended to be helpful; if it isn't, don't do it."

The questions could keep an analytical, introspective person occupied until the day she dies. "My attitude towards this illness is . . ." "Being sick has taught me . . ." "My life has meaning and purpose because . . ." True or false questions are designed to produce a personality profile: "I enjoy being alone," "I'm afraid of being alone." Others encourage the patient to express emotions: "I feel overwhelmed by . . ." Questions relating to family relationships give clues to their strengths and weaknesses: "Something I need to hear from my family is . . ." By sharing this information, a patient can indirectly open up channels of communication no one knows exist.

Victoria Hospice has a permissive attitude to both patients and their families. It's okay for everybody to be angry and frustrated, lonely, frightened, sad, exhausted and confused, and you can express these emotions in ways that work for you, crying, yelling, walking, pounding, dancing. "Remember that all your feelings are valid simply because you have them," says the manual. "Everyone is different and will react in their own way. Each of them is doing the best they can under the circumstances." The hospice manual even instructs caregivers about a patient's right to be at risk: "Refusal to take medications or accept personal help may be very difficult for you to deal with. It is important to recognize that people have a right to make choices that may put them at risk. Their choices should not put you at risk."

These views reflect the philosophy of the manager of Victoria Hospice's team of counsellors, Wendy Wainwright. "I don't want *fixers*," Wainwright says. A freckled redhead with a penetrating gaze, Wainwright speaks bluntly. "This idea of the 'perfect death' is very arrogant as well as being impossible. I see a lot of people who have never gone into anything gently. So why do this gently? We ask ourselves, 'Why are they confused, not able to articulate?' They may need to be restless, agitated, confused, angry, and profoundly sad. We see people for a *fraction* of their lives. We need to help them in the way they *need us* to help them. If we bring in our own shit, we start monkeying around with their lives."

In the counsellors and the volunteers she trains, Wainwright is looking primarily for self-awareness and a high level of comfort with themselves, with life. "They have to have an ability to be with pain," she says. "When you see so much disarray, confusion, despair, and pain, how do you support someone else? Is it an honest, respectful relationship? Are we part of this person's *process*? I work from that place."

Victoria Hospice works on the theory that confusion and disarray can be minimized by providing patients and families with useful tips on how to deal with scary things like loss of appetite and short-ness of breath, and by educating them to anticipate the normal physical changes that occur as a body dies. Dying is, as Wendy Wainwright says, a process, and the hospice's little pamphlet *When Death Occurs* is, Tolstoy excepted, the most honest, simple, and fear-less description of the final act of dying I have ever read. We sleep, perchance to dream, lose our ability to swallow, become confused, pluck at our bedclothes, "see" things or have visions of people not present. We begin to breathe in shallow, irregular spurts, and as our heartbeat slows, saliva and mucous collecting in our lungs and throat may cause the familiar "death rattle." When we slip into a coma, our eyes may be open or shut. Can we still hear? Perhaps. Our arms and legs become cold, the skin there a dark, mottled purple. As our last act, before or after our heart stops, we may void our bladder and bowels.

Victoria Hospice's information packages are wise, practical, well-designed, and free of jargon, but they assume a rational reader who is able to *read*. I'm not talking about illiteracy, I'm talking about fatigue. When I started off on this journey, I naively assumed that dying people, given encouragement, would write their stories. When I broached this insight to Larry Librach, he snorted, "Write! They're too tired!" One of the rewards of my death trip so far has been discovering the extent of my own arrogance and ignorance.

When we start dying, we begin to suffer from cardiac, respiratory, and renal failure. Our chemical soup is going sour, and toxins in our blood may lead to cognitive failure, confusion, and dementia. Our eyes may become sensitive to light, or unable to focus, and we may be unable to concentrate for more than a few minutes at a time. The medications we are taking for pain, depression, and other symptoms will affect our behaviour, and answers to questions about our thoughts and feelings may reflect nothing more than the effective-ness of our prescription drugs. A workbook is most useful to someone in the earliest stages of a terminal illness, but Victoria Hospice tends to get patients in the final, critical stages.

Like the Fowlers' nanny, Mary, many are transferred to the hospice unit from surgical beds or Emergency. Mary had been registered with hospice, but Jim Wilde has made it his personal crusade to persuade the ER physicians routinely to refer patients to hospice if they are inoperable, untreatable, and incurable. Almost all of them are patients with end-stage cancer who have been discharged home without a hospice referral, and their families, at their wits' end, are desperate for help.

The old man in the smoking room is a case in point. Later, I see him pacing furiously up and down the hall, face flushed scarlet, eyes staring, unfocused. He has a brain tumour. At home, he had been awake all night, pacing, and had fallen several times. His wife couldn't cope, and he was admitted this morning. Hospice decides to let him pace while they get him settled down. "You can't get somebody to sit still twenty-four hours a day," quips Dr. Wilde. Wilde also has to settle the family, frantic that the Old Man has gone out of his mind. That afternoon, as I pass the solarium, I see Wilde holding an X-ray up to the light. He is showing the brain tumour to the family and explaining its effects.

The rooms at Victoria Hospice, all single, are big enough to accommodate a couple of sofas, including a pull-out bed, to allow family members to spend the night. Doors may be closed, although a nurse makes regular rounds. Husbands and wives, sons, daughters, and friends will often camp out for days at a patient's bedside, offering love and companionship, fearful that death will come if they leave. Others are welcome to bring food and keep them company. Having families milling around gives the hospice team an informal opportunity to answer their questions and calm their fears, and it seems to work. When I first arrived, two shaking, sniffling young women with tear-stained faces were waiting to take the elevator to the rooftop garden. The next morning, they were sitting in the lounge, sad, but composed.

By no means everyone, however, wants to sit by a deathbed. How often we hear, "Oh, I'd rather remember her as she was when she was well!" Even close family members may not be able to bring themselves to go into the sickroom. If friends and relatives don't visit the dying, it's easy for those of us who do to criticize and condemn, but I'm beginning to see avoidance more as a question of aesthetics than of ethics. People may feel overwhelming physical revulsion, or fear of losing self-control, or worry about their memory being imprinted for life with the indelible image of a cadaver. I don't blame them, and I am learning that we cannot predict who, if anyone, will be with us at the end.

Our sons and daughters may grow tired, and go home for a night's sleep. Some people seem to prefer to die alone. One old man dies at night, alone, an hour after his daughter has left. She returns immediately, sits comfortably with his body for a while, then gathers up his personal possessions. Down the hall, an old woman within hours of death plaintively calls out a friend's name. She's not here, and won't be, but another woman friend sits patiently by her bedside for hours. Some are called, others come. Her son has left word to be notified after his mother's death.

During my few days in and out of Victoria Hospice, three patients die and two are admitted. Patients' names are handprinted in black marker on erasable cards by their doors; it's disconcerting to see a name erased, the room empty and a cleaner swabbing the floor. The name, however, is printed on a small card and placed in an alcove with vases of flowers and a stained-glass lamp. The week has been hectic. One dying patient experienced intractable pain, a nine out of ten on Victoria Hospice's pain scale, and Jim Wilde had to struggle to bring it under control.

For extreme pain, Victoria Hospice has developed a method called "double stacking," doubling the dose of narcotics every twenty minutes until the pain is relieved, then reducing the added dose by 50 to 30 per cent on the regular four-hour schedule. If the pain remains controlled, the dose can be reduced; if it breaks through, stacking starts again. "Douse the pain with the Dose that Does it," is the hospice's motto. In cases of severe shortness of breath, or air hunger, the hospice uses narcotics, as well as fresh air, sedatives, and relaxation techniques, to calm the patient's panic reflexes. Says *Medical Care of the Dying*: "It is unethical to withhold the appropriate dose of medication which would ensure comfort just because this will cause sedation or jeopardize the respiratory drive when no other active measures are available which will provide relief." Drowsiness, it adds, is unavoidable and often welcomed by the patient.

When I see Jim Wilde's drawn, tired face – he has been monitoring the pain crisis, calming the frightened family, for many hours – I understand that this *is* acute care. "We are seeing more complicated disease," Wilde says. "People with cancer used to die of their primary disease, now we see brain and bone metastases. We are more crisis-oriented." Living longer with disease can make dying more complicated and unpredictable. To help chart its patients' decline, Victoria Hospice has developed a Palliative Performance Scale. On a scale of one hundred to zero, each patient is ranked according to mobility, progress of disease, self-care, intake of food and fluids, and level of consciousness. Once the PPS score falls below fifty, the patient is lying down, with extensive disease and some confusion, and needs assistance; at twenty, the patient is moribund; at zero, dead.

The PPS scale is a handy guide for the hospice's small army of caregivers, but by no means infallible. A cancer patient ranked forty on the PPS died that same night; another, ranked ten, has been hanging on for ten days. When relatives ask Jim Wilde the inevitable question, "How long do you think?" Wilde replies: "How was your dad a month ago? A week ago? This week?" If, by reviewing the evidence, relatives are able to visualize the speed of decline, they work it out for themselves.

Usually when I arrive at the door to the Richmond Pavilion I pass one or two forlorn cancer patients sucking on cigarettes in the January cold, IV poles in their hands. One day, I decide to enter via the cancer clinic. A sign, Victoria Hospice, points left down a hall. As I turn the corner, the shiny marble/granite/concrete of the cancer centre turns into an old corridor. Its antacid pink walls are broken by a stretch of open doors. Inadvertently, I peer into shabby pink rooms, each room with two or four beds, each bed occupied by an old, sad, white-haired person. They sit or lie there, sometimes barely covered, their only privacy the undrawn curtains around their beds. Their windows look out on the entrance driveway, and through the door they are exposed to the curious eyes of all the people who pass by in the course of a day. Perhaps watching the traffic in the hall is their recreation.

This, I discover, is an oncology ward. Many of these patients live up Island. They have come here for treatment. Their oncologists think they are too sick to go home, or their families and communities lack the resources to care for them. Families who can afford it might come and stay in a local motel, and the hospital will provide a cot in the room. With two or four beds per room, however, visits are constrained. Patients who are dying, or who have come here to die, can ask to see Dr. Wilde at Victoria Hospice upstairs, but their doctors have to make the formal referrals. Oncology patients are welcome to enjoy Victoria Hospice's roof garden, but the nurse I speak to can't remember anyone ever going there.

The ward, she tells me, has one private room. The only private room I pass has a sign on a closed door that reads:

Dear Visitor:

The patient you are visiting is presently receiving treatment with a radioactive substance. Certain precautions must be adhered to for your protection.

Persons under 18 should not enter the room.

A pregnant woman should not enter the room.

The maximum time limit is one-half hour per person per day. This means that if you should plan to visit more than once per day, your total time should not exceed one-half hour.

A distance of two metres or more from the patient should be maintained throughout your visit.

Do not sit on the bed or use the patient's bathroom.

No direct contact with the patient or the patient's items.

Wear plastic covers on shoes when entering the room.

You are asked to respect these regulations. Your cooperation is appreciated.

As I pause to read these words, I overhear a nurse and a volunteer across the hall gossiping loudly about a patient. I turn and glare at them. They glance at me, and gabble on. Riding the elevator to the hospice's roof garden, only four floors above, I am sick with horror at the thought of dying an institutionalized, imprisoned death, and when I step out into the soft, salty January air, I remember that you can't freeze to death in Victoria in January. Hi Mum, go for it.

Dismay over the treatment of elderly people dying in hospital is one reason why Victoria Hospice has four hundred and fifty dedicated volunteers. One of the originals is Eileen Rutherford, who had been a member of a hospital auxiliary. "I visited people who didn't have family," Eileen says, "and I saw many things I thought were not correct in the care of the terminally ill. I found one lady, appallingly thin, sitting on her bed trying to get washed. Her tube had come out and the bed was soaking wet. She was shivering with cold. 'You need to be tucked in,' I said. 'I'll ring for the nurse.' 'They don't like being bothered,' she said. I stripped off the wet sheet, put a flannel sheet on the bed, got her into bed and covered her up. When the nurse came in, I was *furious*. 'Do you realize she was freezing cold?' I said. 'Why was nothing done?' 'It was my lunch hour,' she said. 'You are a disgrace to your profession,' I told her. The head nurse complained to the auxiliary and I got hell. I said, 'So what?'"

Hospice unit volunteers help the nurses turn patients and get them in and out of bed, wheelchairs, and commodes. "You have to guard against treating patients as children," Eileen says. "Give them as much independence as possible. It's a mistake to try to do too many things. One man liked to get dressed and take a walk. He couldn't get his socks and shoes on, so I helped with that and tied his shoelaces. He was having difficulty with his buttons, so I reached out to help. He took my hand and put it down. 'For God's sake, don't mother me!' he said. 'Let me do it for myself.'" One woman, who could no longer speak, angrily wrote on her notepad, "*You fuss too much.*" Eileen burst out laughing, and so did she. Eileen likes to be addressed as "Mrs. Rutherford" by people she doesn't know well, and she returns the courtesy.

"Don't barge in on a family," she says. "We have some very private people. Try to be with the person in the same place. If they are sitting forward, sit forward; if they're leaning back in the chair, lean back. Be with them in *their* space. Don't get all hand-holdy." If someone reaches out a hand, okay, but a person staring out the window may be sending a "don't bother me right now" message. Uninvited hugging is intrusive and dangerous if the patient has brittle bones or papery skin.

The lack of fussing, the absence of typical hospital *busyness*, gives Victoria Hospice an atmosphere of serenity even in the midst of crisis. It's not creepy or gloomy, it's *quiet*. No intercoms blare. Telephones and pagers are muted. Nurses, volunteers, and visitors don't stand around in little knots, twittering or griping. Nurses record patients' information on a tape at the end of their shifts, and the incoming shifts of nurses and volunteers listen on headphones. Conferences are held in conference rooms, not in halls. No residents or interns flap about, white coats flying. Dr. Downing, the medical director, wears a white coat, but his manner and expression are as stolid as the Buddha. The nurses, like the doctors, move at a deliberate pace, covering ground quickly with long, silent strides. Even bodies seem to disappear as if by magic, and I wonder if an empty gurney I see wheeled into the elevator has a false bottom.

The tricky task of creating a "milieu of spirituality" falls to the hospice's coordinator of spiritual care, Michelle Hogman, an ordained minister in the United Church of Canada. Hogman, a bouncy, articulate, rosy-cheeked young woman, was hired only two months ago and she is still feeling her way. Many, but not all, patients and members of the hospice care team are Christians, and the

Christians are not of the same denomination. Hogman, however, is a resource for staff members suffering from disillusionment, and her presence in the unit is a constant reminder that there is more to hospice care than good medicine. Hogman posts appropriate poems and quotations on the staff bulletin board and raises families' spiritual concerns at staff meetings.

"When a patient arrives," she says, "I go into the room and say, 'Hi, I'm Reverend Michelle. I'm spiritual care. I visit. Would it be okay if I sat with you?'" She usually doesn't have a lot of success on the first visit. "A lot of people think, when the minister comes, that's it, or, gee, we gotta talk religion now. But once I make a connection, people often ask for me to come back." Hogman is confident about reassuring people who share her own beliefs about God and an afterlife, but she is expected to minister to anyone in need of spiritual solace. Her most meaningful relationship has been with a young Buddhist.

Reverend Michelle is a resource for grieving families who have lost touch with a church, but who would like a minister to say a prayer. The Lord's Prayer is comforting, as are many psalms. A prayer often opens up discussion about spiritual beliefs patients and families might otherwise be embarrassed to talk about, and Hogman says her role is to be a listener. "I don't need to dispense wonderful information about the afterlife," she laughs. "You have no idea what's going to hit you." She also facilitates discussion about funeral planning and memorial services at family conferences, especially if opinions are divided and feelings are running high.

Spirituality is a sensitive topic, and beliefs are often expressed obliquely. A dying woman sobbing uncontrollably fell silent as soon as Hogman placed a cross in her hand; her daughter held her other hand and they said the Lord's Prayer together. If patients feel uncomfortable about a cross, Hogman suggests Buddhist prayer beads. "Prayer beads are a tactile way of centring yourself," she says. "You can make your own prayer beads. There are many different ways of expressing spirituality."

Hospice patients dying at home, where most of them are, may request visits from Reverend Michelle, and their families, usually managing without twenty-four-hour nursing support, are in even greater need of consolation, ritual, and reassurance. Victoria Hospice's manual for patients and families deals bluntly with some, but not all, of the emotions aroused by exhaustion, terror, and grief. We may not be prepared to experience guilt and depression, but if they come, these emotions are socially acceptable. What about anger, jealousy, greed, hatred, indifference, or relief?

We know the horror stories. A husband screams at his wife, "Your cancer is your own damn fault! You smoked!" Sisters sit around their dying mother's bed yelling at each other about who will get her silver and china. An estranged daughter arrives home while the rest of the family is at the hospital, stuffs her suitcase with her mother's jewellery, and says, after the funeral, "Mother told me she *wanted* me to have these things." Weepy relatives move in, hoping for a reward in the will. Sons refuse to visit their dying father. Friends angrily accuse cancer patients of "giving up," or say, as they get up to leave, "You can let go now. I forgive you."

It all looks callous. It's human. The ancient Hebrews didn't invent the seven deadly sins, they codified them. If we die as we live, and our deaths reflect our lives, we might as well expect to encounter vice as well as virtue. Honesty too. One wife, separated from her dying husband, crisply informed his doctor that she would not visit her husband in hospital because she had no feeling for him. The nuclear family has blown up. Why bring it back together? Parents lose contact with their children, and their children may have distanced themselves for good reason. The myth of the happy family is as pervasive in our society as the myth of the peaceful death. Family members whose behaviour towards the dying seems to be cruel or indifferent may only be taking revenge for hurts inflicted on them in the past.

"Requests for euthanasia are always from families," says Jim Wilde. "It is *their* suffering projected on to a patient. Rarely do we have a patient ask for euthanasia. Rarely do we have a suicide."

But the dying, too, may be selfish, rude, vengeful, and cruel. They may shut their families out, or favour one child over the others. I met an Asian man with prostate cancer, by no means at death's door, who insisted that one of his three adult daughters be at his bedside twenty-four hours a day. The daughters all had jobs and families, and within weeks they were worn to a frazzle and exasperated with their father. Cancer patients are living longer with metastatic disease, and caring for them can become an intolerable burden for their relatives.

In a rare study of the quality of life of cancer patients in palliative care and of their families, Canadian psychologists Robin Cohen and Anne Leis uncovered a hidden story of family caregivers troubled by financial worries, fatigue, loneliness, frustration, and resentment. Caregivers who take time off work may lose their jobs, or they may quit. The patient may not have been earning a salary for years, and benefits and unemployment insurance may have expired. Medicare doesn't cover the incidental expenses of being sick, and if savings run out families have to borrow. Since only family members can give medication if a nurse is not present, they may have to get up several times during the night, night after night, month after month. Some, fearful of leaving the house in case something goes wrong, lose touch with their friends. Life becomes quietly desperate, and if patients undergo changes in personality, or shocking physical deterioration, they may turn into strangers, skeletons, the living dead. The higher the quality of life for the patient, the lower it may be for the caregiver. "It's a sacrifice," one wife responded. "You're tied down and the responsibility is all yours," said another. "Solely *mine*. It's very hard to do, emotionally as well as physically. I would like to wake up one day and not be responsible for that person."

Wishing a loved one dead is not socially acceptable, but martyrdom is. Caregivers make themselves sick and distraught by trying to do heroic, impossible tasks. "Families minimize their own needs," says Wendy Wainwright. "They are not in the same place psychologically as the patient, and they are all coming at it from different angles. There's a lot of energy moving around, a lot of tension. It brings out the best or the worst, and coming together as a family often makes it worse. Many families disintegrate."

While visiting volunteers and home care nurses, along with Dr. Braithwaite, can effectively assist families in most situations, families are ill-prepared to deal with a medical crisis, and a crisis, as Victoria Hospice well knows, usually happens at 2:00 a.m on a weekend. By 1989, the hospice was responding to so many crisis calls on its twenty-four-hour hotline it created a permanent mobile Palliative Response Team – a nurse and a counsellor – to visit critical cases in their homes. The nurse carries an Old Pal fishing-tackle box filled with essential drugs, and a suitcase full of medical supplies. The trunk of the car is packed with diapers, drinking straws, catheters, gowns, gloves, urinals, and anything else that might come in handy. Equipped with a cellphone, the PR Team handles incoming calls while it's on its way to house calls already scheduled.

"We deal with big-time pain, spontaneous fractures, a bleed that comes without warning," says Victoria Hospice's clinical resource nurse Linda Cliff. "Some people don't take their medications. They're reluctant to accept their disease. Families' inclination to feed the patients is a big problem. Patients vomit the food, suffer from bowel obstruction. They have to be in a crisis state to get them to accept the situation. There's nothing like a crisis. It's a very teachable moment."

A medical crisis sends waves of panic through a family, and while the nurse works quickly to get the patient's symptoms under control, the counsellor tries to get a bead on the social dynamic. "I have to read it in each place," says Eve Joseph, one of the PRT counsellors. "It's a matter of being present, an availability to speak fearlessly about anything. There is nowhere that you are afraid to go."

The presence of the team itself resolves much of the anxiety. With a standing order, the nurses can administer drugs, including opioids, without summoning the family physician, and a hospice doctor is only a phone call away. Once the patient is settled, the hospice team reviews the crisis with the family. What happened? Why? How did it feel? How can we prevent this happening again?

"I ask them, 'What is your worst fear if the patient dies at home?'" says Cliff. "What is the worst that might happen? They might say, 'Bleed to death.' So then we go through what it might look like, normalize the situation. If they say, 'Drown,' we explain, 'We can do *this*.' We also say that doing nothing is okay. Once people work through their worst fears, this situation isn't half bad. We provide a supportive presence so people can reorganize their strengths. We've done a good job if we've empowered people to manage a difficult death at home."

Any family within the Capital Region can call the PRT hotline, but they have to register with Victoria Hospice to receive the service. The success of PRT partly accounts for Victoria Hospice's growth, since 1990, from an average of forty to fifty registered patients to two hundred. PRT serves four hundred and fifty, with two hundred and eighty deaths a year.

"They *know* we will respond," says Linda Cliff. "There *is* someone on the end of the telephone line." Sometimes the patient dies before the PR Team makes it to the home. One family had called the police, and the house was surrounded by squad cars. Eve Joseph noticed a young teenaged girl hovering in the background, the dead woman's daughter. "I asked if I could speak to her," Joseph says. "There was a lot of resistance from the family, but we went into the kitchen and sat at the table. She was shell-shocked. Her mother had died very quickly. She wanted to know if there was anything she could have done. I assured her that there was nothing more she could have done. She'd held her mother's hand, that was all she could have done. I asked her if she had something she wanted to say to her mother. Did she want to do it? She went in to the bedroom and talked to her mum, held her. Death is seen as a physical issue, but it's not over. There's value in attending to the time after."

When panicky families can't get through to their doctors late at night or on weekends, they call 911. The police may arrive first, followed by a fire department rescue truck and an ambulance. Even if the patient is dying, or dies, the paramedics are legally obliged to attempt cardiopulmonary resuscitation unless a physician instructs otherwise. On occasion, they attempt to revive a dead body.

This is how *The Right to Decide*, a guide to advance directives or living wills distributed by Victoria Hospice, describes CPR: "CPR involves applying pressure and electrical shock to the chest, inserting a tube down the throat and into the lungs in order that breathing can be carried out by a respirator (breathing machine), and giving drugs through a needle into a vein. Usually, CPR is followed by unconsciousness and several days of treatment in an intensive care unit."

It goes on: "CPR is a procedure which, while often saving lives, is very hard on the body. People with other illnesses, or whose strength has already deteriorated, are unlikely to recover. Attempts to restart the heart may initially be successful, but many people develop post-CPR complications such as brain damage or infection that lead to prolonged hospitalization, disability, and in many cases death."

Victoria Hospice's *Medical Care of the Dying* notes that 70 per cent of advanced cancer patients die of infection or organ failure. The national success rate for CPR is about 1 per cent.

Paramedics may ignore the fact that a Victoria Hospice registration is a de facto Do Not Resuscitate order, and they may ignore Victoria Hospice. One ambulance crew, dispatched by the hospice to bring in a registered patient, became so upset by the man's bleeding tumour they unilaterally rerouted him to Emergency. For the dying, the Victoria Hospice's Palliative Response Team is a pre-emptive, preventive alternative to the Emergency room. Twenty-five per cent of the PRT patients do die in hospital or hospice, but it's how they get there that matters.

One night shift PRT nurse, responding alone to a call, was confronted by a family who told her that if she didn't do something to settle the restless patient, they would kill him. She settled him, but it took her four hours, and when she'd answered the call she had been coming off a twelve-hour shift.

"It's a very difficult kind of work," says Linda Cliff. "We've had nine deaths this week. The nurses often go to three deaths a day, then do that again the next day." They often cry. "It's sad," says Eileen Rutherford. "I often cry, we all do. But it's not depressing." Nurses can pronounce death, but a doctor has to sign the death certificate. Family doctors charge a fee, and the cynical among them call it "ashes cash." Crying is one way the hospice team avoids the contempt bred by familiarity that can insidiously creep into institutional medical practice. Laughter is another, and Jim Wilde is prized for his wry jokes.

I notice Linda Cliff's broad shoulders, strong arms, and kind, craggy face. Yes, doctors may open the door to Ali Baba's pharmaceutical cave, but nurses deliver the goods. Toronto hospice nurse Kit Martin, a specialist in pain management, calls hospice nurses *sherpas* after the native guides who accompany mountain climbers in the Himalayas. We will map your route, carry your baggage, make camp, and point the way, Martin says, but you have to go to the summit yourself.

By the end of the week, the old man in the smoking room is no longer smoking. He is quiet, lucid, and learning to manoeuvre his wheelchair. As he wheels himself aimlessly down the hall, an old woman, bent double over her walker, comes briskly up behind him, gives him a bump, and pushes him along. He looks around, surprised. "I don't know where I'm going," he says. "Am I going the right way?"

"You're okay," she replies.

They proceed for a few feet, both grinning, then he jumps out of his chair and pushes it along beside her, pretending it's a walker. "I think I'll do it this way," he says. "My bum is sore." They carry on companionably, side by side. Old people, new friends.

XVII

"TOO OFTEN WE DEAL with people who do the squeaking, who cause trouble," says Victoria Hospice counsellor Wendy Wainwright. "Normal people are ignored." Wainwright's insight is illustrated by the story of Bill Neal, who died at age sixty-eight in London, Ontario, on June 4, 1995. His children's story also reveals that normal people who cause trouble in our health care system may get themselves into even more trouble.

Bill, self-employed as an investment adviser and amicably separated from his wife, Joan, was deeply attached to his three grown children, Joanne, Tom, and Dave. Joanne, married with twin sons, lived in Stratford; Dave, with his wife and four sons, in Oakville; and Tom in Toronto. The Neal children were all in their forties, slim, handsome, and dark-haired, almost elfin in appearance, and so close to each other Joanne says they think almost as one. Their values are simple: honesty, healthy living, generosity, and love. When their dad became sick, Joanne was already caring full-time for their mother, who was becoming frail, forgetful, and confused.

Bill Neal was a husky six feet tall, active, sociable, and self-sufficient. Bill lived for golf, and in 1993, a few months after he had suffered a mild heart attack, he began to feel numbness in his feet, accompanied by a stabbing pain that shot down his left leg from his lower back. He hoped the symptoms would clear up with exercise – he could ride his stationary bike for an hour with no ill effects – but by the spring of 1994 he was dragging his left foot when he walked, and he had to stop to rest every two or three blocks. The possibility that he had ALS, Lou Gehrig's disease, crossed his mind.

Apprehensive, Bill went to his family doctor for a checkup on April 5, 1994. Years before, the doctor had put Bill on a drug, metoprolol, to reduce his high blood pressure. Bill had also been a diabetic for more than twenty years, but he wasn't on insulin and didn't stick too strictly to his diet. After an electrocardiogram eliminated Bill's heart as the possible culprit, the doctor, suspecting neuropathy, a degeneration of nerve and muscle tissue caused by diabetes, sent Bill to a neurologist. The neurologist, finding that Bill's symptoms did not completely conform to a diagnosis of diabetic neuropathy, ordered a CT scan of Bill's lower back. The scan, taken on July 15, was negative. The neurologist referred Bill to the local diabetes clinic. The clinic prescribed tolbutamide to control Bill's blood sugar and warned him to watch his diet.

Bill was rapidly losing weight, but his doctor brushed aside his fears. Bill's health was still deteriorating when his doctor moved to the United States, and Bill was desperate to know what was wrong with him. He had no appetite, and growing weakness in his hands and arms made it hard to even open a can. He was having trouble getting up and down the stairs in his townhouse, and he often fell and bruised himself. He suffered severe, chronic insomnia, with nightmares and hallucinations. Bill began experimenting with herbal remedies and alternative therapies. To help him sleep, a friend in the pharmaceutical industry supplied him with a powerful hypnotic, zopiclone.

Bill's new family doctor assured him that his weakness and weight loss were nothing to worry about. The diabetes clinic considered him to be stable. Intelligent and inquisitive, Bill pestered his doctor and the clinic with questions about the weakness in his legs, but he was not referred for more neurological tests. Bill's dentist had replaced all the gold fillings in Bill's teeth at the time his symptoms appeared, and Bill developed a fixed idea that he was being poisoned by mercury from his new fillings.

Bill didn't want to burden his kids with his worries, and it wasn't until a family gathering on Christmas Day, 1994, that they noticed his condition. "It was warm," says Tom, "so we went out for a game of golf. At the fifth hole, Dad took a swing and fell down. It was getting chilly, so we came home. He'd told me earlier, 'If the day comes when I can't play golf, I'm not going to hang around long.' That was his last golf game."

"We were shocked!" says Joanne. "Dad was emaciated, and he couldn't manage to get across a room without grabbing all the furniture, counters, and walls to support himself. He told us of having to crawl upstairs on his hands and knees to get to his bathroom. Suddenly, Dad was an old man."

Joanne and Dave had to intervene personally and repeatedly with Bill's family doctor before they persuaded him to apply for home care so Bill could get help with his meals and housecleaning. The home care investigator was so impressed with Bill's neat personal appearance, intellectual competence, and ability to drive a car, she rejected him. Bill explained that he could drive because he was *sitting down*, but Joanne had to appeal to the placement service herself before her dad was accepted. Bill found a new specialist in diabetes who put him on insulin a few days later. "I'll have you golfing by the summertime!" the specialist told him.

By March 1995, Bill had lost so much weight his worried friends commented that he looked like a concentration camp inmate. In January, on his way to lunch, he had fallen in the snow outside his golf club. Alone, and unable to get up, he had dragged himself by his arms to a glass door where he could be seen. Now Bill could no longer make it across the driveway to his car, and his wrist lacked the strength to turn the key in the ignition. He spent most of his time sitting in a chair. Conversation was an effort. His voice was sinking to a whisper.

Far from being able to follow his diabetic menu of three small meals and two snacks a day, Bill ate almost nothing. Food revolted him. At Easter dinner, Joanne noticed: "Food had to be gulped down due to aversion and nausea. A glass of water was too heavy for Dad to pick up. His hand shook, and he could no longer use his thumb and forefinger to grasp. He seemed close to starvation."

Exhausted and debilitated by a painful barium enema and CT scan for possible cancer of the colon – the problem turned out to be hemorrhoids – Bill began looking for a long-term care home. He decided on Parkwood, a huge, brick veterans' hospital and chronic care facility on London's south side. "I offered to have him come and live with us," Dave says, "but he said he'd rather not impose himself on his family. He was looking forward to Parkwood. He had served in the United States Army in the Second World War, but he had been born in Canada, and he was thrilled to be considered a veteran in Canada." Dave drove his dad to Parkwood for assessment on April 4, 1995. One Parkwood physician who examined Bill on admission suspected that Bill's symptoms might be ALS. The diagnosis was far from certain, however, and for confirmation the medical team arranged for a consultation by a neurologist from Victoria Hospital across the road.

During the four weeks that Bill waited in the assessment wing for the neurologist's tests and report, he was repeatedly examined by specialists in internal medicine hoping against hope to uncover a treatable illness. Bill was also enrolled in a rehabilitation program involving physiotherapy he found strenuous. Bill tried hard, but the physiotherapy was stopped when his condition worsened.

The Neal children, upset by their dad's continued sickness and suffering in the face of repeated promised of recovery, became concerned by his deterioration during the delay. What was a man as frail and feeble as their dad doing in a rehab program? Was he going to be sent home? Where would he go? Joanne had given to Parkwood menus of snacks she had been able to get her dad to eat, and Dave, fearing that Bill might conceal his history of self-medication, had made the doctors a list of all the drugs he'd found in his dad's medicine cabinet. They were disappointed that Parkwood did not acknowledge their assistance.

Bill, in limbo, afraid for his life, adopted a subtle strategy of self-defence. "He played things politically," Dave says. "It was an upbeat, always joking, social approach. Fit in, be congenial. He was looking forward to getting a permanent bed. He saw the assessment as an audition for residence, and he wanted to qualify."

Dave spent a couple of days a week in London cleaning up his dad's home office and visiting him at Parkwood. He'd massage the sore muscles in Bill's legs, play the piano for him in the lounge, or just sit and shoot the breeze. Joanne or Tom came every other day of the week. Walking into her dad's room one day, Joanne saw him slumped in his wheelchair, his face yellowish, his head lolling to one side.

"Oh Dad, you're dying," she thought, "You're *dying*, Dad!" In the hall, Joanne asked the head nurse if this was true. Says Joanne: "The nurse turns to three other staff members and says, 'Your dad is just fine. Don't you think so?' They all agree and nod their heads. The head nurse says, 'Your dad is managing quite well. *We* don't think there is a problem. Why do *you*?'"

"I'm sorry," Joanne retorted. "You'll never get me to say my dad is fine because he's not." Later, she privately approached another nurse, saying, "I think my dad may be dying." The nurse laughed and said, "No, Joanne, your dad is *not* dying."

Joanne, fearless about asking pointed questions, demands truthful answers. "I told them, 'Let's not pretend. I know it's not pleasant, but just spit it out.' Their attitude was, 'We know what we're doing.' They shut down everything I had to say. If you talk about dying, people think you're a terrible person. People think you're *wishing* death on them. Can you believe the horror of the patient, as well as the family, when his condition is not even *recognized*? All of his struggling and effort are not appreciated, and his suffering cannot be alleviated if it is not *seen*. Dad knew this. We could see fear and helplessness come into his eyes when we talked about his deterioration."

Bill Neal avoided confrontation. He'd grumble, and he asked a lot of questions, but if he wasn't satisfied he'd let the issue drop. The Parkwood staff, including Bill's social worker, found Bill cooperative, pleasant, a terrific guy. Bill confided his worries and grievances to his children and trusted them to do battle for him.

"We acted as his 'advisory council,'" Dave says. "He'd voice his complaints, but he didn't communicate fully. He'd leave out half, and expect you to read his mind. They'd give him peanut butter on bread with no butter. He had a very dry mouth, and the peanut butter would stick to the roof of his mouth. He'd complain about the peanut butter, but not explain *why*."

"He leaned on me," Joanne says. "I'm an organizer, a doer. He'd say, 'Joanne, you're my tiger.' Dad needed me to be brave." Joanne's first fight was to get her dad a television set. Bill loved to watch TV, especially golf, but he had been told he was not allowed a TV in an assessment bed. Food was a big irritant. Parkwood's dietician drew up a menu for Bill she considered nourishing and appetizing, but Dave noticed that his dad often left his food uneaten. Nauseous, with a mouth that felt like the Sahara, Bill gave food away and hid his dry cookies in his night table. The nurses, having denied to Joanne that her dad was dying, were in no position to explain that loss of appetite is a normal, expected part of the dying process.

Unaware of the tentative diagnosis of ALS and alarmed by the pharmacopoeia of pills they had found in their dad's medicine cabinet, the Neal children began to wonder if Bill's deterioration was caused by the drugs he was taking. Joanne checked every pill Dave had found in Bill's medicine cabinet against the drug manufacturers' guidelines. She learned that metoprolol was not recommended for diabetics and it could increase the risk of cardiac arrest if it were suddenly discontinued. Both metoprolol and zopiclone, Joanne found, carried warnings about hallucinations, nausea, dry mouth, tiredness, weight loss, and sleep disturbances. When the Neals learned that Bill, hallucinating, had jumped out of bed in the night and grabbed the man in the bed next to him around the neck, they confronted the Parkwood doctors.

The doctors explained that they were reducing the zopiclone, a drug recommended for use for no more than ten days. Bill had secretly been taking zopiclone for weeks, possibly for months, and while the drug may have been causing Bill's restlessness, confusion, and nocturnal hallucinations, he had become psychologically dependent on it. Metoprolol had been reduced but it would have to be discontinued before a substitute could be prescribed. Since Bill was capable of making his own decisions about his care, and he agreed with his doctors, his children's concerns about the pharmacological origins of his mysterious illness carried little weight with his medical team. Bill's doctors did make conscientious efforts to explain and justify the reasoning behind their prescriptions, but the Neal children, anxious, upset, and in the dark, felt that the doctors were brushing aside their concerns. When one doctor, with the kindest intentions, stated that it might be for the best if Bill died of a heart attack, Joanne was offended. Her dad would still be dead, wouldn't he? Was the manner of dying an *option* here? And who made *that* decision?

By May, when Bill was finally examined by a neurologist, Joanne was becoming distraught. "I was exhausted. Dave was designated as the primary family contact, but Dad would call me. He loved to talk, and I'd try to keep his spirits up. He'd say, 'Keep asking questions.'" But nothing Joanne did for her dad, or tried to do, seemed to make any difference. "I was run to death," she recalls. "I was beside myself. I kept thinking, 'I can't fix anything.' I kept trying to push it out of my mind, but my heart would sink."

Since Bill's medical team was not aware of Joanne's role as her dad's designated investigator and advocate, Joanne was easily dismissed as a "difficult" daughter trying to interfere in her father's decision-making. Had Bill's social worker, a young woman he liked very much, included his children in her circle of care, she might have unsnarled the lines of communication and made life less frustrating for everyone. The social worker, however, had only a brief interview with Dave and a phone conversation with Joanne shortly after Bill was admitted.

On May 8, 1995, at Parkwood's first and only Neal family conference, Bill and his children were told at last that Bill almost certainly suffered from rapidly progressing ALS. The neurologist had scheduled an appointment with a colleague for confirmation later in the month, but he was not optimistic. The Neals knew that ALS was terminal and untreatable. Bill's hopes for a cure were shattered, his children were furious that it had taken the doctors five weeks to discover that their dad was dying. Bill understood that he was going to die, but he was apprehensive about *how* he was going to die. He didn't mind dying of a heart attack, he'd had one of those, but he had a horror of suffocating. Bill Neal presented a brave face to the world, but his children knew that he often felt frightened and tearful. Now he needed time to think things over.

During the next week, Bill's breathing became laboured. He hallucinated and grew restless. He tried to walk leaning on a wheeled table, fell, and bashed the back of his head. The doctors talked to him about signing a DNR order. Bill was ambivalent. He didn't want to be maintained indefinitely on a ventilator in a paralyzed or vegetative state, but he didn't want to die if resuscitation could give him a little more time. Hell, he wanted to live!

But live where? Bill was absolutely determined to move into the veterans' residential wing where he'd applied to go in the first place. Bill feared being sent home again, and while he understood his prognosis intellectually, the imminence of his death and his need for continuing medical care had not registered psychologically or emotionally. "Dad figured he had a year to live," Dave smiles. "He'd lost money on the stock market and he was waiting for a market boom to recover it." Bill's doctors agreed to the move. In preparation, Bill's hypertension medication, metoprolol, was being withdrawn with his consent. No substitutes were prescribed. On May 18, the Thursday before the long Victoria Day weekend, Bill Neal was admitted to 3 Kent West in the veterans' residence.

The status of Bill's DNR order remained confused. He did not sign a form, and his sometimes conflicting verbal instructions were interpreted differently by the family and various members of his medical team. His children's understanding of their dad's wishes was that DNR applied only in the event of cardiac arrest. Bill had not prepared an advance directive in the event he became unconscious or mentally incompetent, and in the absence of a signed DNR, Parkwood's policy was to transfer residents in a medical crisis to Emergency at Victoria Hospital.

In 3 Kent West, Bill Neal's new doctor examined him and then left for the weekend. Bill was assigned a new social worker. He was dismayed to find himself sharing a room with three strangers. His roommates were able to shower and dress themselves, walk or wheel up and down the halls, and eat their meals together in the dining room. Bill couldn't get out of bed without help. Joanne noted in her journal: "Dad slumps to the left while in his wheelchair and can no longer hold up his head. His eyes roll back in his head every few minutes, and he appears to sleep in nodding fashion in the midst of sentences. He describes seeing things at times, like vegetables floating in the air. His voice is barely audible."

On Saturday, alarmed by Bill's restlessness and confusion, Joanne pleaded to speak to a doctor. The doctor on call refused to come in. The head nurse listened sympathetically, and suggested that her dad might be transferred to a floor with more complex care resources. The nurse apologized that she couldn't ask for a transfer until after the weekend. "I don't think my dad is going to make it through the weekend," Joanne replied.

Bill's blood pressure was spiking. On the following day, Sunday, May 21, when Tom was there, the doctor on call came in to give him an injection. Bill was seeing carrots and making chopping motions with his hands, but he was conscious. Shortly before 11:00 p.m. Sunday night, a nurse from 3 Kent West called Joanne at home to say that she was sending Bill by ambulance to Victoria Hospital. He was suffering from severe hypertension. When Joanne and her mother arrived at the hospital from Stratford a little after midnight, Bill was awake and attached to monitors. His blood pressure was stabilizing but he looked ghastly. Joanne noted in her journal: "He is constantly agitated, restless and anxious, every moment or two needing to change his position. Wanting to sit up, to dangle his legs over the bed, wanting hoisting up, shifting of pillows from one side to the other, needing his feet, legs, and arms rubbed because they bother him, seeing vegetables and other things in the air. His voice is a whisper, very hard to understand."

Joanne phoned Tom and Dave. Tom had just got home from visiting his dad, but he and Dave promised to drive to London as soon as they could. Joanne and her mother sat by Bill's bed, holding his hand. Victoria Hospital would not admit him – they said he would be returned to Parkwood as soon as his blood pressure stabilized – and the doctors on duty had four other critical cases. About 4:00 a.m., Bill, fighting for every breath, began to lose consciousness. Joanne was frantic. Why didn't somebody pay attention? Bill was given oxygen. Oxygen seemed to make his breathing worse, and Joanne removed the mask. Bill suddenly sat up, a peculiar pinched grimace on his face. A passing medic stopped and began shouting orders in medical code. The only words Joanne clearly understood were, "Right now! I mean RIGHT NOW!" The ER team swarmed around Bill's bed.

A medic took Joanne aside. Was there a DNR order? If not, a resuscitation decision might have to be made soon. Yes? No? What was it? This was a decision Joanne did not expect to have to make, but she did. "I didn't expect Dad to regain consciousness," Joanne says. "I wanted him to live until Tom and Dave arrived. I wanted them to be able to say good-bye to a *living being*." Joanne gave permission to resuscitate. Bill Neal stopped breathing. He was attached to a respirator and admitted to Victoria Hospital's Critical Care Trauma Centre.

The Neal children were in complete agreement that if their dad failed to regain consciousness, his respirator would be turned off. By the next day, however, Bill Neal was wide awake. The tube in his windpipe made it impossible to talk, but he could understand and communicate by nods and squeezing hands. He gave Joanne a thumbs-up, and when Tom asked if he wanted to turn the respirator off, Bill shook his head, no.

On Tuesday, May 23, Bill asked for his glasses so he could write notes. He was glad to be alive. He told his neurologist that he wanted to stay on the respirator. He was given nutrition and medication by tubes, morphine by injection. He sucked on ice chips. He was in no pain. On Thursday, he was transferred to a private room with a TV. Joanne wrote on Friday, May 26: "Dad's attitude has become a strong one, to live as long as he can. He asks that the no resuscitation order, in the event of a heart attack, be reversed."

Bill Neal's rising from the dead astonished the medical staff in the Critical Care Trauma Centre. How did this dead man not breathing get in here? The CCTC is designed to save the lives of healthy people badly injured or sick people suffering temporary physical trauma. One Victoria Hospital physician expressed his opinion that if Bill Neal's terminal ALS diagnosis had been fully confirmed on his admission to Emergency, he would never have been resuscitated. Joanne was angry. She felt that she had correctly expressed her dad's wish, and it was hard enough for her to bear his suffering without being made to feel responsible for it.

Attempts to wean Bill off his respirator failed. He could not breathe on his own. Relations between the Neal children and Bill's medical team – the third team they'd had to deal with within six months – became tense. When the Neal children were asked to enrol Bill in a respirator tube experiment, they refused, disgusted that researchers would suggest an experiment on a dying man. They became more vigilant about the quality of care their dad was receiving. Drugs, including Gravol, Valium, Tylenol, and Aspirin, as well as morphine, seemed to make Bill confused, and sometimes he became hyperactive. Was he getting the wrong kind of drugs? Was he being overdosed? Unable to get satisfactory answers to their questions, in spite of frequent conversations with the doctors, Bill and his children became fearful and uncertain about his future.

After Bill's ALS diagnosis was confirmed on May 26, the question of how Bill Neal was going to die was put to Bill himself. The script, as Joanne calls it, proposed two options: a miserable, lingering death, probably from infection, if he remained on the respirator, or, if he agreed to go off the respirator, a peaceful passage, heavily sedated, surrounded by his family. Certainly Bill's doctors were obliged to consult with him about his grim prognosis, and since they could prescribe no treatment, it may have seemed to them to be in Bill's best interest to offer him an opportunity to put an end to his suffering. An ALS patient like Sue Rodriguez would have leapt at the chance to orchestrate her final exit, but to Bill Neal, euthanasia sounded like suicide. Bill had no intention of committing suicide, assisted or not. He was making up a lot of lost time with his kids, and his brother Ralph had come from the States. Bill scrawled on his notepad, "No, stay on respirator."

Says Joanne: "The same message was repeated again and again by various doctors and nurses in the CCTC. They would tell a different anecdote each time, but they all used the same words and phrases. The intention was always the same: Dad should go off the respirator. What a sad, dangerous attitude, that Dad should end his own life."

Unable to speak, fearing to sign his own death warrant with an unintentional gesture, Bill Neal responded to the script by staring into space. His doctors, thinking he didn't understand, tried to recruit Joanne. Her dad talked to *her*, didn't he, so maybe she could get through to him? On Saturday, May 27, Joanne was confronted. "This doctor's approach," she says, "was that Dad might suffer in a crisis if weaned off the ventilator and not die comfortably. Dad should also understand that he could become unconscious and the decision would pass to us to end his life. It would be best if he did it because he could then say his good-byes and have us near him. The doctor said it was 'better coming from a family member,' and we should 'just make him understand.' He had a kind demeanour and seemed sincere when he said that this was difficult for him to say."

The doctor's request was difficult for Joanne to hear. She didn't want her dad to die horribly, as the doctor had implied, but what kind of daughter counsels her dad to kill himself? Why was he asking this of her? What a terrible choice to have to make! Reluctantly, she agreed:

"I asked Dad if he wanted the tube taken out. He nodded, 'Yes.' Then I went on with the words, 'I mean to take the tube out and then pass away . . . then die, Dad?' He shook his head vehemently, 'No, no!' I had to reassure him not to worry about it, we would follow his wishes and leave him on the machine. I felt sickened."

A week after he had been admitted to the CCTC, Bill was feverish and disoriented. His neurologist diagnosed pneumonia. During the next two nights, Bill was wakeful, confused and agitated. By Thursday, June 1, Joanne saw death in his glassy eyes. "Dad knew too," she says. "On his notepad he printed, 'WAKE PARTY.'"

The medical staff of the CCTC continued to raise the issue of the respirator. When Bill finally wrote, "too weighty a decision now," a nurse pressed Joanne to explain the situation to her dad in the hope of getting a definite answer.

Joanne called her brothers. They had no idea of the pressure that Joanne was under. Neither Tom nor Dave, the primary family contact with power of attorney, had been approached to intervene. They were shocked and suspicious. Was Joanne being pressured because, as a woman, she was seen to be a weak link? What if the doctors made the decision to remove Bill's respirator themselves? Did they have the right to do that? The Neal children appreciated the hospital's predicament. Yes, Bill's respirator might be needed to save a child's life. If and when that became the case, they were confident Bill would agree. But what about *his* life? "*They* resuscitated him," Tom says. "It's their responsibility to have policies about resuscitation. It's a bad position to put the family in. Dad was dying. The end was imminent. Why push him faster? Why bring up euthanasia at such a tender moment?"

At Bill's request, one of his children now sat by his bedside night and day. On June 2, Joanne wrote: "Dad can no longer move his hands or his head. His eyes are staring out most of the time and are beginning to look cloudy. He can't write any more. He can only blink and furrow his brows in response."

Bill had developed an infection in his lungs. Fluid had to be suctioned from his respirator tube, and foul-smelling green slime oozed from his mouth. Even so, a day nurse reported to the Neal children that their dad might have to be moved to a public ward and his visitors restricted. They were speechless. Says Joanne: "It's almost beyond belief that a dying man and his family could be treated in such a callous manner." Two more doctors came to counsel her about turning off her dad's respirator. Joanne replied: "Listen, I've said it before. Dad understands everything. We understand everything. What *else* is there to understand? This seems like suicide to Dad. It's not his way. He just needs time."

Bill was promised that he could take his time to die. Joanne was grateful, but why did he have to suffer so much? Couldn't the doctors do anything? Wait a minute, maybe they could. A phrase from the past came into her mind. Palliative care. Two years before, after a friend's husband had died right here in the CCTC, her friend had investigated palliative care. Joanne approached a nurse. Did Victoria Hospital have palliative care? The nurse assured her that the CCTC nurses knew the stages of dying. They knew how to do palliative care. Joanne disagreed, and the nurse eventually admitted yes, the hospital did have a chaplain and two nurse specialists.

The next day, Lynda Warder, the hospital's nurse clinician for palliative care, had a long talk with Joanne. "I thought I was crazy," says Joanne. "Lynda told me I was coming from a good place. My behaviour was appropriate. I was doing what I was doing and that was okay." Lifting the burden of advocacy from Joanne's shoulders, Warder persuaded the CCTC staff to treat the Neal family with compassion and kindness. "The difference was immediate and amazing," says Joanne. "All was cooperation and friendliness." The Neals were also deeply grateful for the support of Bill's neurologist, a physician who respected Bill's right to make his own decisions and who reassured them all that they were coping well in difficult circumstances.

On Sunday evening, June 3, Joanne and her mother headed home to get some sleep. They entrusted Bill to the care of Paula, his night nurse. Paula assured them she would call if there was any change in his condition. Shortly after midnight, Paula called Joanne to say that Bill's blood pressure was falling and he no longer responded to a light shone in his eyes. Joanne and Joan arrived back at the hospital at 1:00 a.m. Paula sat with them as they watched the monitor by his bedside. The blips on the monitor screen gradually flattened, then became a straight line. Bill Neal died at 4:00 a.m. Paula turned off his respirator.

"It was dark and raining when Mum and I left the hospital," Joanne recalls. "There was nobody around. We felt so alone. When we got home, I couldn't move. I could hardly breathe. I couldn't speak, I could just make a little squeaking sound. I felt I was trapped in heavy armour, ready to explode."

Joanne had helped her dad die the way he'd chosen, but she had paid a hard price. "I'd had so much horror, such fear," she says. "I felt I had to be strong for Dad, but I felt such grief at his suffering, I'd burst out crying. His death was horrifying. He did not want to go. *He did not want to go!* I wanted to shake him and say, 'Come back! Come back!' but he was in another place. I couldn't fix it for him."

Joanne recovered from her shock, but she was angry at the way her whole family had been treated. As Joanne reviewed the catastrophic course of their dad's illness with Tom and Dave, they became unanimous in their belief that their dad, who revered doctors, had been the victim of neglect and maltreatment. The Neals didn't hire a lawyer. They didn't sue. They didn't want vengeance, or money. They wanted accountability and improved standards of care for the mortally ill.

In July 1995, they registered an official complaint with the Ontario College of Physicians and Surgeons. It cited "systematic neglect by the medical establishment" leading to Bill Neal's increased suffering, and they asked that four doctors involved "be investigated for misconduct and reprimanded for their lack of patient-centred response." The Neals' complaint included Bill's family physician and his multiple encounters with the health care system during the year before his death. The college initiated an internal investigation.

A year after Bill died, Joanne, reading up on palliative care, borrowed from her library *The Heart of Hospice* by Dr. Dorothy Ley, completed, after her death, by Harry van Bommel, and published in 1994. "As I began to read," Joanne says, "I came across a tribute to Dr. Ley written by Dr. John Swift, medical director of palliative care, Parkwood Hospital, London, Ontario. Parkwood? There was palliative care at *Parkwood*? I was blown away!"

Parkwood Hospital had not told the Neal children about its ten-bed palliative care unit, one floor above Bill's bed in Admissions, or about the outreach consulting team that visited patients and residents in their rooms. Joanne couldn't remember seeing a sign in the hospital reception area or on the grounds indicating that Parkwood offered palliative care, no arrows pointing directions in the halls, no pamphlets displayed in the information racks. "Nobody mentioned palliative care," she says. "We didn't know it *existed*!" Although a Parkwood doctor had suspected Bill Neal's terminal ALS diagnosis on his admission, the Neal children had never met Dr. Swift, and as far as they knew, Parkwood had not included their palliative experts in discussions about Bill's care or end-of-life prospects.

There are many reasons. Bill may have been dying before his children's eyes, but without a firm diagnosis of a terminal disease there was no medical reason for the doctors to involve palliative care. The neurologist who diagnosed Bill's ALS early in May wanted a second opinion, but Bill was on a respirator in the CCTC before his scheduled appointment with the second neurologist. This hesitancy, and the fact that the cause of ALS is unknown, fuelled the Neal children's conviction that their dad was really dying from toxic drug-induced nerve damage.

A firm diagnosis of ALS would not necessarily have warranted a referral to palliative care. Reena McDermott, the nurse who founded the Parkwood unit in 1982, left Parkwood a few months before Bill Neal arrived, but McDermott considers ALS a chronic disease. "Palliative care was not necessarily appropriate," she says, "not unless something indicated he was dying. Going into the palliative care unit is a frightening experience. You go to palliative care when you're *dying*. The appropriate thing was done. He was transferred to hospital."

McDermott's views reflect the common assumption that palliative care is for patients *in extremis*, and only recently have hospice and palliative care practitioners themselves begun to recognize the needs of patients with degenerative diseases. London doesn't lack resources for the dying. Hospice of London and the London Health Sciences Centre offer palliative care, and King's College, affiliated with the University of Western Ontario, is internationally recognized for John Morgan's Centre for Education about Death and Bereavement. Dr. Morgan has written and edited numerous scholarly books, the Centre has taught accredited courses in palliative care and thanatology, the study of dying, for many years, and it hosts a popular annual conference. In a facility for the aged and infirm like Parkwood, why shouldn't palliative care be the institutional standard of practice?

But when I spoke to Parkwood executive Gillian Kernaghan in 1997, she said, "We don't refer everyone who is dying to the palliative care service. Many of our staff here are skilled in palliative care. Our staff have looked after people who are dying for years. Palliative is a word a lot of people don't necessarily understand. We don't necessarily use that word. We use 'comfort care.'" Kernaghan said that Parkwood had no identified procedure for the dying, and that care was "very much the patient's choice." There was no necessity to consult Dr. Swift, she said. Patients in veterans' care, or their families, would have to ask for palliative care. Most of Parkwood's palliative beds were filled by patients who came directly from the community. Life expectancy was less than two weeks.

Had Bill Neal been admitted to Parkwood as a dying man, not as a veteran with an undetermined, degenerative neurological disease, palliative specialists may have had the skills to alleviate the symptoms of physical, psychic, and emotional suffering that caused Bill Neal and his family so much distress. They might have recognized Bill's children as key players on his medical team, given them information about treatments and medications in ways they understood, and explained their dad's frightening agitation and confusion as normal, predictable aspects of the dying process. As it was, the Neals learned from experience.

When Joan Neal's health failed in the spring of 1998, Joanne was able to get her mother admitted to a quiet, beautifully decorated room in the palliative care unit at Stratford General Hospital. During the twenty-five days before Joan died, Joanne and her brothers felt welcomed, respected, and comforted by the medical staff. They were not frightened by their mother's loss of appetite, confusion, or strange sayings, and they were talking with Joan on March 25 when she crossed her hands over her breast and died.

Acknowledging Bill Neal's suffering would have validated his children's concern and calmed their anxieties. Their emotions would have been recognized as anticipatory grief, not repudiated as denial, hostility, aggressiveness, or hysteria. By treating the Neal family as a unit, palliative care might have avoided the emotional strife, caused by misunderstandings and differences of opinion, between Bill's doctors and his children. Bill, an Anglican, had read a great deal about previous lives and other spiritual beliefs. He appreciated the volunteer who dropped off literature with scriptural quotations. With a counsellor like Victoria Hospice's Michelle Hogman, Bill might have explored his spiritual self and become less fearful. He might have completed an advance directive and signed a DNR form. Not long before Bill died, Tom, who believes in reincarnation, whispered in his dad's ear, "You have to be willing to let go of the body. It's a leap of faith you have to make yourself."

Could the whole traumatic trajectory of Bill Neal's dying have been prevented? The answer depends on the question hidden at the heart of the Neals' complaint to the Ontario College of Physicians and Surgeons. If a physician causes a patient to suffer, whether physically, mentally, or spiritually, tolerates his suffering or fails to treat his suffering, does this constitute medical malpractice? Within the hospice and palliative care community, the answer now is yes. This view is supported by medical ethicists, but in 1995 the issue of suffering, as old as humankind, was so peripheral to conventional medicine in Canada it virtually didn't exist.

The Neals submitted their complaint to the Ontario College of Physicians and Surgeons before Joanne became aware that Parkwood had a palliative care team, so the lack of referral was not at issue. After a three-year investigation, the college's complaints committee replied in April 1998. The committee found no evidence of neglect or increased suffering and no grounds for concern about Bill Neal's medications. The problem of the transfer of an unstable, terminal patient to a long-term care residence on the eve of a long weekend was not addressed because the doctors named in the complaint had not been responsible. The committee found that Bill's family physician, by referring Bill to specialists, had not fallen below the standard of practice, and praised the Parkwood physician who originally diagnosed Bill's ALS. All in all, the report said, fine physicians were doing their very best to provide excellent care with sensitivity, compassion, and expertise. Although there was never any suggestion that Bill Neal had become mentally incompetent, the committee placed all blame on the decision to resuscitate, a decision which, unfortunately, they said, led to tremendous grief for all concerned.

The decision to resuscitate, however, may not have been Joanne's to make. "There is no statutory or ethical obligation to provide futile interventions when no medical justification exists," Dr. Howard Ovens, director of emergency services at Toronto's Mount Sinai Hospital, observed in 1998. "Patient autonomy properly extends to the rights of patients to refuse treatment, not to the right to demand useless treatment. On the advice of lawyers and ethicists, many hospitals have required physicians to obtain patient consent to writing a do-not-resuscitate order. This is a unique requirement among medical procedures. It is not a benign one. Participating in this decision can be anxiety-provoking for families and can produce significant and long-lasting guilt. The decision to provide or withhold resuscitation is a medical one and should remain in the hands of physicians."

In 1995, bioethicists, a burgeoning substratum in our health care system, were only beginning to grapple publicly with these decisions, and since Canadians, given our doctors' publicly funded deep pockets, are reluctant to sue for malpractice, there were no legal precedents. It was 1998 before the multidisciplinary, multi-institutional University of Toronto Critical Care Medicine Program/ Joint Centre for Bioethics Task Force on Ethical Issues in Critical Care came up with a "Model Policy on Appropriate Use of Life-Sustaining Treatment."

The policy defines the goal of intensive care as preventing "unnecessary suffering and premature death by treating *reversible* illness for an appropriate period of time." Intensive care, the task force decided, should not be provided for patients with lethal, progressive, unrelenting terminal disease incompatible with survival longer than three to six months. However, the task force made exceptions for "an experimental treatment which may cure or alleviate the underlying condition, or to help the patient achieve a personal goal (e.g., seeing a loved one for the last time who is flying in from afar)."

This policy is so open to interpretation that the task force concluded that the process of decision-making may require mediation, arbitration, lawyers, and the courts. Sounds like a good way to hasten death, for sure. Who needs this bureaucratic interference? Have we all become incapable of ethical decisions? Dr. Eric Cassell, an American physician and an authority on medical ethics, puts the issue simply: "The most important determination to be made before starting a respirator is the degree of probability that the patient can ever be successfully removed from it."

The Neals, highly critical of the college's investigation, asked for a review by the provincial Health Professions Board. Since the medical profession is provincially self-regulating, it's no wonder that for all the thousands of complaints Canada's colleges of physicians and surgeons receive every year, doctors are almost never found at fault. The benchmark for evaluating performance, standard of practice, means essentially doing what reputable doctors are doing. What if their practice isn't very good?

As I write this in the spring of 2000, the review board has yet to report, but in March 1997, Joanne received a letter from Gail Crook, manager of family medicine and palliative care for the London Health Sciences Centre. Crook wrote that she was working to identify palliative care service gaps in their system. "We are very aware that there is much to be done to improve the palliative care process," she said. "I would like to commit to you that I will use the information you have sent to me to share with the healthcare providers as an example of where we might have done things better and where we need to improve our process in the future." Crook closed by saying she would invite Joanne to join a focus group. Joanne is still waiting.

XVIII

BILL NEAL CHOSE the way he died, and he died more peacefully than sixty-five-year-old Paul Mills, a cancer patient in Halifax, Nova Scotia, whose family gave the hospital permission to withdraw his respirator under heavy sedation.

In April 1996, Mills was diagnosed in Moncton, New Brunswick, with cancer of the esophagus, the tube that connects the mouth to the stomach. Mills underwent two major surgeries to remove his esophagus and reposition his stomach so food could pass into it directly from his mouth. Serious complications, including infection, led to two more operations in Moncton, and on September 29, 1996, Mills was transferred to the Queen Elizabeth II Health Sciences Centre in Halifax. Surgeons at the hospital operated on Mills six times, leaving him in the ICU with a gaping, pus-filled wound in his chest. On November 6, Mills's doctors conceded that he was incurable. On November 9, when he had become unconscious, his family agreed that life support should be discontinued the following day. They said their good-byes and went home. A priest gave Mills last rites.

At 12:30 p.m. on November 10, Paul Mills, sedated with synthetic morphine, Dilaudid, was taken off his respirator. Mills should have died within minutes, but he struggled to keep breathing, writhing and thrashing, every muscle visible in his open chest. His nurse, Elizabeth MacInnis, increased the doses of Dilaudid to one hundred milligrams per hour, then to five hundred. The drug had no apparent effect. When Mills had gasped and struggled for more than two hours, a scene MacInnis later described as "horrible and hideous," the most agonizing death she had ever witnessed, MacInnis asked the unit's respirologist, Dr. Nancy Morrison, if there was anything she could do. Dr. Morrison injected nitroglycerin into Mills's IV line to lower his blood pressure, and when that had no effect, she injected a concentrated solution of potassium chloride. Concentrated potassium chloride stops a heart cold. Paul Mills died within a minute.

Witnesses reported Morrison's lethal injection to the medical director of the ICU. In Canadian law, physicians may administer megadoses of drugs intended to relieve pain and suffering, even if they hasten death, but they cannot administer drugs intended to kill. Nancy Morrison had acted out of compassion in a desperate situation. Had she murdered a dying man? A peer review committee at the hospital found Morrison's conduct unacceptable, and the hospital suspended her from the ICU for three months. She subsequently resigned from the unit.

Paul Mills's family found out how he had died six months later when the media called to ask if they knew that he'd been murdered. On May 6, 1997, swarms of Halifax police, following up a complaint from a doctor troubled by rumours about active euthanasia in the ICU, had descended on the hospital and arrested Dr. Morrison on a charge of first-degree murder. Conviction carried a mandatory life sentence with no parole for twenty-five years.

Once the circumstances of Paul Mills's death became known, the punishment Nancy Morrison faced on conviction seemed so extreme that public opinion swung overwhelmingly behind her. Crown prosecutors proposed to reduce the charge to manslaughter, but at a preliminary hearing in February 1998, the judge threw the charges out, ruling that there was insufficient evidence to persuade a jury to convict. It was a peculiar judgement since the evidence had not yet been heard, but the judge's right to make the ruling was upheld on appeal. Charges against Morrison were dropped in December. In April 1999, following an investigation by the Nova Scotia College of Physicians and Surgeons, Morrison admitted she had made a "mistake" and that she had used potassium chloride to hasten death. A reprimand was placed on her file.

Nancy Morrison overreacted in a crisis, but how did that crisis arise in the first place? Dr. Charles Wright, a Vancouver expert in evaluation of medical practice, chaired a scathingly critical external review of how the Queen Elizabeth hospital handled Paul Mills's death. Wright believes that Mills was in the wrong place to begin with. "He could have been looked after more appropriately in a non-surgical environment," Wright says. That place could have been the hospital's palliative care unit. The unit's director, Dr. Ina Cummings, is one of Canada's most respected and experienced palliative specialists. Paul Mills's physicians did not consult Dr. Cummings during his five weeks of excruciating surgery. They did not consult Dr. Cummings when they realized Mills was dying, nor when they decided to remove his life support.

Experts on pain know that an occasional patient will suffer from intractable pain, pain so unresponsive the only solution is anaesthesia. Since Paul Mills had been on high doses of opioids to control the pain of his cancer surgery, the amount required to sedate him may have been much higher than even the gorilla-sized doses he was given. Some people can regularly handle one, two, three thousand milligrams of morphine and still be walking around. Changing from an ineffective narcotic to one that works, a standard practice in palliative care, might have solved the problem quickly.

"It's a tragic thing," says Dr. Kenneth McKinnon, a member of the QEII external review committee. "It could all have been prevented." McKinnon, the retired director of palliative care at Halifax's Camp Hill Medical Centre, believes that consultations about Paul Mills's care could have started during his surgery: "It's not a question of frightening patients, but of being included as part of the medical team. Mills was weeks in the ICU. There was lots of time to deal with his distress. Palliative care is a doctor's obligation. It should be as important as any other type of care."

McKinnon's views are reflected in the committee's unanimous recommendation that the QEII facilitate the process of providing patients with palliative care when appropriate: "Such good, normal, usual and ethical care includes withholding futile interventions, withdrawing interventions that would prolong the dying process (such as respirators and various other life support treatments) and the administration of sufficient pain and sedative medications to ensure the patient's comfort. Meticulous titration of opiate and sedative drugs is required and if distress continues, drug doses are increased until relief is obtained. There is no upper limit to the dosages of opiates and sedatives that may be required."

Wright admits that during the years he was director of epidemiology and evaluation at Vancouver Hospital, he was unable to change pain control practice. "The medical culture rewards the misapplication of life-sustaining technologies," he says, "while slighting the prevention and relief of suffering." Wright's classic example is cardiopulmonary resuscitation. During the 1960s, it was discovered that the acute arrhythmia characteristic of some heart attacks might be stopped by a sudden electric shock. Although the success rate with arrythmia was 20 per cent, zero if the technology was not immediately available, CPR became a miracle cure for heart attacks.

Then, Wright says, "In spite of the fact that there was neither any theoretical basis nor any successful experience, the use of CPR was extended to patients dying of overwhelming infections, cancer, and patients at the end stage of chronic irremediable diseases of all kinds. Almost imperceptibly, and in many cases without any definitive written policy, the situation was reached in our hospitals in the 1970s where the staff were expected to perform CPR on all patients dying unless a specific order to the contrary were written in the chart. Death in hospital became increasingly labelled as 'cardiac arrest,' thus transforming it into a medical and potentially remediable condition."

The death-defying drama of CPR, he says, masks the reality that few CPR recipients, including heart patients, live to be discharged from hospital. There is no report of success with CPR for metastatic cancer, a 5 per cent success rate with other cancers, and a 2 per cent rate of success with infections. "When patients die, they are dead," says Wright. "It isn't a cardiac arrest." When CPR does work, survivors may suffer broken ribs and breast bones, massive bruising, and severe brain damage. "A persistent vegetative state is a condition feared much worse than death by a huge majority of normal people," Wright says. CPR can be so violent that families and friends are usually ushered out of the room, leaving their dead and dying to be beaten up alone.

When we consent to treatment, do we always understand the consequences? Charles Wright and his committee did not investigate the history of the ten drastic surgeries, with their complications, that had brought Paul Mills to die in the Queen Elizabeth's ICU. Did Mills's surgeons confidently expect a cure, or did Mills and his family insist on life-saving treatment? Did surgery lengthen Mills's life, or enhance its quality? Was surgery justified in the first place? Could Mills have lived his last months without pain, and died a natural death?

Paul Mills's medical records described him as being depressed and confused in mid-October, nearly a month before his life support was withdrawn. He told at least one nurse he wanted to die. "He was an incredibly sick, critically ill gentleman," Elizabeth MacInnis told the court. "The last few weeks of his life were certainly tortuous."

Tom Neal now sees dying as the tail end of a medical catastrophe. How often is he right?

XIX

ON JULY 27, 1998, I am sitting in the crowded headquarters of Hospice and Palliative Care Manitoba, talking with its executive director, Margaret Clarke. I found out about the hospice from Larry Librach in Toronto. Did it exist in 1995? I asked. Oh yes, he said, it's been around for years. The hospice address, 2109 Portage Avenue, was unfamiliar to me, so when I phoned Margaret Clarke I asked for directions. "We're in the Deer Lodge Centre," she replied.

Three years ago today my father was dying on the sixth floor of the Deer Lodge Centre. The weather is exactly the same, clear sunny skies, a warm breeze. The city is almost deserted. Everybody's at the lake. I have driven in myself. It's disconcerting to turn down the same street west of the big brick building and park in the same place where I had parked during those four harrowing days. I had used the rear entrance, but the entrance to Hospice and Palliative Care Manitoba is through a nondescript little side door on the street where I had parked. How many times had I rushed in and out, bringing mail, newspapers, television sets? Imagine, if only I had one day used the side door . . .

Would it have made any difference? The Manitoba hospice is, like Hospice King, essentially a volunteer visiting service. An independent charity founded in 1986, it has no in-patient beds, and its only formal connection with Deer Lodge is the office space, housekeeping, and maintenance the centre provides. Harry already had a bed in Deer Lodge, and while he was at home there was no reason for anyone to recommend a visiting volunteer.

But, Clarke tells me, Hospice and Palliative Care Manitoba is also an educational resource and a referral centre. I sure could have used its pamphlet *When Someone You Care About Has a Life Threatening Illness*, with its plain talk about grief, fear, and emotional pain. "If you are the caregiver," it says, "giving care to someone else takes a lot of energy, emotionally and physically. It's alright to ask for help." The hospice phone number, 889-8525, is on the back of the pamphlet. I knew I needed help, but how could I have found the hospice phone number without a hospice pamphlet? I didn't know enough about hospice to look in the phone book, and I may not have found it listed under hospice anyway. It was then changing its name from the Manitoba Hospice Foundation.

Are there hospice pamphlets in the Deer Lodge day hospital? Margaret Clarke isn't certain. My father had gone there for his checkups every six months or so. However, his cancer hadn't been diagnosed at the time of his last visit, so why should he pick up literature about life-threatening or terminal illness? Information posted in medical facilities isn't necessarily going to get into the hands of the people who are looking for it. Why is it the medical establishment expects sick and frightened people to *ask* for information when we don't know what to ask for or where to go to find out? Who ya gonna call, ghostbusters?

How could hospice have helped? "We could have helped you navigate the system," Clarke says. She could have walked around the corner at Deer Lodge and found Dr. Rosenberg in the day hospital. With encouragement from hospice, he might have brought in a pain and symptom specialist and arranged appropriate home nursing. Failing that, hospice could have sent one of its own nurses to do an assessment, and, if Harry had agreed to a second opinion, brought in a hospice-trained doctor. We could have had a twenty-four-hour hotline and a nurse to explain what to expect. But Harry, tired and distressed as he was, would have had to make all these decisions himself. He might have said no. Sometimes all a daughter can do is stand and wait.

And although we could have afforded twenty-four-hour home nursing for the few days it was needed, would the nurses have been trained or skilled in care of the dying? The VON did not set up its palliative care team until 1996, and while some community nurses may have taken training in the palliative care unit at Winnipeg's St. Boniface General Hospital, I had at that time no way of knowing how good they were. Harry may have been happiest seeing Diane's familiar face in Deer Lodge.

Hospice and Palliative Care Manitoba has no equivalent to Victoria Hospice's Palliative Response Team, and the entire province of Manitoba, with a scattered population of one million, has only two full-time palliative physicians, Dr. Mike Harlos at St. Boniface Hospital and Dr. Hubert Marr at Winnipeg's Riverview Health Centre. A third Winnipeg physician, Dr. Janice Mulder, who is a pharmacist as well, includes palliative patients in her practice at Grace General Hospital and Jocelyn House hospice. Hospice and Palliative Care Manitoba's sixty-five volunteers serve only the Greater Winnipeg area, and while for $300 the hospice will provide rural communities and institutions with an intensive, twenty-hour volunteer education video, *A Friend in Hand*, it has no direct connection or follow-up with the people who take the course.

The organization, funded entirely by private citizens and foundations and agencies such as the United Way, struggles along on $200,000 a year. This is less than a lot of Winnipeg doctors pocket annually from medicare, and I notice in the hospice's annual report for 1997 that out of the one hundred and four new referrals it received for volunteer visiting during the year, not one came from a physician. Most referrals came from the VON, followed by an increasing number of requests from families and patients themselves.

Hospice resources outside Greater Winnipeg are limited to part-time palliative nurse coordinators in two regions and a patchy, self-organized, grassroots mixture of services that varies from one community to the next. Some areas are well served by doctors and nurses who have trained and practised at St. Boniface Hospital, but much of the province is in limbo, including remote Aboriginal communities for whom life-threatening illnesses include diarrhea, influenza, malnutrition, alcoholism, and suicidal despair. "The Manitoba government has declared palliative care a core service," says Margaret Clarke, "but it hates to allocate the resources. I don't think palliative care will ever be fully funded."

Winnipeg, fragmented into feuding medical fiefdoms, has been struggling for four years to implement a coordinated palliative care program. A lot of Winnipeggers have died in needless pain and suffering during that time. A 1995 study by University of Manitoba psychiatry professor Dr. Harvey Chochinov concluded that if pain and clinical depression among the terminally ill were treated, fewer patients would express a wish to die quickly. As it was, only seventeen of the two hundred patients Chochinov interviewed expressed a wish to die quickly at all. Four of the six he interviewed after they received palliative care had changed their minds.

If Dr. Mulder is a Grace Hospital doctor and a hospice doctor, why couldn't Deer Lodge have referred my father to Mulder right away? But Mulder, I learn, was hired by Grace Hospital only this spring. Too late, too late. What about Jocelyn House hospice? How long has it been around? Margaret Clarke thinks that Jocelyn House, which opened in 1985, may be the oldest free-standing hospice in Canada. I've never heard of it. I'll have to go and have a look.

Jocelyn House, once a private family home, is an unobtrusive suburban split-level set in a large, leafy lot on the banks of the Seine River. A cathedral ceiling and open-concept design make it appear larger than it is. The maximum number of residents it can accommodate is five. When I arrive, it has only two. Three died the week before. The experience has been tough on the staff and survivors, and they are glad to have some quiet time.

Deaths at Jocelyn House average only five a year out of twelve or thirteen admissions. It is not designed for acute palliative care, and residents are often transferred to St. Boniface or Riverview when their conditions deteriorate. Advertising itself as providing "personalized hospice care for those living with terminal illness," Jocelyn House offers a safe, homelike environment for people who are "presently in a stable state requiring minimal care." The majority of the residents are over seventy, and a few of them live at Jocelyn House for several months. One ninety-year-old woman with breast cancer stayed for a year. She moved to a long-term care home because she found the deaths of the friends she made in the hospice too hard to bear.

More of a way station than a journey's end, Jocelyn House is an alternative to institutional care for patients, too sick to live alone, who have been discharged from hospital with those famous last words, "There is nothing more we can do." Residents pay $750 a month for room and board in addition to the costs of their medications. Nurses are on duty day and night, and either Jan Mulder or Hubert Marr at Riverview is on call. Volunteers assist with fundraising, maintenance, entertainment, excursions, and errands.

The house is attractive, and Giselle Lapointe, the acting director, invites me to join the residents for lunch. The man with a brain tumour is uncommunicative, the woman on my right subdued by the recent death of the resident in the next room. Seeing the body being taken away on a gurney, she had commented, "That's what I'm here for, isn't it?"

One of the drawbacks of an intimate environment is intimacy. Loud, bad-mannered, ill-tempered, and emotionally distraught residents are no more welcome here than they are in most other homes. "We can't handle confused or agitated patients," Giselle tells me.

"Delirium makes it difficult for the other residents." The hospice also cannot cope with residents in unmanageable pain or who require more than one person to move them. Says Giselle: "People with less than two weeks to live should be in acute care."

No room for Harry at this inn, after all. Everywhere I turn in Winnipeg, palliative care recedes like a watery mirage on a prairie highway. Why can't the Jocelyn House residents stay in their *own* homes, I'd like to know. The main reason, Giselle says, is that Manitoba Home Care may not be able to guarantee the long hours of consistent care needed by an increasingly helpless patient. If a home care worker fails to turn up, a family member has to be available to pick up the slack. Aged terminal patients, usually widowed, often have no relatives in the city, and their faraway kids worry that Mum or Dad will not have help to bathe, make meals, or clean house. They worry too that Mum or Dad might fall, or forget to take medications. Residents may come to Jocelyn House to give their children peace of mind, but it also helps that their room and board here is cheaper than an apartment and a fraction of the cost of a room in a good retirement home.

The cost is subsidized, that's why. Even if Jocelyn House were at capacity all of the time, the residents' fees would amount to less than one-quarter of its $200,000 annual budget. The balance comes from private donations, fundraising, and grants from government and charitable agencies. The citizens of Winnipeg, who, like other Canadians, are paying about $2,500 per year per capita for health care, are digging into their pockets to provide thirteen Jocelyn House residents a year with care that costs more than $15,000 apiece.

Good for them, but what about all the patients who don't qualify, or have never heard about the place, or really do prefer to die in their own beds? What would I have done if my father *had* lived three months? Six months? My life would have unravelled. How many adult children are free to transform themselves into full-time personal caregivers for a month, six months, a year? How many *want* to do this? In hospice and palliative care there is a sentimental assumption that families should, or want to, look after their dying relatives. But I have spoken with a lot of people, good people, who can't, or don't. That's why we pay nurses.

Why in Manitoba, or any other province, should the mortally ill be expected to *buy* basic, compassionate care? If palliative care is not free, equal, and universally accessible, why not? It's paid for, why isn't it there? How can the Manitoba government endorse one small Winnipeg hospice and not provide high quality care to all dying patients? Fifteen thousand dollars spent over three or four weeks at the end of a life can buy a lot of comfort.

Jocelyn Hutton died in this house of bone cancer at the age of seventeen. It was the Huttons' own home, and after Jocelyn's death in 1980, her parents, Bill and Miriam, donated their home as the foundation for a hospice. Jocelyn had the same kind of cancer as Terry Fox, in the same place, the right leg above the knee, and, like Terry, she'd had her leg amputated. Thanks to his Marathon of Hope for cancer research, Terry Fox is a name recognized everywhere in Canada. Jocelyn Hutton is remembered by a small circle of people in Winnipeg.

It's depressing to find hospice and palliative care so impoverished and fragmented in Manitoba, its Canadian birthplace. The St. Boniface General Hospital opened a twelve-bed palliative care unit in November 1974, a month or two ahead of the Royal Victoria Hospital in Montreal. Neither hospital knew what the other was up to. Both are still in business, and St. Boniface's palliative care is not to be confused with its pastoral care. Should I have called St. Boniface after all?

I see no nuns or priests in the ward's narrow hall, and it is cluttered with the usual medical paraphernalia. The ward is in an old part of the hospital, and the walls are painted the dismal, indeterminate shade of *blech* some crafty paint manufacturer must have unloaded cheap on every hospital in Canada. The nurses, looking frazzled, wear pastel uniforms. Joan Honer, the clinical nurse specialist in charge of patient admissions, is in white, as is Mike Harlos, the unit's physician.

Harlos is young, tall and muscular, a good thing too since he is the only palliative specialist for twenty ward patients, about four hundred admissions a year, and a home-based patient population that averages one hundred and forty. He is on call two nights out of three. The nurses look frazzled because, as a consequence of budget cuts, there's not enough of them. I see a lot of people who look like family milling about, but no volunteers smocked or unsmocked. The unit uses few volunteers, Joan Honer explains, and volunteers are not to touch or feed the patients. No hospice hugs here, but when I think about it, Winnipeggers don't go in much for hugging. Patients can use a smoking room and a whirlpool bath, a group of singers and a music therapist come every Wednesday, and the Humane Society brings pets for a visit. There isn't a piece of stained glass in sight.

"People think they can set up a bed with a stained glass window and put a pot of flowers on the table and call it palliative care," Joan Honer says scornfully. "Everyone wants to donate a picture." No warm fuzzies here. No pictures. Send money, please, for education and patient comforts. This is a *hospital*, she is saying, not a hospice. Joan Honer has been here since 1980. She has a soft voice, a quiet manner, and gentle brown eyes, but I get the impression it is Joan Honer who keeps this place running. It is intensive care. The median length of stay is six days, the mortality rate 80 per cent.

Honer and Harlos are vigilant about the patients they admit into the unit. A man who decided to stop his kidney dialysis arrived with two suitcases and announced, "This is where I'm going to die." Not all cases are so straightforward. They do not admit cancer patients on chemotherapy. Harlos will consult in the oncology ward, but he and Honer believe that it is the responsibility of the oncologists prescribing chemotherapy to deal with its potentially complicated and lethal side effects. And a patient on chemo, however futile the treatment, may not be ready to face the harsh reality of dying.

"We don't stop people from dying," Harlos says. "If people hemorrhage, get pneumonia, that terminal complication will not be stopped." Harlos *will* treat a secondary, curable illness in a home-based patient who has come in temporarily for symptom control, but he and Joan Honer screen out terminal patients who insist on useless or harmful technology.

The St. Boniface palliative care unit is the end stage in a journey that must begin with a referral from a physician. That physician has to be on staff at St. Boniface Hospital, have admitting privileges here, or care for a patient who has had an extended period of treatment at this hospital. No room for Harry here. When I ask Joan about this exclusivity, she retorts: "Why don't other hospitals open palliative care units?"

As it is, the St. Boniface unit has all the patients it can handle, and to maximize its stretched services, patients are streamed according to their level of need. The first phase is home care, nursing and support services for patients looked after by their family doctors. In the second phase, outreach, patients and families can consult the unit by telephone, attend the outpatient symptom control clinic, or, if necessary, be seen by Mike Harlos at home. Admission to the in-patient unit is reserved for patients in crisis or those who require institutional care. The majority of the one thousand people who call the unit for help every year do not qualify.

Getting registered and classified with the palliative care service is only the first hurdle. Patients assessed as *first phase*, relatively stable, are not automatically admitted to the ward even if they turn up at Emergency. An advance phone call from their physician explaining their deteriorating condition is required to move them into *second phase*, with full access to all services, including the in-patient ward.

The gates to the underworld in Winnipeg are few, I find, and guarded by many-headed doctors. No doctor, no referral. No referral, no palliative care. Unlike Victoria Hospice, which got the attention of Victoria's family physicians by sending its nurse/counsellor Palliative Response Team into their patients' homes to deal with medical crises, St. Boniface has not established an effective working relationship with Winnipeg's family doctors.

"We have terrible trouble with family physicians here," Mike Harlos sighs. "Ninety per cent of the physicians say they do good palliative care. It's not their fault. They don't know what they don't know. I had an eighty-year-old surgeon say to me, 'When I slow down, I'll do palliative care.' I say to these guys, 'I'll bet our ward is more acute than your ward!'" Nobody in Winnipeg, he says, expects a family doctor to come to a home at night. Some won't show up for days, if ever. If Harlos makes a crisis house call and leaves a prescription, a family doctor may ignore it because he didn't write it. Harlos finds that many of the patients he visits don't have family doctors. If they have been seeing a specialist for many years, why go back to a doctor who may not remember them? Tough it out alone. Looking back, Harry's bed at Deer Lodge was a great blessing.

The highlight of the St. Boniface palliative care unit is the obstetrics ward I have to pass through to reach it. How lovely to leave life with the bawling of newborn babies in your ears! I'm not going to check out Riverview Health Centre's palliative care unit. The beds had been full three years ago anyway, with a waiting list, and the receptionist hadn't bothered to ask why I was calling, or if she could help me. Another dragon lashing her tail at the gate, a consequence, I understand now, of physician referral *only*, please.

So, I will go see the physician who goes back to the beginning of palliative care in Manitoba, Dr. Paul Henteleff. Dr. Henteleff retired as director of the St. Boniface unit in 1991, and I find him riding a lawn tractor on his rural property east of Winnipeg outside the village of Dugald. Crossing the CNR railway tracks, I had glanced about for a plaque, a monument, something to commemorate the passengers who had died there in the wreck of the Campers' Special on September 1, 1947. I saw nothing resembling a memorial until I arrived at the Henteleffs' driveway. It was lined with flower beds, and more flowers, massed in beds covering an acre or more to the east, have transformed their property into a prairie version of an English country garden. The Henteleffs' private garden is not related to the Dugald wreck, but, to the south, farmers' fields are golden with sunflowers, the international symbol of hospice. We push up the daisies, and cover the dead with flowers as symbols of life.

Dr. Henteleff and I sit in the screened gazebo. He is much younger than I had anticipated, quiet, reflective, rather melancholy. I had assumed that Henteleff had founded the program at St. Boniface, but no, he says, the idea came from a British doctor, David Skelton, appointed in 1973 to head the hospital's new two-hundred-bed geriatric ward. Skelton, converted to hospice principles by Cicely Saunders in England, asked St. Boniface Hospital to designate twelve of the two hundred beds for care of the dying. The Grey Nuns agreed immediately.

Skelton quickly found that doctors in other wards, eager to admit new patients, yet embarrassed to send dying patients home, were happy to use a transfer to palliative care as a station stop for patients with a one-way ticket to the morgue. The unit grew to twenty-eight beds. Skelton couldn't handle it all, and Henteleff, prodded by his conscience, volunteered his services. He became fascinated by the challenges in this experimental field, and took over as director in 1979 when Skelton moved to start palliative care in Edmonton, Alberta.

Years before, Paul Henteleff had watched Elisabeth Kübler-Ross interview a couple of terminal patients at St. Boniface Hospital during a Grand Rounds presentation. "I was *enthralled* at how she could later deconstruct an interview with a patient," Henteleff recalls. In practice, however, he learned that talking with a dying patient was not necessarily the doctor's job: "I had this man who kept saying to me, 'If you can get my bowels fixed, I'll be okay.' I thought he meant he'd get better, and I worried that he wasn't facing his death. When I spoke about this to the nursing sister, she told me, 'Yesterday we were planning the details of his funeral.' I thought, 'Why should he talk to *me* about that stuff? Bowels are all I have to do for him. I don't have to be open and talk.' It can be a terrible burden."

Henteleff learned to rely on the nurses for up-to-the-minute, hands-on information about his patients. It was the nurses, he realized, who bathed, fed and sat with them, got them up to the toilet, turned them, examined them, and, alert to subtle changes, knew when to call him. "Nurses are far better than doctors at recognizing imminent death," Henteleff says. They were also better at charting pain. Henteleff was shocked when a study of his patients' records showed that 10 per cent were in severe pain. "The nurses had made the record," he says, "but I was failing to see it as *right now*. The ritual of being committed to the relief of pain was convincing me everything was okay. Was I blinded by my confidence and hope that tomorrow would be better?" Henteleff told his nurses, "Anything you do, I will back up." Like doctors at Victoria Hospice, he developed protocols for drug doses the nurses could follow in his absence, and introduced the practice of having nurses and other staff record reports on audiotape. "I gave *them* the power," Henteleff says. "I was free."

Introspective and self-critical, Henteleff broods about the subtle, unspoken, and unrecognized psychological power medical caregivers have over their patients. "Scientific research needs to be done in palliative medicine," he admits, "but it is very burdensome for some patients. You're giving questionnaires to people every day, and *they don't have many bloody days left*. And how powerful is the role of the *questioner*?" Henteleff became sensitive to the fact that patients put on many faces, Doctor Smiley Face, Nurse Pain Face, Family Happy Face, Best Friend Weepy Face, Stranger Brave Face, Writer Talking Face, Researcher Serious Face, and that they adopt these masks to protect themselves from the irritatingly nosy, bossy, healthy people looming over their beds. The best defence may be to play along.

"*Never* start by asking patients about their pain," Henteleff says. "If you talk pain, that's what you expect. Ask how they're feeling. Are they comfortable? Let the patient say." He dismisses complementary therapies as "hobbies" that suit the caregiver, but St. Boniface nurses have an arsenal of skills, including one nurse trained in massage, Shiatsu, visualization, aromatherapy, and a therapy I have never heard of, tragering.

The dying process subjects us to so many indignities that Henteleff learned respect for "the invisible dome" of a patient's private space:

"I had a very strong-minded young woman with a brain tumour. She was outspoken, angry, suspicious, turbulent. I introduced a tranquilizer into her drugs. 'What's that?' she asked the nurse. When the nurse told her, I got a strip torn off me! She wasn't taking any of that shit from me. She had a business being angry. I was producing *war*. I apologized for doing something without her consent. She was right."

Henteleff gets very angry with romantics who portray dying with dignity as an ethical and intellectual achievement, our finest hour. "Dying is inevitable," he says. "It is not *achieved*. Disintegration is the norm, and communication is often undermined by the very disintegration of life. Are these ordinary deaths undignified?" In 1986, Henteleff was asked to find participants for a psychiatry study of terminal patients' attitudes towards death. He found that two-thirds of the nearly two hundred patients he screened were not mentally competent or able to communicate, or too sick and weak for a short interview.

"It was not, I passionately hope, their finest hour," Henteleff says. "See the dying as they are. I am not accountable for the dignity of their dying if the standard of dignity is raised to a level beyond *their* capacity at the time of dying, possibly beyond their capacity at any time in their lives."

Henteleff has condensed his philosophy as a physician into five "warnings of hateful action." Do not deceive. Do not mistreat, and mistreatment includes inaction in the face of suffering when relief is possible. Do not abandon. Do not exploit. "The dying can be prey," he says, "not only to the greed of charlatans, but also to the caregiver's zeal to demonstrate 'involvement,' manipulate symptoms, recruit for research, or to impose beliefs and solutions." A St. Boniface nurse once found the husband and daughter of a semiconscious patient berating each other across her bed. When the nurse disapprovingly pointed out that the woman could probably hear everything they said, the daughter replied, "Well, we're always like this and she knows we're here." When a social worker proposed to a dying father that he achieve a reconciliation with his estranged son, the father replied, "Bugger off!"

Do not exalt. "Treating a dying patient on a level above the human caricatures their humanity," Henteleff says. "It is an indignity. The action of exalting another human dooms the caregiver to failure, and that, too, is an indignity."

Dr. Henteleff retired at sixty, frustrated by financial cutbacks, political inaction, lack of medical school education about pain and symptom control, and the indifference of family physicians. He felt too that he might not have long to live. "I have angina," he says. "I am very aware of the risk of sudden death." Henteleff belongs to a funeral planning and memorial society, but when he tried to write an advance directive, he found he couldn't do it.

Henteleff doesn't envision himself dying in the St. Boniface palliative care program. "It's not the kind of death lined up for me," he shrugs. Nor does he want it. After a pause, he confesses: "I don't like the idea of someone bathing me, massaging me. I have an aversion to being handled." Henteleff speculates that people fundamentally reject palliative care. "It doesn't fit in with any of our normal desires. We have a lifetime of experience getting sick, moments of panic or concern, and we react with denial. Oh, it's just the flu. When we see changes in our condition, we don't necessarily assume that this is the last straw. We figure, 'I'll be as well tomorrow as I was yesterday.' *Accepting* palliative care is the hardest part of dying. If you deal only with people who have done that, you're leaving the hardest part for someone else to do."

Palliative care is simple and easy to learn, he believes. "We are more sophisticated in our methods now, but the results are ever so slightly better." He learned by trial and error, critically reviewing every death, observing and listening to patients, their families and the nurses. St. Boniface Hospital's inventive young clinical pharmacist, Elliot Fingerote, taught him what to expect from the drugs he prescribed and suggested alternatives when they didn't work. If necessary, Fingerote manufactured what they needed in the hospital pharmacy. Speaking of Fingerote, Henteleff's face brightens with a nostalgic smile. "We had *such a good time*."

I am intrigued by Fingerote. Pharmacists, unduly fearful of being prosecuted for supplying narcotics to addicts, are scarce in palliative care circles. I had never heard of Elliot Fingerote. If he has been so influential in establishing the practice of palliative care in Manitoba, I'd like to meet him. Where is he now? Dr. Henteleff writes down Elliot Fingerote's phone number. Fingerote is director of pharmacy services at the Deer Lodge Centre.

So the next day, the third anniversary of my father's death, I'm back at Deer Lodge talking to the creator of the morphine suppositories that had seemed to give Harry some relief from pain. I am so grateful to Elliot Fingerote I could hug him. Articulate, energetic, and opinionated, Fingerote tells me his story:

"I became clinical pharmacist at St. Boniface Hospital in 1970. When Dr. Skelton arrived in 1974, he worked on building a team. He brought the team idea with him, it was unknown here at the time, and I liked it. It was a comfortable, patient-oriented way to work. I didn't know what palliative care was, and we didn't know what a pharmacist would do. I would define the role."

At the time, Fingerote says, it was believed that morphine taken by mouth didn't work, yet patients in a wasted condition could not tolerate the pain of repeated injections. Skelton had been accustomed to the use of suppositories in Britain, but there were no suppositories in Winnipeg. The hospital had a methadone withdrawal program for drug addicts, and Skelton suggested Fingerote make some methadone suppositories with cocoa butter.

"They failed with the first patient," he says. "His pain was not relieved. With the second patient, they were a success, so I went to talk to him." Over time, the nurses alerted the team to the miserable side effect of constipation, and Fingerote added bowel stimulants and stool softeners to the medication menu. He had almost no literature to refer to, and the team's closest colleagues, equally new to the job, were at the Royal Victoria Hospital in Montreal.

"Skelton wanted to convert to oral medication," Fingerote recalls. "He asked me, 'What have you got?' 'Morphine.' 'How much should I use?' *'I don't know.'*" The only test Fingerote knew of was the "rat tail squeeze," giving a rat morphine until it stops squealing when you squeeze its tail. But how to compare rats to human beings? The St. Boniface unit stuck to a Winnipeg version of England's Brompton's cocktail: rye whisky, cocaine, a phenobarbital sedative, and morphine.

"Our colleagues complained," Fingerote says, "and we started asking, 'Why are we using Brompton's?' In 1976, Balfour Mount in Montreal published a paper saying that morphine *alone* was effective. We could leave out all that other stuff and the patients didn't notice any difference." Fingerote added morphine to chocolate syrup to mask its bitter taste. It worked.

His first challenge was to get patients off the prescription drugs to which they had become addicted. "There were relatively few drugs in the 1960s," he says, "and we knew nothing about drug interactions. Valium was coming on the market, antidepressants, diuretics, antibiotics. People were taking barbiturates, long-term, addicting sedatives. They were taking stuff that was inappropriate and taking it inappropriately. It was hard to get them off."

Fingerote believes in using a few basic drugs well, and narcotics are basic drugs that are generally not used well. "We have fears, and we have little to base those fears on," he says. "We always have an antagonist drug that can reverse the effect of the narcotic. You won't kill anybody with narcotics. I *hate* any reference to a pain scale. Does it matter if it's a six or a five? It hurts. *I will do something.*"

Fingerote came to Deer Lodge from St. Boniface in 1994. "This is one big terminal care unit," he says. "Your last stop." Maybe not quite. Fingerote is flabbergasted to learn that Harry Robertson had been admitted here to die. Had Harry been a long-term resident, Fingerote says, Deer Lodge would likely have discharged him to an acute-care bed in Grace Hospital. "We lack physician input here," he says. Family physicians are not paid to visit the institutionalized aged and decrepit unless they're sick. Residents' doctors tend to drop by for a chat about once a month.

My curious circular journey around Winnipeg has brought me back to where I began. I'm glad we managed to miss the death train to Grace Hospital. An acute-care hospital was the last place Harry wanted to die. St. Boniface too is an acute-care hospital. Would he have wanted a semi-private room with one nurse for five or six dying patients? And I am tickled by the possibility that Harry's dying may have been an unusual event at Deer Lodge, a learning experience for medical professionals as well as for me. He had taught his last class.

As I leave Deer Lodge, I hesitate and look up at the south windows glaring in the afternoon sun. Should I go back to 6B? No. Let the dead bury the dead. The river of time has flowed on. I'm late. I have to drive back to the lake today.

The next morning, I go to the boathouse and open the wooden box, Lieut. Robertson RCNVR. I had forgotten to make an inventory of the keepsakes I had put in it, and the first object I take out is my father's watch. It's still ticking.

XX

BY DECEMBER 1998, I am halfway through the Advanced Issues in Palliative Care course sponsored by York Region's palliative care services in Newmarket, Ontario. This is the most education I can get without enrolling in a community college or John Morgan's course in thanatology at King's College in London, Ontario. I am beginning to doubt the value of lectures. New research is showing that it is futile to educate people on the lower rungs of the health care pecking order if they lack the power to change the structure. Nurses who acquire more education about opioids than the doctors they work with may find their knowledge repudiated because they are nurses, and if they are bold enough to question doctors' prescriptions, they risk making the doctors even more reactionary. Knowledge gained at workshops and seminars is soon forgotten if not put into practice.

I have in my hand a blue binder full of handouts that include, among the conceptual foundations of palliative care, "a multidisciplinary team of professionals and volunteers." There's not much doubt in my mind where the volunteers sit in this locker room. The nurse who lectured us on symptom control began by saying that she was going to keep her presentation simple because "I don't want to make it too difficult for the volunteers."

Excuse me? Another nurse ranked volunteers number five out of nine essential components of palliative care (evaluation of practice was last). "Volunteers are not the trained people you think they are," she warned. (Why am I here, then?) "The volunteer doesn't do the nasty things. Families think that all they do is sit there." She cautioned that volunteers must have mandatory police checks. Why? Volunteers don't administer medications. Patients are in far more danger of being harmed by a negligent nurse or a physician who knows nothing about morphine.

Since I began volunteering at Hill House Hospice, a new four-bed facility in Richmond Hill, I have watched a lot of nurses at work. I have infinite admiration for the nurses who do the nasty things expertly, who brush their patients' hair and give them backrubs, who sit with them at night and lend grieving relatives a strong shoulder to cry on. These women – I haven't met a male nurse in Ontario – are poorly paid, overworked, and often tired, but they are skilled, wise, calm in a crisis, and committed to strangers they see in only a snapshot of time.

At Hill House, nurses are often alone when their patients die at night. "The first time I had to wash a body by myself, it took me a long time to screw up my courage," admits a young community nurse I'll call Rita. "I lit a candle and turned on the TV. At least I could hear voices, see people's faces. The body wasn't stiff, and it took me a while to realize that I didn't have to wash carefully for fear of hurting the patient. I think it's only ethical to wash the body. Hospitals don't always do it, and families usually leave very quickly when someone dies. I make sure the funeral directors handle the body with care and respect when they put it into the body bag."

Rita respects as well the feelings of the living: "I was caring for Barbara, a comatose patient whose husband was convinced she was going to get better. He wanted to have her catheter removed so she could get up and go to the bathroom. You can't just say, 'Look, she's in a *coma*.' I said that she might wet the bed, require changing and moving, and it would hurt her. He bought that."

Quiet, tactful nurses like Rita create a comfortable emotional space that allows families to work through their emotions in their own ways. Barbara's husband finally realized that she was close to death when an air ambulance he tried to charter refused to fly her home. Then, in every Canadian community, there are the nursey nurses who talk about "moving patients to a place where *we want them to be*," the monkey chatterers who gossip loudly and giggle while their dying patient's relatives weep in the next room, and the whiners who complain and kvetch about their personal problems. There are nurses with bad backs who can't turn a patient without help, and exhausted nurses working a second or third consecutive twelve-hour shift with no sleep. Thirty and forty years ago, the dying may have been neglected by not-on-my-shift nurses, but now they are at risk from nurses determined to keep them alive. One woman with end-stage brain cancer asked her nurse for advice about how she should provide for her young child. In reply, the nurse shouted, "The best thing you can do for your child is *survive!*" The woman died soon after.

Before we die, we become dead weights. I have tried to turn on her side an emaciated woman much smaller than I who was snuggled into a mountain of duvets and pillows in the middle of a kingsize waterbed. She was able to hear and understand my instructions, and she still had some muscular energy, but as I floundered about in her bed, I thought, "My god, she's heavy! Am I strong enough to do this?" I did, but I made a note to keep my eye out for nurses with long, sinewy arms, strong hands, and powerful body language.

Sherpa-nurse Kit Martin is one of these. She's the nurse who ranks volunteers five out of nine. Maybe she's right, but since she ranks evaluation dead last, we may never know. But Kit Martin has packed a lot of people up their mountains, and she's the first person I've encountered who takes a serious historical and archaeological interest in the origins of hospice. I sit enthralled as Kit tells us about the oracle at Delphi, and how *oracle* means a structure, a courtyard, as well as the cryptic prophecies of ecstatic priestesses. Pilgrims who came to Apollo's oracle at Delphi were on a healing journey, and Martin speculates that the priestesses, with their arcane knowledge of herbs and drugs, manipulated a prescribed process of healing and killing.

I'm so excited by this unexpected connection with contemporary medicine I rush off to my library to read up on Delphi. I'd gone to Delphi years ago as a typical young romantic North American tourist. All I remember of Delphi is an Israeli couple on the bus yearning for the McDonald's hamburgers they had left behind in Tel Aviv, and a tiny rivulet of water trickling down a dusty, disappointing mountain called Parnassus. Could the oracle have been a spring? I stopped, dipped my fingers in the stream, then, hesitating, put them to my lips. I may die of typhoid, I thought, but this is Delphi.

I didn't know then, as I discover now, that the ruined Delphic oracle had been dedicated to the Pythian Apollo, a sun god glorified in Greek mythology for killing Python, the monstrous snake guarding the oracle. *Python?* A python, a huge snake that ingests its prey whole after crushing it in the coils of its powerful body, is a jungle, swamp, and water snake. What is a python doing up here on the dry rocky slopes of Mount Parnassus? Two thousand years ago, before the shrine was plundered and destroyed, Mount Parnassus would have likely been more lush and fertile than it is today, but, still, the Python seems to me to have come from somewhere else.

Once I start rooting through mythology and ancient history, I find that Python is reincarnated as Typhon, the great World Snake slain by Zeus, a legend that inspired the Norse story of Thor's fatal combat with the Midgard serpent that encircled the world, and later, Beowulf's underwater combat with Grendel's Mother. The *Beowulf* poet may have been right in making his snakelike monster female. According to legend, the oracular Delphic python spoke through a priestess, the Pythoness, and scholars of Greek myths interpret the story of Apollo killing the Python as representing the destruction of a prehistoric shrine dedicated to Gaea, Mother Earth, by an invading cult of sun worshippers. Another name for Python in Greek

myth is Delphyne, a name still given to girls. Delphinine, a poisonous drug derived from the delphinium flower, indicates that the site
may have been originally chosen for its herbs and flowers, and the
power to poison would have given the Delphic priestesses a reputation for witchcraft. Their shrine may have been a spring, a cleft in
the rock that emitted volcanic rumblings and vapours, or a cave.
The European cult of the cave bear dates back forty thousand years,
and the bear that was worshipped was Ursa Major, the Great She-
Bear. The presence of bears meant that berries and beehives were
probably close by, and honey was prized as a healing salve, a preser-
vative, a sweet, nourishing food, and, fermented, as an alcoholic
drink. Bees, like bears, were associated with goddess worship. Were
the original Delphic priestesses stoned on mead? Was the golden
bough a honeycomb?

Stories, speculation, myths, but I am more willing to believe in
Delphyne and her priestesses than I am in the Virgin Mary. The
Greeks called Delphi the centre of the world, the *omphalos*, or navel.
A navel is the scar of a severed umbilical cord, and *delphys* is the
Greek word for womb. If the Delphic oracle indeed offered herbal
remedies, drugs, counselling and visualization, it would have been
closer to a hospice in its Gaea incarnation. Dedicated to Apollo, it
became a luxury spa for emperors, generals, and pilgrims wealthy
enough to offer lavish gifts to the god. The babblings and tremblings
of the oracle might have been a touch of theatre to give the pilgrims
their money's worth, and since her prophecies were ambiguous, she
couldn't be held accountable.

The Delphi of Apollo was known as a purification centre. The
serious healing was going on at Epidaurus in the temple of Asclepius,
Apollo's son and the god of medicine. According to myth, when
Asclepius restored a man to life, Pluto, lord of Hades, persuaded
Zeus to kill Asclepius with a thunderbolt. Perhaps this accounts for
the theory that doctors fear death more than the rest of us. Asclepius,
whose staff, or caduceus, has only one entwined snake, has not survived in legend as well as Hermes, with two snakes, who carries

on as St. Christopher, patron saint of travellers. One of his shrines, of course, is St. Christopher's Hospice in the London suburb of Sydenham, presided over by the Great Mother of the modern hospice, Dame Cicely Saunders.

One look at Medusa, a she-monster whose hair was a mass of writhing snakes, turned Greeks to stone, and, according to the Old Testament Book of Genesis, it was a subtle little snake in the grass that, tempting Eve with the knowledge of good and evil, persuaded her to eat the forbidden fruit of the Tree of Life in the Garden of Eden. Why Eve, I wonder, not Adam, and why should eating a fruit doom humanity to sexual shame, suffering, pain, and death? Was it mere disobedience, or did the angry god of the Hebrews expel Adam and Eve from the garden because the Tree of Life was sacred to his archrival, the Assyrian and Babylonian goddess, Ishtar?

The Hebrews emerged as a people with a distinct culture and religion about 1200 B.C., relatively recently in human history, and as the Old Testament relates so eloquently, they were in constant conflict with the older, wealthier, and powerful civilizations around them. Much of this conflict involved religion, since the Hebrews' belief in monotheism, one god, was a unique concept. Other cultures had pantheons of gods and goddesses associated with the sun and moon, sacred animals, hills, groves, and streams. Ishtar, known to the Phoenicians as Astarte and to the Semites as Ashtoreth, was by 1200 B.C. a popular goddess of love, war, and fertility. Figurines found in Mesopotamia show her with broad hips and fat thighs proffering her bare breasts, a characteristic, as well, of the Minoan goddess figurines on the island of Crete.

For patriarchal Hebrew theologians, Ishtar, associated with the worship of bulls, the Golden Calf of the Old Testament, must have been a fearful and formidable incarnation of female eroticism. Ishtar herself was a reincarnation of Inanna, a powerful fertility goddess worshipped in Sumer, a pre-Babylonian Mesopotamian civilization that emerged in the fertile valley surrounding the Tigris and Euphrates rivers about 4000 B.C. Sumerian clay tablets covered with cuneiform script were unearthed in what is now southern Iraq at the end of the nineteenth century, but they were not pieced together, translated, or published until the 1970s.

The Sumerians are credited with inventing writing, the wheel, codes of law, and cities. The worship of Inanna, the Whore of Babylon herself, predates by millennia the Hebrews' Jehovah. In a book by Sumerian scholars Diane Wolkstein and Samuel Noah Kramer, *Inanna, Queen of Heaven and Earth, Her Stories and Hymns from Sumer*, I find a practical story, deciphered from the clay tablets, of Inanna's descent to challenge the Queen of the Underworld, her sister Ereshkigal.

The frontispiece to the book is a portrait of Inanna carved on a stone vessel about 2400 B.C. Inanna has a round, girlish face, big cow eyes, and an enigmatic smile. Masses of ringlets surround her head and reach to her waist. She wears a crown shaped like a crescent moon or a pair of horns, and carries a date cluster. Sumerian scholars believe that the *huluppu*, Inanna's sacred tree, was a date palm.

On earth, Inanna, the Morning and Evening Star, sister to the sun and daughter of the moon, was a vegetation fertility goddess united in divine marriage with a shepherd-king, Dumuzi. Inanna and Dumuzi are depicted on clay tablets lying in bed in close, sensual embraces. In the poem "The Courtship of Inanna and Dumuzi" Inanna praises her lover:

> He shaped my loins with his fair hands,
> The shepherd Dumuzi filled my lap with cream and milk,
> He stroked my pubic hair,
> He watered my womb.
> He laid his hands on my holy vulva,
> He smoothed my black boat with cream,
> He quickened my narrow boat with milk,
> He caressed me on the bed.
> Now I will caress my high priest on the bed,
> I will caress the faithful shepherd Dumuzi,

I will caress his loins, the shepherdship of the land,
I will decree a sweet fate for him.

This story of Inanna's descent was written about 1700 B.C. The
Sumerians did not believe in an afterlife or in individual reincarnation, and when Inanna, Queen of Heaven, descended to the Great
Below and returned, she became Queen of Heaven and Earth. The
poem begins with the pomp of a royal progress: "From the Great
Above she opened her ear to the Great Below. From the Great Above
the goddess opened her ear to the Great Below. From the Great
Above Inanna opened her ear to the Great Below. My Lady abandoned heaven and earth to descend to the underworld. Inanna
abandoned heaven and earth to descend to the underworld. She abandoned her office of holy priestess to descend to the underworld."

To challenge her ugly, ill-tempered sister, Ereshkigal, Inanna gathered all her spiritual powers. She placed the *shugurra*, the crown of the
steppe, on her head, fastened two bead necklaces around her neck,
and slipped a gold ring over her wrist. She wrapped herself in her
royal robe, and bound over her chest her breastplate named "Come,
man, come!" In her hand, she carried her royal symbol, a lapis measuring-rod and line. Inanna instructed her servant, Ninshubur, that if
she did not return, Ninshubur was to weep at the temples of the gods
and plead with them not to let her die.

When Inanna knocked loudly on the outer gate to the underworld
and demanded to be let in, Neti, the gatekeeper, reported her arrival
to Ereshkigal:

> When Ereshkigal heard this, she slapped her thigh and bit
> her lip. She took the matter into her heart and dwelt on it.
> Then she spoke:
> "Come, Neti, my chief gatekeeper of the *kur*, heed my
> words. Bolt the seven gates of the underworld. Then, one by
> one, open each gate a crack. Let Inanna enter. As she enters,

remove her royal garments. Let the holy priestess of heaven enter bowed low."

Neti heeded the words of his queen. He bolted the seven gates of the underworld. Then he opened the outer gate. He said to the maid: "Come, Inanna, enter."

When she entered the first gate, from her head the *shugurra*, the crown of the steppe, was removed.

Inanna asked: "What is this?"

She was told: "Quiet, Inanna, the ways of the underworld are perfect. They must not be questioned."

When she entered the second gate, from her neck the small lapis beads were removed.

Inanna asked, "What is this?"

She was told: "Quiet, Inanna, the ways of the underworld are perfect. They must not be questioned."

At the next gates, Inanna was stripped of her second strand of beads, her breastplate, her gold ring, her measuring-rod and line, and her royal robe.

Naked and bowed low, Inanna entered the throne room. Ereshkigal rose from her throne. Inanna started towards the throne. The Annuna, the judges of the underworld, surrounded her. They passed judgement against her.

Then Ereshkigal fastened on Inanna the eye of death. She spoke against her the word of wrath. She uttered against her the cry of guilt.

She struck her.

Inanna was turned into a corpse, a piece of rotting meat, and was hung from a hook on the wall.

When Inanna did not return, her servant Ninshubur, wailing and tearing her flesh, pleaded with the Air God, Enlil, and the Moon

God, Nanna, not to let Inanna die. They coldly replied: "She who goes to the Dark City stays there." But Enki, God of Water and Wisdom, was grieved. Fashioning two flylike creatures from dirt under his fingernail, Enki gave to one the food of life, to the other the water of life. The flies slipped into the Great Below to sympathize with Ereshkigal, who was moaning and groaning like a woman in labour, and when Ereshkigal offered them a gift in return for their commiseration, they asked for the corpse hanging from the hook on the wall. Ereshkigal gave the corpse to them. Sprinkled with the food and water of life, Inanna arose.

But the judges of the underworld refused to allow Inanna to ascend unless she provided someone to take her place. On her way home, accompanied by a bodyguard of death demons, the *galla*, Inanna encountered her two grieving sons and her loyal servant, Ninshubur. Dressed in soiled sackcloth, they prostrated themselves at her feet. No, she told the *galla*, I won't give them to you. Then, in her holy city of Uruk, Inanna found her husband Dumuzi, wearing shining robes, seated contentedly on his magnificent throne under a big apple tree. When Dumuzi saw Inanna, he did not move.

"The *galla* seized him by his thighs. They poured milk out of his seven churns. They broke the reed pipe which the shepherd was playing.

"Inanna fastened on Dumuzi the eye of death. She spoke against him the word of wrath. She uttered against him the cry of guilt:

"Take him! Take Dumuzi away!"

Has a wife ever lived who has not at some time consigned her husband to perdition? Inanna, however, relented. She missed sex with Dumuzi. She arranged a compromise. Dumuzi's sister Geshtinanna would take his place in the underworld for half the year.

The story of the death and rebirth of Dumuzi is repeated in all the myths involving sacrificial kings or bridegrooms – Tammuz, Adonis, Osiris, Dionysius, Jesus – that James Frazer collected in *The Golden Bough*, and by the time the story of Inanna and Ereshkigal travelled to Greece, Rome, and Europe, their multiple personalities included

Isis, Demeter, Persephone, Venus Aphrodite, Artemis (Diana), Hecate, and Freya, all goddesses associated with sex and death. Styx was a goddess who presided over a poisonous river, and our word Hell comes from a Norse goddess, Hel.

I like to think of Inanna twinkling in the sky morning and evening, keeping watch, and the story of her descent makes psychological and spiritual sense to me. Birth star, death star. Sunset and evening star, Lucifer, Lucy in the Sky with Diamonds. The Beatles' song was blasting out of archaeologist Don Johanson's tape deck on the night of November 30, 1974, as Johanson and his team of French and American archaeologists celebrated their discovery of the fragmentary skelton of an early female hominid. They named her Lucy.

Lucy, age twenty, had died at Hadar in Ethiopia's Rift Valley about three million years earlier. The shape of Lucy's pelvis was human, not chimpanzee, and she had the thigh bone of a walking woman. Johanson's discovery was confirmed four years later when archaeologist Mary Leakey, working at Laetoli, Tanzania, discovered a trail of hominid footprints preserved in ash from a volcano that had erupted 3.5 million years ago.

The theory that humankind originated in Africa is now generally accepted by archaeologists and anthropologists, although there is controversy over whether it was the relatively primitive *homo erectus* who walked out of Africa and dispersed around the globe as early as one million years ago, or whether *homo sapiens* evolved in Africa and left as recently as ninety or one hundred thousand years ago. If it was *homo sapiens*, thinking man, who departed from Eden, the emigrants would have carried with them their myths, stories, songs, and religious beliefs. Almost nothing is known about how, when, or why this dispersal took place, but the Noah's Ark theory, as the archaeologists call the late dispersal hypothesis, might help explain how a mythic oracular python made it up a mountain in Greece.

In *Ancestors: In Search of Human Origins*, Johanson and other archaeologists explore a theory that our ancestors were scavengers, not hunters, and that our fear of death is rooted not in the act of killing, but in a fear of being eaten. The popular image of a Stone Age hunter spearing a mammoth or sabre-toothed tiger runs counter to archaeological evidence indicating that our early ancestors lived on shellfish and small game, turtles, reptiles, insects, eggs, nuts, fruits and roots, supplemented by marrow sucked from the bones of carrion. It made sense, Johanson argues, for relatively small, slow, two-legged creatures to watch for vultures circling a kill, wait for the big carnivores to eat their fill, then move in to carry off what was left. Men may have made weapons to chase away other scavengers, and the small game our ancestors killed likely included each other.

Fear of being eaten helps explain ritual cannibalism, a rite that transforms the act of eating human flesh into a sacrament, or, in other cultures, a taboo against eating human flesh under any circumstances. Both the Old Testament and Greek literature describe an apparently common and widespread practice of child sacrifice. In *No Go the Bogeyman*, Marina Warner explores children's fears of being snatched and eaten by ogres and bogeymen, and using Goya's horrific painting, "Saturn Devouring His Child," she examines the myth of Kronos, Father Time, who eats us all. "EAT ME" said the sign on the cake that Alice ate to continue through Wonderland, and in Carroll's sequel, *Through the Looking-Glass*, the Walrus and the Carpenter eat all the plaintive oysters. Those of us who grew up with Grimms' fairy tales read about children who had to use their wits to avoid being abducted, cooked and eaten.

We shrug off myths and fairy tales as child's play, so what do we do with *real* ogres? Dictator Idi Amin, who held the African nation of Uganda in his murderous grasp from 1972 to 1979, threw corpses to crocodiles and joked about practising cannibalism. Amin may have been satirizing American cartoons of Africans with bones through their noses boiling missionaries in iron pots that I remember seeing as a child, but was he being funny ha, ha, or funny serious?

I hadn't thought about Amin, now in exile, for years. But since 1997 I have been sending money to Uganda to enable a village girl to attend school, and I am intrigued when, in September 1998, I see listed among the speakers at Montreal's International Congress on Care of the Terminally Ill, Dr. Anne Merriman, director of Hospice Uganda.

How does a hospice deal with mass death from infectious diseases? The leading cause of death in Uganda, I discover, is malaria. Close behind are yellow fever, dengue fever, typhoid, cholera, diarrhea, polio, worms, and AIDS. Life expectancy in Uganda is about forty years, half the Canadian average. Does familiarity with death make it easier to bear, or harder? It struck me that Uganda, like Canada a post-colonial relic of the British Empire, might have something to teach us about dying. Hospice Uganda, based in Kampala, had e-mail, and Dr. Merriman welcomed me to stay for a week at the hospice's residence. I booked my flight for the dry season the following February. My family and friends said, *"Uganda?* Are you *crazy?"*

XXI

MY FLIGHT TO UGANDA in February 1999 requires a stopover in England. Taking an extra day or two in England gives me a wonderful opportunity to visit St. Christopher's Hospice, and, with boldness and luck, I might be able to meet Dame Cicely Saunders. My e-mail request for a tour of the hospice is denied, but I am free to use their library. The librarian suggests that if I write directly to Dr. Saunders she may agree to see me. I do this with some trepidation. Dame Cicely, now eighty, has a reputation for being abrupt, autocratic, and dismissive of fools. She loathes being treated like a cult figure. To my astonishment, I receive by return mail a personal invitation, signed simply "Cicely Saunders," to see her at St. Christopher's on a Wednesday afternoon.

I take a train on a chilly, damp morning. The trip to the London suburb of Sydenham takes about twenty minutes. From the station, Penge East, I walk to the hospice through quiet streets of brick houses framed by gardens. St. Christopher's sits on a rise beside a railway track, a fitting location for life's last station, and its glass verandas are angled to catch the sun. The garden is a sea of mud. A pond and stream are being installed near a summer house, but the hospice grounds are as quiet as the neighbourhood.

I find the library in a former laundry building next door. The Education Centre, an old brick house, is being renovated to accomodate the hospice's expanding teaching role. As it is, four thousand people visit every year. The library has most of Cicely Saunders's speeches and articles dating back to 1957. I find that it was Cicely Saunders, not Elisabeth Kübler-Ross, who introduced the idea that medical professionals might learn from their patients, and as a nurse and social worker before she became a physician, Cicely Saunders legitimized the practice of sitting by a dying patient's bedside, often in silence, as an expression of solidarity and compassion.

Cicely Saunders, an evangelical Anglican, at first envisioned her hospice as a religious community, and it is she who originally popularized the goal of dying in a state of peaceful acceptance. As a hard-headed physician, however, she abandoned the Brompton hospital's bizarre cocktail in favour of plain morphine, pioneered the concept of team medical care, a team that included therapists and volunteers, and launched home care for the dying in 1969. Cicely Saunders is as committed to scientific research as she is to the comfort of her patients. Her frequently updated textbook, *The Management of Terminal Malignant Disease*, is a classic reference, and the short paperback version, *Living With Dying*, is the wisest book any lay person could expect to find about hospice philosophy and practice. Cicely Saunders is as clear and pithy a writer as she is a thinker.

I am to meet her in her second-floor office at St. Christopher's. Most of Sydenham is poor, and on the train I have passed grimy wastelands of industrial parks and public housing. As I walk over to the hospice, I am impressed that the outside of this plain, five-storey brick building is spotless, as if washed with rain, and when I enter the spacious lobby, there is no trace of the cluttered, noisy, antiseptic environment I have found in some Canadian palliative care units. The walls, the yellows and blues of spring flowers, are covered with bright, impressionist paintings. Everything is simple, immaculate, and, considering that the hospice has sixty beds, serene. Such a relaxed ambiance could only be achieved with the planning, discipline, and attention to detail for which Dame Cicely is famous.

Visitors are coming and going, and since nobody seems to mind, I walk into one of the wards. It is sunny and open, the four beds, widely spaced, separated by floral print curtains that can be drawn around. Patients are reading or sitting in chairs, looking out the windows. In the lunch room around the corner, a young man is smoking. St. Christopher's offers more freedom, including the right to drink liquor, but less privacy than Canadians might expect. Dame Cicely believes in hospice as "a community of the unlike," and she practises the principle that the dying should not be isolated. I have a hunch, given the unusual quiet, that she believes the dying should contemplate the trees, not the television.

I am apprehensive as Dr. Saunders's secretary leads me upstairs. After my morning in the library, I realize that almost everything I have been taught about hospice, Dame Cicely has created. What if I say something gauche or ignorant? Will she cut me off at the knees?

Dame Cicely, chair of the hospice's foundation, is sitting behind her desk, and as she looms out of her chair to greet me, I understand why people find her so formidable. Cicely Saunders is tall, much taller than I had guessed from her photographs, so tall that with her sharp nose, bright blue eyes, and white halo of hair she reminds me amusingly of Big Bird. Broad-shouldered and deep bosomed, she wears a dark grey, exquisitely tailored chalk-stripe suit with a crisp white blouse buttoned to her neck. As I sit, a hospice volunteer and humble scribe in my cheap Cotton Ginny library-grubbing clothes, Cicely Saunders describes in a businesslike way how St. Christopher's has evolved over forty years.

"We've spread!" she says, opening her arms to take in the world. There are now about 5,400 hospices and palliative care units in more than eighty countries, most of them thanks to trips Cicely Saunders made many years ago to Canada, the United States,

Europe, Southeast Asia, and to cities and towns throughout Great Britain. Palliative care has become a medical specialty in Britain, and home visiting teams and day hospices are integrated into the National Health Service. St. Christopher's researchers estimate that 75 per cent of British patients dying of cancer die in the care of a hospice or a palliative hospital unit. This success is phenomenal by Canadian standards, but not good enough for Cicely. Although she has become stooped, and walks with the aid of stout canes, she has no intention of retiring. She has too much to do.

"There is an unmet need in the field of non-malignant disease," she says briskly. "Twenty-five per cent of these patients aren't being served in hospitals." St. Christopher's, like other hospice services in the United Kingdom, was developed primarily to treat cancer pain, but Dr. Saunders is broadening her horizon to include heart failure, multiple sclerosis, ALS, and Alzheimer's disease.

And she is expanding St. Christopher's home care service. "We care for eight times as many people at home as in the hospice," she tells me, and the proportion is likely to grow. St. Christopher's, serving a population of 1.2 million, cares for four hundred patients a day, fifteen hundred a year, and since most people want to die at home, home care is the only way to go. St. Christopher's beds can still be used for respite, teaching, or for people unable to remain at home, but as Cicely Saunders has learned, running an independent hospice costs a fortune.

St. Christopher's has an annual budget of about $22 million Canadian, and more than half of that money is spent to maintain the in-patient hospice. The National Health Service contributes 30 per cent of the budget; all the rest comes from legacies, gifts, charitable trusts, investments, educational fees, and fundraising. St. Christopher's Hospice exists because, among her multiple talents, Cicely Saunders, wealthy and well-connected from birth, has the charm and persistence to raise $15 million a year.

Because of the costs, her dream of a free-standing hospice may no longer be viable. Cicely Saunders is reaching out into the medical establishment by setting up satellite hospice services with local hospitals, and St. Christopher's has joined with the school of medicine at King's College, London, to create an international centre for research and policy in palliative care. St. Christopher's Hospice is renowned, but not rich. It is less overtly Christian than it was, and it has not become a shrine. Cicely Saunders says that her philosophy of care remains unchanged, but she has moved away from her earlier ideal that death should always be peaceful.

"I have people say to me, 'I thought you never had pain in a hospice,'" she scoffs. "People have exaggerated expectations of a peaceful death. People need to have their own deaths. If they are fighting to the end, that's them."

I have the feeling that it will be her too. "I've gone on learning," she says. "I started from traditional Christianity, but I've branched out to wider spiritual issues. I've been reading astrophysics, learning about the mind of God. I've got more confidence in God because I know Him so much better. The less I know about the world, the more I believe."

Do you think about your own death? I ask.

"I *presume* St. Christopher's will look after me," she says tartly. "I've selected some ideas for my memorial service. This year I will tidy my office. I *don't want* resuscitation."

Have I been impertinent? Dame Cicely abruptly observes that I am keeping her from her Ash Wednesday service. Later, she must give a speech to a large audience. A question of raising money, again. As I gather my things to leave, I remark that in Canada it seems to be difficult to interest audiences in speeches about hospice. Dame Cicely gives me a cutting glance. "Not if you speak *well*," she says.

I fly into Uganda's Entebbe airport from the south across the vast blue calm of Lake Victoria. As the plane descends, it circles north over tree-covered volcanic hills broken by papyrus swamps and meadows. The green of the Ugandan landscape is brighter, more luminous than the evergreen of northwestern Ontario, but I feel that I could be flying across Lake Superior into Thunder Bay. When I see plumes of white smoke rising from dense bush, I think *forest fire* and peer about for water bombers. All is calm.

I am met by Anne Merriman, a blithe spirit in her early sixties, and Tim, a priest in shirt sleeves, who is visiting from Kenya. The tropical vegetation reminds me of Cuba, but the air smells of fresh water, and the February heat is similar to Winnipeg's in summer. A long drought in the western provinces has raised fears of famine. I am in Africa, where people routinely die of hunger. The Ugandan government admits that 40 per cent of the country's twelve million children, 60 per cent of the total population, are stunted by malnutrition.

Hospice Uganda is located in Makindye, a suburb of Kampala, and as we drive through the city's sprawling outskirts I see one reason for the plumes of smoke. Garbage. It seems to be the practice to pile loose garbage at an intersection, or in a convenient vacant lot, then, when the stench becomes intolerable, to toss gasoline on it and set it alight. Better than not burning it, I guess, but the acrid smoke from these fires reminds me of the Old Testament Valley of Gehenna, Jerusalem's garbage dump, where, according to legend, children had once been burnt as sacrifices to Moloch. Hairy black marabou storks, huge, hideous carrion birds, festoon the trees near the dumps. At some corners, skinny cows tethered atop piles of fresh garbage browse for something edible. The goats nibbling grass in the roadside ditches look fat and juicy.

Kampala is a city of ruins occupied by refugees from impoverished rural villages. Before 1967, when president Milton Obote precipitated Uganda's "troubles," to use Anne's tactful Irish word, Kampala, built, like Rome, on seven hills, was the most beautiful city in Africa. Now Kampala is a dusty, clay-brick version of downtown Detroit. Crumbling buildings, once apparently intended for offices or shops, look as if they have been bombed, or perhaps they were abandoned unfinished. They have no windows, or the glass has been replaced by boards, metal, and cloth. These derelict places are occupied by thousands of villagers who have come to seek a living in the city. The homeless who can't find shelter construct their own one-room shanties in vacant lots out of mud bricks, boards, and scrap metal scavenged from the rusted-out vehicles I see abandoned everywhere. As we head down the dirt road towards the hospice, I think, god, what do all these people use for toilets?

Hospice Uganda is housed in a big, white ranch-style bungalow set back from the road behind a tall hedge. I'll be staying in its visitors' residence, Kateregga House, named for Henry Kateregga, a wealthy Ugandan businessman who gave the hospice its first permanent home. It is clean and comfortable, with small private bedrooms, a sitting room, a dining room, and two housekeepers, Christine Nelima and Juliet Mutonyi, who cook our meals and boil our drinking water. Christine is away. Her brother's son died this morning and she has gone to his village for the funeral.

Hospice Uganda's two doctors and four nurses visit patients in hospital and at home within a twenty-kilometre radius of Kampala. With an average caseload of twenty to thirty patients, nearly four hundred a year, home visits mean a lot of driving over rutted, hilly mud roads full of potholes in the hospice's fleet of three Suzuki 4X4 trucks. On Monday, I'm going out with Dr. Henry Ddungu and a nurse, Bernadette Basemera. All of the hospice's employees are African. Anne Merriman, funded by the Irish government's Agency for Personal Service Overseas, would like to train a Ugandan doctor to replace her.

Our first call is down the road in Makindye. I follow Dr. Henry into a gloomy decrepit building that looks as if it might once have been a store, a service station, a garage. It appears to be empty, but in an inner room we find a family squatting around a kerosene burner. They have a few brightly coloured plastic dishes laid out on a woven palm-leaf mat, a dishpan, a cooking oil container for water, and, in a corner, a stalk of green bananas. Dr. Henry speaks to them in an African language I don't understand. A man points to a curtained doorway. Behind the curtain, in a room hardly bigger than a closet, an old woman, curled into a fetal position, lies on a pile of bedding on the floor.

Dr. Henry bends over her, asking her how she is. She seems comatose, but she eventually mumbles words he translates as "Not too good, doctor." She is dying of melanoma, and Dr. Henry has been giving her morphine. She has stopped eating and drinking and has been unresponsive for three days. As we leave, helpless to do more, I wonder if this impoverished family is relieved to have one less mouth to feed.

At the next home, a neat, sunny concrete townhouse in a hillside suburb, we are warmly greeted by plump, healthy-looking women, the patient's aunts. "You are welcome," one of them says to me, gently taking my hand in both of hers. I like this solemn, formal phrase. Julia, a highly placed civil servant before she became too sick to work, is lying on a couch in the living room. She is emaciated, delirious, groping the air and moaning, "Don't go, don't go." Julia is dying of AIDS. She is thirty-two. Her son, who seems to be about five, is curled up at her feet, his face the picture of utter desolation.

Dr. Henry saw Julia for the first time four days ago. She has tuberculosis, neuropathy, and possibly meningitis, in addition to her dementia. Her son too has all the symptoms of AIDS, skin rash, lethargy, speech impairment, and stunted growth. He is ten years old. Julia's husband died of AIDS three years ago. Didn't she get tested? I ask Henry later. No.

Twelve years ago, when HIV was first found in the blood of Ugandans suffering from a mysterious wasting disease called "slim," it seemed impossible to them that heterosexual Africans with children could suffer from a disease believed to be restricted to gay, white men. In North America AIDS was described as originating in Africa, but in Africa it was explained as a white, European disease contracted from prostitutes. Uganda uncovered its secret epidemic when Cuban officers began testing army recruits for HIV. President

Yoweri Museveni organized an aggressive safe-sex public education campaign, but for married couples the implications of homosexuality and prostitution make condoms a touchy or taboo topic.

Dr. Henry can help Julia with the pain associated with her neuropathy and meningitis, and he will be able to enrol her son in the children's outpatient program at Mildmay, a new British AIDS treatment centre on the road to Entebbe. One of Julia's aunts will take him in until he too dies, but orphans with visible AIDS run a high risk of being mocked and shunned.

Most of Hospice Uganda's patients have AIDS-related cancers, Kaposi's sarcoma and cancer of the cervix, and the hospice's main mission is to educate Uganda's doctors about treating cancer pain. Anne describes one of the first patients she saw after she arrived in Kampala in 1993, a woman with pain in her hip and multiple abscesses:

"We could hear her screaming from the car. There was a nurse holding her down, and another nurse with a probe, and they were sterilizing an abscess on the part of the buttock you avoid because of the sciatic nerve. I was nearly crying. I nearly beat the nurse up. We told them to stop it. Then they told us they had stopped the morphine. She would become addicted. They were answering me back like crazy, so I said, 'I'm going to ring the doctor in charge.' Do you know what his answer was, 'We are used to looking at pain.' You either leave the profession if you're sensitive, or you carry on and do damage by being insensitive to the pain."

All her life, Anne Merriman had wanted to be a medical missionary in Africa, but it was while she was practising in Singapore, Malaysia, in the 1980s that she discovered palliative medicine. Hired as the director of a new Nairobi Hospice in Kenya in 1990, she encountered the suffering of untreated cancer patients:

"What hit me in Nairobi was the terrible extent to which cancers went. The patients we were seeing hadn't ever seen *anybody*. They had no chance of therapy, or they came too late. The wounds and everything we saw, it was desperate." Merriman, a dynamic, decisive personality, grew frustrated with the bureaucracy in Nairobi and returned to England. On the advice of Cicely Saunders, she wrote an article in *Contact*, a magazine distributed free in Africa, offering to set up a model hospice in an African country. Her most enthusiastic response came from Uganda, and Uganda, a single-party state governed since 1987 by the National Resistance Movement, was the safest of the countries that expressed interest.

In September 1993, Anne opened for business in a borrowed house with one nurse and a second-hand Land Rover. Today, Hospice Uganda has nearly thirty employees, satellite hospices at Mbarara and Hoima in the west, and an annual budget of $225,000 Canadian. A little more than $30,000 is raised locally through public concerts and an annual walkathon. The remainder comes from charitable foundations based in Great Britain and Ireland. Anne is trying to persuade British banks in Kampala to become long-term corporate donors. Her goal is to make the hospice entirely Ugandan.

While the Ugandan government does not contribute a penny – total annual spending on health care is seven dollars per capita – its political seal of approval has helped Hospice Uganda's doctors get a foot in the door as consulting physicians at Mulago, the state hospital in Kampala. On Tuesday, I join Dr. Henry for rounds at the lymphoma clinic. The clinic, buried in the sprawling hospital complex, is an old, decaying building on the crest of Mulago hill. I can't believe my eyes when I see the rusty corrugated iron roof, rusted-through eavestroughs, peeling paint and dirty, broken screens. The sign by the door reads: "UGANDA CANCER INSTITUTE. The Lymphoma Treatment Centre is a joint effort of the Makerere College Medical School and the National Cancer Institute of the United States."

Inside, the stained concrete walls are plastered with warnings about pneumonia and diphtheria, and a welcoming sign reads: "AIDS IS GUARANTEED DEATH." The posters are not as dismal as the wards, with their bare, concrete floors, streaked walls, ancient iron beds, and mattresses horribly stained by body fluids. I can understand why Ugandans sometimes steal their relatives from hospitals, and I notice families with portable cooking braziers, pots and dishes, camped vigilantly on the lawn outside. The patients look terrified.

Our first patient suffers from "cancer with no specific site" but, more urgently, from an impacted bowel, the consequence of having been prescribed codeine with no stool softener. I am impressed when Dr. Henry, one of the most stylish and immaculately dressed young men I have ever met, whips out his surgical gloves, and with a cheery "No problem!" volunteers to remove the impacted poop manually. It's a great lesson in preventive medicine – if you don't want to do messy stuff, guys, don't let it happen – and I am amazed to see that the oncologists *take advice from a hospice doctor.*

There are few patients here, all from rural areas. Wealthy urban Ugandans seek cancer treatment overseas. The sick in Uganda have to buy all their drugs, including chemotherapy, and for most patients, drugs of any kind are unaffordable. A breast cancer patient at the hospital has stopped her chemo because her family can no longer pay for it. She has relapsed.

Chemo may be futile anyway. As we move from bed to bed, I hear the same diagnosis repeated, "cancer of unknown origin." These patients have metastatic cancers, that's true, but they also suffer from anemia, congestion, emaciation, fever, dehydration, and oral thrush, all symptoms of AIDS. Henry Ddungu suspects that Burkitt's lymphoma, relatively common in Uganda, may be AIDS-related, and the last patient we see, a sorrowful boy of about twelve, has a bulging Burkitt's tumour on the side of his jaw. A doctor puts his hand gently on the boy's shoulder, looks at us and sighs. No treatment.

The boy will be sent home. Where is home? I ask the young oncologist standing beside me. "A refugee camp," he replies. A bitter edge to his voice prompts me to ask about the sign at the door. Where's the American money? "*Ha!*" he laughs. "We haven't had money from the United States for *years.*"

I have the ghastly feeling as I leave the Lymphoma Treatment Centre that cancer, like typhoid and tuberculosis before it, may have become a code word for HIV/AIDS. According to Hospice Uganda's published figures, about four million people, 20 per cent of the population, have HIV or AIDS, but Anne Merriman estimates that it could be as high as 30 per cent. Uganda, with no proper system of birth registration, doesn't even know how many people it has, much less people with HIV/AIDS. Children, including AIDS orphans, are not routinely tested for the disease, so when they become sexually active there is no way of knowing whether or not they were born with the virus. Well, what can you do about it? Create modern-day leper colonies of the infected? Call the disease something else, and *poof*, it's gone. A war on cancer in Africa would make AIDS disappear overnight. Yes, I am told, the HIV/AIDS infection rate is dropping in Kampala, but not in the rural villages. Ninety per cent of Ugandans live in the villages.

The first person most Ugandans consult about their disease is their local herbalist and shaman, the witch doctor. Rural Uganda may have only one university-educated physician for forty-eight thousand people, but every village has a traditional healer, as the witch doctor is now called. Healers are a respected and influential people in their communities, and patients who go to hospitals continue to seek their advice and use their remedies. As African scholar John Mbiti explains in *African Religions and Philosophy*, traditional medicine has ethical and spiritual dimensions:

> A bereaved mother whose child has died from malaria will not be satisfied with the scientific explanation that a mosquito carrying malaria parasites stung the child and caused it to suffer and die from malaria. She will wish to know why the mosquito stung her child and not somebody else's child. The only satisfactory answer is that 'someone' sent the mosquito, or worked other evil magic against her child. This is not a scientific answer, but it is reality for the majority of African peoples.

The "someone" might be a witch, sorcerer, disgruntled neighbour, or the offended spirit of a deity. Eighty per cent of Ugandans are Christian, predominantly Roman Catholic, but before the relatively recent arrival of Islam and Christianity in the nineteenth century, the countryside was sacred to a host of gods and goddesses – a temple consecrated to a river fertility god, Python, was located on the swampy north shore of Lake Victoria – and society was organized into clans named for totem animals. Spirits communicated through temple priests and priestesses who acted as oracles or mediums. While Ugandans may now go to a mosque or a church, their traditional beliefs have not disappeared. On Friday, February 26, my morning edition of the Kampala newspaper *The New Vision* has a feature about a former banker, Sarah Nsubuga, who claims to be a medium for Nakayima, an ancient female spirit living in a sacred tree on the top of Mubende hill in western Uganda. Although Nsubuga says Nakayima's message is for the president's ears alone, *The New Vision* takes Nakayima's existence seriously enough to give Sarah Nsubuga a full-page feature story with a photograph of a carved statue of Nakayima.

Traditional healers frequently attribute sickness and death to the malign influence of the *baalubaale*, the restless spirits of the dead who intervene actively in human affairs. The dead, according to John Mbiti, do not die completely as long as they are remembered by the people who knew them. If these "living dead" have children and grandchildren, they remain members of the family, for good or ill, for as many as four or five generations before they disappear into the spirit world.

In a culture where sickness and death come from invisible parasites and bacteria, a spiritual explanation provides a logical answer to the patient's perennial question, "Why me?" By assigning blame elsewhere, the healer relieves the patient of responsibility, and the healer's prescription of medicines and rituals to propitiate the spirit is no different from North American physicians and psychologists who steer cancer patients into meditation, guided imagery and psychotherapy, or the healers who specialize in shark cartilage, magnets, massage, macrobiotic diet, raw juice cleansing, chakra balancing, ear candling, aromatherapy, the radiance technique, or whatever else, however misguided, gives the sick comfort and hope.

Ugandan witch doctors are not trained or licensed. Once ostracized by the British, today they are criticized by the Ugandan medical establishment for sorcery and superstition, overdosing, misdiagnosing, and uncleanliness. The newspapers carry scary stories about witch doctors who abduct children for sacrifice, or demand sacrificial children from their parents. Establishment medicine, however, is so inadequate and unaffordable it is not a realistic alternative. Dr. Andrew Ndamira, medical director of Mobile Hospice Mbarara, describes a typical hospice predicament:

"Imagine a forty-five-year-old widow with seven children who, after several years of seeking remedies for a chronic illness from various healers, finally ends up in hospital, only to be told she has cancer which is too far advanced to be cured. While still assimilating this sad news, she is served with a discharge form to vacate the bed because there are many emergencies coming in. She is, however, referred to Hospice Mbarara. Imagine also that you are the health worker at the hospice on duty when the patient arrives.

"The approach, as you can guess, is nothing short of difficult. 'When am I going to die?' is likely to be her first question. 'Why me?' or 'Where will I leave my children?' are other common questions. One needs to learn skilled ways of sensitively dealing with such questions. Many people wonder why a group of health professionals should devote their energies to caring for such patients. My answer is that somehow someone needs to care for these patients. They are by no means useless, miserable rejects waiting for 'their day.' Some have contributed a great deal toward the well-being of our great nation. Others have been skilled professionals or even national heroes. The rest are destitute paupers with nothing obvious to sing about throughout their lives. All, however, must die with their full honour and dignity."

A hospice patient in the village of Kabamwerere tells his own story in the Hospice Mbarara newsletter:

When I first got to Mbarara Hospital they told me it was tuberculosis. I'd known that already, after I coughed up the blood. My uncle did too and died within a year. So I sold two goats and came to hospital. A few days after arriving, the doctor drew out a basin full of bloody water from my chest. Laazimah, it was a bad situation! Then I got sent to the TB ward. We swallow enough medicine to supply my village for a year. But I began to improve. Then the cough started worsening. My feet and then my stomach got swollen. I couldn't swallow. That man who is after my land, he's behind all this, also sent rocks to lodge themselves in the back of my throat. I can see them in the mirror. I couldn't sit or lie, I couldn't eat. I couldn't stop coughing. I couldn't breathe. The day I thought I'd die, the doctor came, looked and prodded a bit, wrote in the file as usual and disappeared. Somehow it got to be morning.

Then two ladies came. With a suitcase. It was that bad, I wasn't interested to know what they were up to. They politely insisted that it was me they had actually come to see. So that was how I got to be under the care of Hospice Mbarara.

It is a miracle! Laazimah! The first time, there were many questions but less poking and thumping than the young doctors. And medicine! God is great! Some liquid medicine, so many tablets my wife gets confused. But things are undoubtedly better! I get to the gate now and the terrible pain that I couldn't escape has gone. The hospice team comes regularly and takes time. You know, it's a relief to be really listened to. By the way, I was rather surprised that they understood that I needed sugar for my tea! Now I have quite a negotiating edge in ward affairs!

I have cancer. I still think the land issue may have a role but since I called for the priest I've left that to God. My son is here now and I have made a will. But I do appreciate the time I've had to get myself in some order, and, well, at the end of the day as usual enjoy a good round of the news!

The lady with the suitcase was a hospice nurse, and the suitcase, a portable pharmacy, is Hospice Uganda's version of Victoria Hospice's fishing-tackle box. Hospice Uganda's home visiting team usually includes a doctor, and its staple narcotic is liquid oral morphine made from powder in its own pharmacy. The nurses do the counselling and they work on the same principle as Victoria Hospice's Palliative Response Team: empower the family. The family will have to administer the medications and do the home nursing. They may not have a phone, or access to a phone, and there's no point in leaving leaflets and workbooks for people who can't read or write.

When it comes to dying in Uganda, as in Canada, family usually means the women of the family, and as we drive from home to humble home, we are welcomed with grave courtesy by daughters, aunts, sisters, granddaughters, daughters-in-law. Most wear loose, sari-like dresses in brilliant colours, or a crisp cotton *gomesi*, a scoop-necked, ankle-length dress with short, pointed sleeves, a style derived from the gingham gowns Victorian missionaries insisted their converts wear. A chair is produced for the *musungu*, the white woman, who, to her embarrassment, is wearing Gap khaki pants, and the women, with a graceful fluid motion, ripple into sitting positions on a palm-leaf floor mat. They listen attentively, nodding, as the nurse gives them instructions. The nurse is calm, but forceful. These women will have a lot of information to remember. I am struck by how quiet they are. "Those who have lost are more able to cope," Dr. Henry tells me. "They have lost so many brothers, so now they *know*."

Two sprightly elderly widows, both dying of cancer, insist on having their pictures taken with me. I feel more embarrassed. "They are glad to see you here," Dr. Henry reassures me. "It shows you care." Come to think of it, if I had cancer of the esophagus and an African witch doctor walked through my front door, I'd have my picture taken too.

These brave old ladies are enjoying a "tame death" at home in the bosom of caring, healthy, and relatively prosperous families, but they are in good spirits today because the hospice team has come with morphine. The opium poppy is not in a traditional healer's herbal pharmacopoeia, and university-educated doctors still ignore their patients' pain.

"People's biggest fear is dying in pain," says Racheal Dipio, the hospice's nurse coordinator. "All the family is in pain. Women are worried about their children. They need to identify people who can take care of their children. One lady I cared for had lost ten of her eleven children. Their father had died. '*I am going to leave my child alone in this world!*' she cried. It was helpful for her to have somebody to talk to. If I talk to them with understanding, they open up and you discuss what comes out."

Racheal's problems sound familiar: patients who have been deceived by their oncologists, who refuse to hear their diagnosis, who expect a miracle cure. Racheal speaks three languages, but in a country with fifty-three ethnic groups, plus refugees, communication can be a problem. "Carers don't always translate what you explain," she says. When patients live "up country," beyond the hospice's twenty-kilometre radius, relatives come in once a month, often on foot, to report changes and renew medications. "It's working very well," Racheal says. "No one has run off with the morphine."

Hospice assesses its patients on a social and spiritual scale from one to five. Nurses need to know patients' education, family situation, expectations, and how much, if anything, they can pay. The spiritual scale begins with patients unable to distinguish good from evil, escalating to those who feel united with God in a personal, mystical relationship. Racheal says that with a combination of faith and drugs, pain can be controlled in all patients at the top of the spiritual scale. Most, however, are at level two, an affiliation with a religious structure. "There is no patient without a spiritual belief," Racheal says. "If a patient asks, we pray with them."

Hospice Uganda's contact with the family ends with the patient's death. "We could spend all week taking bodies home," Anne Merriman says briskly. "We don't want to get into all that. The families are much stronger about it than we are. They have to be. They're too busy. They have to get back to work and get ready for the next one."

The dead are customarily buried in their ancestral village garden following a funeral attended by the entire community. "The dead body is much respected," says J. M. Waliggo, a Ugandan Catholic priest, educator, and member of the human rights commission. "It is the person that has been. All rituals are meant to show that respect. Keep the body intact, clean, composed, well-arranged, gently handled. The person is still around, but in a new way. He or she still 'sees' what is done or omitted. People respect very much the desires of the dead – how to be buried, where, when, and by whom. Once these are fulfilled there is a harmony between the dead and the family and community as a whole. It is the entire community doing this work to bid a solemn farewell to one of its members." The period of mourning ends when an heir to the dead person is officially designated.

"Weeping stops," says Father Waliggo. "Joy is restored. Funeral rites complete the circle of life, and so life goes on as before." Failure to perform these ceremonies would disrupt the entire social fabric of the community, but how many funerals can a village afford? Kampala's carpenters have switched from making furniture to coffins, and on the city's outskirts their workshops line the roadsides. The coffins, usually equipped with a window to see in, or out of, are beautifully made, but expensive by village standards. A crowd of mourners has to be fed, and those who have jobs must take time off work. Even in death, AIDS poses a threat to mourners who clean the body. Father Waliggo himself admits: "We need to teach new ways of showing that respect so that any danger of infection is avoided."

Ugandan villages are sprawling communities of adjoining family compounds, each surrounded by small, carefully cultivated plots of banana and coffee trees, jack fruit, bread fruit, yams, potatoes, and ground nuts, with chickens pecking in the dirt and a goat nearby. Driving through the countryside around Kampala, we are almost on the equator, and the noonday sun seems not to be above us, but around us, blazing up through the fiery orange soil and iridescent greens of the vegetation. Dylan Thomas expressed it perfectly: *The force that through the green fuse drives the flower*. Lake Victoria is a cool breeze, a scent of moisture, a felt presence. The land is fertile, and with a little pruning and hoeing, families can live on the produce of their own gardens.

Here in the kingdom of the Baganda, an ancient, powerful tribe that gave its name to the entire country, the staple crop is the banana, and *matoke*, a tasty steamed banana mash, is the national dish. Given its reputation, I'd expected a big tree, like a palm, but the banana is a squat, bulbous stalk with a dishevelled topknot of long, shaggy leaves. There are, I am told, twenty-eight different kinds of banana in Uganda, including bananas for roasting, eating raw, steaming, making into wine, and brewing into beer. Banana leaves are used to wrap food, make baskets and clothes, and before coffins became fashionable, the dead were buried in shrouds of banana leaves. Buried beneath a banana to become, in time, another banana. The tree of life, the banana. Inanna. *Inanna Banana*.

Am I maddened by the noonday sun or have I traced my spiritual roots to a garden in Africa? It makes sense that mythology would express experience, and the expulsion from the Garden of Eden may be a late metaphor for a forced flight from the African garden when *homo erectus* first stood up. The word banana is Congolese. When it flowers, the banana produces a single, drooping stem with a big, pulpy, red bud having the look and texture of a placenta, or the engorged head of a penis. The bud opens to produce yellow flowers, stamens, and seeds that ripen into a thickly clustered stalk of bananas. At the end of the cycle, the plant dies, but a new one springs up from the rhizome at the base. Could Virgil's golden bough have been, originally, a stalk of bananas? Makes sense to me. Inanna may have become a date palm or fig tree in Asia, but it would have been more practical for Adam and Eve to plait banana-leaf skirts than to try to hide their nakedness behind fig leaves.

What does Baganda myth say about the banana? In an essay in *Uganda, A Century of Existence*, Kasalina Matovu, a professor of languages at Kampala's Makerere University, analyses the one hundred names the Baganda have for the parts and uses of the banana plant. Matovu says that the banana names, typically beginning with a feminine prefix, "nna," are the most distinguishing feature of the names the Baganda give to girls. The "nna" prefix, she continues, characterizes the names of sacred hills and rivers around Kampala. Lake Victoria, the source of the Nile, renamed for an English queen, is Nnalubaale, the mother of all spirits.

Nana, nanny, maman, Anna, St. Anne, patron saint of pregnancy, the mother of Mary, the Christian incarnation of the bisexual banana plant's virgin birth. Uganda is ravaged by HIV/AIDS because sex is not shameful, fertility is celebrated, and many children assure the living dead of several generations of immortality. Polygamy is legal, multiple and serial sexual relationships are common. "When a man talks about his family, we don't know what he's talking about," says Abby Sebina-Zziwa, a sociologist at Makerere University. If a man dies and leave his land to one woman, Abby says, this wife will be expected to raise his children from all his liaisons. It is not uncommon for a village woman whose sons have all died to be supporting as many as twenty grandchildren on her few acres of land.

"Thirty per cent of Uganda's population is supporting the rest," Abby says, "and that 30 per cent is *dying*." Many of Hospice Uganda's patients, women widowed by AIDS, are dying in their thirties, cared for by their teenage children, and those relatives who survive find themselves financially crippled by dependent orphans. The strongest people in Uganda are the old. They've made it through the British occupation, torture, terrorism, thirty years of civil war, and the diseases that are destroying their families. What happens when they die of old age?

I worry about the very old caring for the very young when Dr. Henry and I visit Sally, an AIDS patient abandoned by her husband, who has returned to her father's house to die. Dr. Henry has been treating Sally for bone pain, TB, and confusion. Her father has land, and his neat, swept yard and spacious clay-brick house are shaded by trees. Coming out of the sun into the darkness, I spy a tiny girl with bright button eyes peering shyly at us from the shadows. She looks to be about four or five, and her legs and white dress are covered with dust from playing in the yard.

Her mother is curled up on a mattress in an inner room, skeletal, her mouth open, moaning. As Dr. Henry kneels and leans over to examine her, the child hustles up to the side of the mattress and peers solemnly at her mother, leaning over exactly like the doctor. The hospice nurse, Mwasi Batuli, talks to the girl in a joking way. The child smiles and peeps at me, seated on my inevitable *musungu* chair. She sidles over to me, her eyes downcast, holds out her hand and kneels at my feet, her face against my knee, her hand in mine. This curtsy is a traditional Baganda greeting that predates the British. I ask her her name, and she whispers something I don't understand. As soon as Dr. Henry puts down his stethoscope to talk to her grandfather, hovering anxiously in the doorway, she hops up and darts over to the bed. She picks up the stethoscope and, with a mischievous grin, holds it to her eye.

As we climb back into the Suzuki, the child clings to the passenger door. It's all I can do not to scoop her up and tuck her under my arm. Her grandfather will take care of her, Henry assures me. What is her name, I ask.

"Happiness."

Mourning is another woman's name I have heard. Or maybe it's Morning. "Illness and death have been here in Africa since Africa existed," says Father Waliggo. "People have had a very rich experience of both. People have learned how to confront both and how to cope with both. Despite the long history and experience of these two realities, there has never been a people or a society that has become accustomed to illness and death. Every illness and each death is unique and new and brings about new shocks and fears."

By the end of the week I am becoming fearful. In Kateregga House, three British women, working and studying for a period of several months at Hospice Uganda, discuss where to go, in an emergency, for safe refuge. What about me? Canada's presence in Uganda is so small we share diplomatic quarters with the Swiss. Our expert Ugandan drivers, alert, muscular young men, may, I realize, be bodyguards. Kampala, at first, had seemed perfectly safe. I have been able to walk alone through polite crowds of street vendors in the market areas unmolested by beggars, and the only soldiers I have seen were washing their clothes outside their tumbledown barracks on the way to Makynde. Every family, however poor, has a washtub and a clothesline, and it's a common sight to see men and women crouched over their tubs, vigorously rubbing clothes with a bar of soap. Then I began to notice the high, strong concrete walls, topped with barbed wire, that surrounded many of the homes we visited, and realized that the brightly painted slabs propped up for sale by the roadsides were solid steel gates.

Hospice Uganda's compound is surrounded by a chainlink fence topped with barbed wire, and the gate is locked at night by the watchman. The shuffle of his footsteps as he makes his rounds wakes me, and I listen to the howling of Kampala's guard dogs. Not long before I arrived, a restaurant popular with foreigners was bombed; last year it was the Speke Hotel downtown. I don't know whether to be thankful that the American Club across the road will have excellent security, or apprehensive that it is a prime terrorist target.

George, a Dutch doctor based in Kenya, has driven in from the north with a tale of armed bandits who hijacked a missionary truck and killed its driver. Northern Uganda is overrun by outlaws who kidnap recruits from boarding schools, and Yoweri Museveni's refusal to allow any ideological deviation from the policies of his National Resistance Movement, including opposition political parties, perpetuates a cycle of unrest and revolution. Stories of corruption, graft, and embezzlement by politicians and civil servants fill every issue of *The New Vision* newspaper, and this is a government newspaper. This week, the mayor of Kampala has been jailed for fifteen months in the United States for defrauding a Boston bank of $44,000. He has refused to resign.

Ranked officially as one of the world's poorest countries, a billion dollars in debt to the World Bank, Uganda annually sucks in millions of dollars through an international IV line of foreign aid. Where does the money go? Who knows. Imported food, clothing, and drugs intended for licensed pharmacies are sold on the black market. The Americans are keen on condoms and safe-sex videos, China has sponsored a new soccer stadium. In 1998, the British, in cooperation with the World Bank, opened the Mildmay Centre for AIDS Care and Training, a cloister of brick buildings perched on a prominent hill on the road between Kampala and the Entebbe airport.

Mildmay, a specialist referral centre, is open to the general public for only a few hours a day, three days a week, and for sick people on foot, without cars or money for a taxi, it is a long walk from anywhere. If they do get there, Mildmay has no beds, and patients suffering from the severe, persistent, and intractable symptoms of pain, nausea, and confusion Mildmay exists to treat would have trouble making it up the hill. Patients must have a letter of referral from a physician, including a positive HIV test and a medical history, and they have to pay a fee. Almost no one in Uganda can afford the cost of the protease inhibitors that keep people like Joe Maroon alive and active in Canada. Even the indigent pay five hundred Ugandan shillings (fifty cents) for a consultation. Since hospitals in Kampala have AIDS clinics, and there are AIDS information centres, testing centres, and church and charitable support networks in the community, I suspect that Mildmay's chief virtue is its visibility, a Potemkin clinic intended to show foreign dignitaries travelling to and from the airport that Uganda's war against AIDS is being won.

In spite of a World Health Organization directive to integrate traditional healers into health care services, the Ugandan government is showing no inclination to do so. Anne Merriman would like to train traditional healers in rural areas to identify patients in pain, and, through them, get pain control to the homes through a hospice team in every district. These partnerships could be the model for a national system of public health clinics, but disease prevention, free medicine, sewers, garbage disposal, and clean water are not the big-buck projects that appeal to corrupt politicians or imperialist governments eager to manipulate foreign aid for propaganda and political points back home. Just this week, a scientist who tested the "protected springs" from which the majority of Kampala's population draws its water discovered that 60 per cent were contaminated by human excrement draining from nearby pit latrines. Kampala's shanty towns are criss-crossed by drainage ditches and open sewers. Epidemics of cholera are frequent, especially in the rainy season when the sewers overflow into homes and streets. The Uganda Red Cross estimates that, country-wide, there were more than 2,000 deaths out of nearly 48,000 reported cholera cases in 1998.

On Saturday afternoon, as I wait outside Kateregga House for a hospice driver to take me to the airport, I watch a young woman sitting patiently on the ground outside the hospice door. She has a small suitcase, and what seems to be a roll of bedding. The right side of her face is covered by a bulging white bandage and she wears a white-patterned *gomesi*. She sits with the erect posture of a woman accustomed to walking many miles balancing a heavy load on her head. I have seen many of these laden women walking with graceful, undulating strides along the shoulders of the orange dirt roads. Has she walked here? And how far? She waits, motionless.

"The people are suffering and they can't do anything about it!" How often I have heard this despairing cry from hospice nurses and from Ugandans I've spoken to outside medical circles. I have listened, but suffering in Uganda defies my attempts to comprehend it. The voices of African ancestors mutter in the dry, rustling leaves. No rain. Another hot, dry afternoon. Since morning I have had an oppressive feeling of foreboding, of imminent violence. Even Anne Merriman says, "I don't understand what goes on here."

I feel safer at the airport. The next day, as my flight is landing in Toronto, guerrillas from Rwanda abduct and terrorize a party of North American and European tourists tracking gorillas in the Bwindi Impenetrable Forest on the border between Uganda and Rwanda. The Ugandan park warden is killed and eight tourists are hacked to death. Death taught me as a child to avoid impenetrable forests. I'm glad to be home.

XXII

THIRTY-THREE MILLION Canadians spend more than $80 billion a year on health care. This helps explain why, with the exception of Aboriginal communities, we live twice as long as Ugandans, but we're spending four hundred times as much to do it. The population is aging. The incidence of cancer is increasing. Treatment of life-threatening illness causes side effects that have to be treated, and the course of treatment is determined by tests. All this costs money. Attempts to cut costs by closing hospitals and laying off nurses have led to long waits, overcrowded emergency rooms, competitive private clinics, and intense public pressure for governments to pump more money into medicare.

But where is this money to come from? Can we afford to spend 30, 40 per cent of all our federal and provincial taxes on health care? And how will this money be spent? Home care? New hospitals? Long-term care institutions? More technology? The federal and provincial governments have been at loggerheads over these questions for years. Doctors, a self-governing profession, bill the government, and since doctors are paid a fee for every service they provide, they have an incentive to order tests and treatments, prescribe drugs, and refer patients to their colleagues for more tests, treatments, and drugs. Hospitals, independent corporations, are expected to turn a profit. Where is our money going, and is it being spent in the most effective way? We don't know, and we don't ask. The title of a book by Toronto medical reporter Lisa Priest says it all: *Operating in the Dark: The Accountability Crisis in Canada's Health Care System*.

"Let's avoid wasting money on treatments that have been proven ineffective," pleads Larry Librach. "A large percentage of chemotherapy in Canada is estimated to be ineffective with *no hope* of being effective. Why are we supporting that waste of money?" Doctors, he says, are ordering repeated CT scans, at $200 a scan, and serial MRIs, at $500 an image, simply to show that a tumour is growing. "These tests show why people are dying," Librach says. "We *know* they're dying. They just give a better picture of why they're dying."

Only a minuscule amount of the money we invest in medical care goes, even indirectly, to hospice or palliative care, and when governments go on cost-cutting rampages, the dying are the most vulnerable. Nowhere is this illustrated more graphically than at the Royal Victoria Hospital in Montreal. In November 1999, I expected to find its internationally renowned palliative care unit, opened in 1975, a thriving model of success. I find a tragedy.

The hospital itself, a Victorian gothic temple to the Queen Empress and her colonial robber barons, looks like a relic of a vanished civilization. The palliative care unit, on the third floor of the Ross Pavilion, has been reduced from sixteen beds to twelve because a nurse is on sick leave. This is fewer than the number of beds it opened with twenty-five years ago. It lost its home care patients, plus the physicians and nurses who cared for them, when Quebec restructured health care services into regional community access centres in 1997. The PCU's team acts as consultants, but patients have to go through their family physicians or case managers.

"The quality of care patients receive at home has diminished," says the PCU's director, Dr. Anna Towers. "Patients are left alone at home with insufficiently trained nurses. We are not paid to make home visits. The physicians have to call us, but there aren't enough physicians so we don't get called. And it's hard to fix things on the phone." Patients can visit a day hospital at the Montreal General Hospital, which has a palliative care specialist, but they need a doctor's referral. Since Quebec pays doctors in Montreal only 70 per cent of the fees it pays to doctors in rural areas, the city is not an attractive place for family doctors to practise.

The Royal Victoria has been integrated into the McGill University Health Centre complex, and the PCU's psychologist, Dr. Robin Cohen, is participating in a pilot project to create an integrated continuum of supportive care services in the community, a model that should have been in place before the province restructured the system. Anna Towers believes that the government's sole motive in restructuring was to save money, and the effect of Quebec's cost-cutting has been devastating. "We would love to get referrals from the community," she says, "and develop an interface with chronic care. But we need money. We are developing in a field that is shrinking."

Over the last ten years, communities everywhere in Canada have learned that budget cuts can suddenly wipe out hospital services, or entire institutions, that have been in existence for years. The future of palliative care at the Royal Victoria is uncertain. "Five years ago, the hospital said it would close its palliative beds," says Dr. Balfour Mount, now retired as its PCU director but active as a consultant. "But the need for palliative care is going to *increase*. The Royal College of Physicians and Surgeons needs to recognize palliative care as a discipline on a par with cardiology." Health care priorities, he says, provide a microcosm of the society we live in, and we respond to our fear of death by reinforcing our value system. "A society based on scientific materialism," he says, "is uniquely unprepared to deal with death."

It's heartbreaking to see the Royal Victoria's PCU, respected for its education, research, and practice, struggling for breath. By establishing Cicely Saunders's holistic, compassionate model of care, and by advocating for reform, Balfour Mount revolutionized Canadian attitudes towards the care of terminally sick. Mount inspired Canada's first wave of hospice and palliative care practitioners, now dispersed throughout the country, and for twenty-six years he has chaired a biannual International Congress on Care of the Terminally Ill in Montreal.

The holistic, patient-centred model of care, however, is being challenged by what Mount calls "thanatologic fascism." Medical specialists, for instance, may become focused on treating palliative patients as symptoms, much as their previous doctors treated them as diseases, re-creating an interventionist, technological, doctor-driven model of care antithetical to hospice principles. It's becoming easier to bring the hospital to the home, and an "I have done everything" approach makes the physician feel good. If a patient's quality of life lies in simply being alive, it's logical to equate quality with length of life, and it's natural for doctors to look for a scientific solution to spiritual pain. Balfour Mount and Anna Towers worry that sadness, anger, withdrawal, and other behaviour normal in a dying person may be seen as a problem to be "fixed" rather than an emotion to be expressed.

Dr. Towers calls the interventionist approach the "factory conveyor-belt model," but she agrees that, with care, the research needs to be done. "The researchers are getting very good," Towers says. "They are coming up with amazing drug combinations. No one will have to die in pain. But there are things about dying that professionals can't control. What symptoms patients present will never have been presented before in the history of the world. It's a unique experience."

Most of the recent research I've read on pain and symptom management, depression, and other aspects of palliative medicine has been practical and thought-provoking, but how about rating patients on a hope scale? In May 1999, the Cross Cancer Centre in Edmonton hosted Rays of Hope, a national conference of psychosocial oncologists on the theme of hope research. The presentations included "Challenge of Hope Research in a Clinical Setting," "The Challenge of Hope Assessment," "Exploring Hope in Research and

Practice," "Ethics of Hope," and "Hope Changing: The Transition from Active Treatment to Palliative Care."

Whether their treatment is labelled clinical or holistic, palliative physicians constantly face ethical dilemmas. Are they being invasive, or negligent? Here are some thorny examples from one hospice workshop I attended.

An active, middle-aged married woman dying of metastatic breast cancer, which has spread to her bones, falls and breaks her hip. She is rushed to Emergency. Should she have surgery? Surgery might kill her, but, although her pain is under control, without surgery she will be bedridden. Her doctor opts for surgery. She survives, and lives another six weeks, but she never gets out of bed. Her husband, who thought surgery would restore her to her old active self, is resentful and depressed. Was the surgery worth it?

If palliative physicians define quality of life as patient satisfaction, they are under intense pressure to meet their patients' wishes. Jane, fifty-two, has cancer of the jaw. She finds it difficult to swallow, and is terrified of suffocating. She is depressed, but she wants to live six months to attend her son's wedding. Moving the wedding ahead isn't an option.

Her doctor says that a tracheostomy, a tube in her windpipe, would allow her to breathe, but she would lose the ability to speak. Against his advice, she chooses the tracheostomy. The tube has to be suctioned constantly to remove secretions and she requires twenty-four-hour home care. She walks up the aisle at the wedding, but afterwards, unable to open her jaw, she feels she made the wrong decision. She wants to die. Her husband can no longer cope at home. Jane is transferred to hospital and placed on full mechanical life support. She dies in the palliative care unit, sedated, of an untreated infection. Everyone involved feels miserable.

Palliative doctors tend to have a high opinion of their counselling skills, but Balfour Mount has identified the phenomenon of the "patronizing patient," patients who, by reassuring doctors that they're doing a great job, lull them into complacency. I would call these patients placating or appeasing. A relationship of inequality is not conducive to criticism or confession, and family crises, which cause nurses and doctors so much grief, might be prevented by involving social workers and family counsellors, as a matter of course, from the beginning.

Bad news might be easier to break, and to hear, if a counsellor were present. A message that comes from several people, including a volunteer, is stronger than a message from a strange physician the patient might mistrust. A social worker is a better judge of a home environment than a nurse, and hospitals discharge patients home without a clue about what kind of home it is. Is she being sent back to an abusive husband, or is a violent husband being sent home to his wife? Is her husband too frail to care for her? Is an angry daughter kidnapping her mother for revenge? Does the patient want to go home? Should a hospice, under family pressure, admit a patient against his will, or accept a dying patient on a Friday afternoon when her doctor leaves orders not to be called until Monday?

During three years as a hospice volunteer, I have met a lot of friendly, pleasant, rural and suburban families. Some are as orderly, composed, and self-sufficient in dying as they must have been in health. Others erupt into cauldrons of conflict around the deathbed. It's their way, and it doesn't make any difference if they're Asian, Jewish, Italian, or rock-ribbed Ontario. I wonder if Balfour Mount isn't right when he says that turmoil may be a "systems problem," family chaos caused by a dysfunctional health care system. I think we should call it the sickness care system.

Michele Chaban believes that emotional trauma can be prevented if a death, however difficult, is handled so that everyone involved feels they have done the best they can. As long as their behaviour does no harm, it may do good. Bringing food to patients unable to eat horrifies nurses, fearful that their patients will choke, inhale, or vomit the food, but the buying and cooking of the food is an important ritual for the cook. It's not necessary for patients to eat the food.

Feelings are unlikely to be hurt if the patient, giving thanks, puts the dish aside, promising to eat it later, and the nurse can seize an opportunity to allay family fears about starvation. Patients may ask for food to please others, or because they still hope to get better.

Since, in Canada, women have surrendered to professionals their traditional role as nurses of the sick and washers of the dead, they need to be encouraged to help in other constructive ways. As volunteers soon discover, it's family members who often need companionship, moral support, and practical assistance. During my Sunday afternoons volunteering at Hill House Hospice in Richmond Hill, two husbands have busied themselves by fixing light switches and appliances. Children often visit at Hill House, and occasionally large families will camp out for several days. It's a homey place, with toys and TV and computer games, and even when Mum or Nana or Grampa is cadaverous, disfigured, or wrapped in bandages, the kids show surprisingly little fear or revulsion. They'll hop into the patient's bed, much as they must have done at home.

Homeless men, too, have friends. In June 1998, with Dr. David Ouchterlony of the Mount Sinai team, I visited Jim, a homeless man dying of cirrhosis of the liver in a street hospice in downtown Toronto.

Eighteen months before, Seaton House, a hostel for destitute men, had converted an old bath house next door into an annex, an overnight "damp" hostel for men who needed their booze at night. They could bring their bottles in, as long as they drank outside. "These are men who are barred from other hostels," says social worker Jordan Lewis, who came up with the idea for a hospice. "They are alcoholics and drug users with multiple medical problems, HIV, liver disease, and severe psychiatric illness."

When three men died at the annex during its first year, the staff realized that they were unprepared. "They were dying when they came to us," says night supervisor Art Manuel. "We didn't know the causes, or what to do." They also didn't know how to counsel the dead man's friends. In November 1997, a shower room on the top floor was converted into a twelve-bed dormitory for men who would otherwise be dying on the street. Dr. Ouchterlony visits when necessary as part of his rounds.

The annex is quiet in the afternoon. Jim, wearing a bright red sweater, is slouched in an armchair in a corner of the sitting room, his chin resting on his chest. The room is full of men of all ages sitting anxiously on the edge of their chairs. The TV is tuned to World Cup soccer, but these guys, their eyes full of concern, are watching Jim. Dr. Ouchterlony kneels by Jim's side, listening hard to Jim's mumbled answers to his questions. Not much is known about Jim, not even his real name. A couple of his buddies brought him in after they found him slumped on the street. They'd taken him first to St. Michael's Hospital next door, but Jim said, *"Get me out of here!"* His buddies are hanging in with him here at the Seaton House hospice.

"I hate to leave this guy," one of them told Ouchterlony, his eyes welling with tears.

"I don't want to take him with me, either," Jim quipped, and everybody laughed.

Jim has lived six weeks longer than expected, but his legs and ankles are swollen into tree trunks. He is miserable because he can't walk any more. A homeless man, he seems to have been a homeless child, and scavenging on the streets is the only life he knows. He misses it.

A social worker, a young woman, bustles in full of good cheer. She'll get Jim some pressure stockings to ease the discomfort in his legs. In hospice, Jim is eligible for social assistance. He is clean – "No lice here," says Jordan Lewis – and he is offered three hot meals a day. "He's eating and drinking," Ouchterlony says, pleased. "His leg sores are healing. He's down to one or two glasses of sherry a day. He's in much better shape than when he was brought in."

Jim, his friends at his side, died quietly in the hospice two weeks later.

XXIII

I HAVE BEEN TRAVELLING through a changing landscape. By 1999, the groundswell of public support for euthanasia and assisted suicide stirred up by Sue Rodriguez in 1992 has ebbed. The issue became so emotional and divisive that politicians touched it at their peril. "Disabled and institutionalized people are frightened out of their minds," Senator Wilbert Keon told me in 1997. An outstanding heart surgeon and director of the Ottawa Heart Institute, Keon had supported a bill by Senator Sharon Carstairs intended to clarify and protect the rights of health-care providers who, on request, withhold or withdraw life-sustaining medical treatments. The bill died when an election was called, but not before the senators had been swamped with a tide of hysterical mail.

The 1995 report of the Special Senate Committee on Euthanasia and Assisted Suicide had recommended that the Criminal Code be amended to provide a less severe sentence for euthanasia motivated by compassion or mercy. This view is shared by Dr. Charles Wright and the committee that investigated Dr. Nancy Morrison's role in the death of Paul Mills, but when Saskatchewan farmer Robert Latimer used compassion as his defence for murdering his severely disabled daughter, Tracy, juries at two trials convicted him. The second jury recommended, unsuccessfully, a token one-year sentence, a reflection of public opinion polls showing that 73 per cent of Canadians felt Latimer should be treated leniently. Yet there wasn't a peep of public protest in April 1998 when Toronto doctor Maurice Genereux was convicted of prescribing overdoses of Seconal to two depressed, but not dying, HIV patients he knew were contemplating suicide. One man died, the other recovered after a friend found him unconscious. Genereux, the first physician in North America to be convicted of assisting suicide, was sentenced to two years less a day in a provincial jail. The survivor, Mark Jewitt, said he was surprised and disappointed that Genereux didn't get penitentiary time. He sued Genereux for malpractice.

In November 1998, a video of "Dr. Death," Jack Kevorkian, killing an ALS patient from Michigan was shown on the CBS television program *60 Minutes*. Kevorkian, who boasted about his involvement in more than one hundred and twenty deaths, had been acquitted three times of assisting suicide. On television, Kevorkian demanded that the state of Michigan charge him to settle the euthanasia issue once and for all. The state rose to his challenge. Kevorkian was charged with murder, convicted, and sentenced to ten to twenty-five years in jail. Spectators in the courtroom applauded.

The change in attitude is due, in part, to the growth of hospice and palliative care in the United States and Canada. In the U.S., it is standardized through the National Hospice Organization and funded by medical insurance; in Canada, hospice and palliative care is still struggling to be recognized by federal and provincial governments as an essential component of health care. "There should be universal access to competent and effective palliative care," the Senate committee recommended in 1995. "It should be integrated with other health care services, and, ideally, its availability should not vary substantially from region to region. The committee urges governments at all levels to make the development of a comprehensive system of palliative care in Canada a priority."

Five years later, every region in the country has a different combination of hospice and palliative care services, if they have any at all. In Ontario's York Region, where I have lived for more than four years, the territory once served by Hospice King, now Hospice King-Aurora, is divided among Hospices Vaughan, Richmond Hill, Hill House, Thornhill, and Newmarket, as well as Markham-Stouffville to the east. It's great to see more hospices, but each is independent and they are not coordinated by the region's Palliative Care Services branch.

While most hospices are free of charge and not for profit, they represent the privatization of part of our sickness system. A community hospice knows it's doing a good job if it has a high profile, a positive word-of-mouth reputation, and generous donors. But access is far from being equal or universal, and the palliative population is overwhelmingly people with cancer, AIDS, and, increasingly, ALS. Patients with illnesses defined as chronic are usually seen as candidates for therapy and rehabilitation, not hospice, although they may be suffering and dying of their diseases. Our attitudes towards dying are influenced by our preconceptions about diseases. Palliative care for cancer, maybe, but not for heart disease.

"Heart disease is fundamentally a different kind of disease, a totally different paradigm," explains Dr. Keon. "Patients with heart disease don't see themselves as terminally ill. They want drugs to boot the heart along, keep it tuned. A massive heart attack is a nice, clean way to go." Maybe, but in the meantime the patient may be struggling with pain, shortness of breath, fatigue, edema, anxiety, loneliness, and depression. And why aren't hospices serving people incapacitated by strokes, or working with the Alzheimer's Society?

A hundred and fifty years after we built our first lunatic asylums, we are still locking the demented away in institutions. Hospice King-Aurora, like many others, serves people who are chronically ill, like my friend Norma, over eighty now, still ticking along more than five years after she was told she had four months to live, as well as patients with only days remaining, but other hospices will not accept patients whose prognosis is more than six months or, in the case of Hill House Hospice, one month. On the other hand, the Hospice of Windsor and Essex County will register patients on diagnosis and emphasizes its wellness programs.

A long-term relationship can be emotionally rewarding for patients, caregivers, and families. "The women who came to our home became close and invaluable friends to my mother," says Norma's daughter, Kathy. "She looked forward, and still does, to their twice-weekly visits. Each volunteer seemed to develop a 'specialty,' and Mum planned her week around her hospice days – her Scrabble day, her bank day, her library day – and the holidays that the rest of us so looked forward to were disappointing days for her because she might have to miss one of her visitors. It is no exaggeration to say that the hospice and its wonderful volunteers have contributed in no small part to my mother's longevity in defiance of doctors' predictions of a too-early death."

A province can designate palliative care as a "core service" but provide little or no money for it. I am pleased to know Winnipeg's Grace Hospital now has ten palliative beds in its oncology unit, and any patient, relative, or concerned friend who phones nurse manager Laurie Read will get a sympathetic ear. The cost of the beds, however, comes entirely from the hospital's own budget.

"We can't say yes to everybody," Read sighs, "but we make exceptions on compassionate grounds. You can't say to people, 'There is no place for you in the system.'" One hundred and fifty of the five hundred patients who die at Grace Hospital every year are referred to palliative care. It's all the facility can handle. "We're not funded by the province and we likely won't be," Read says. "Manitoba Health doesn't acknowledge us." In spite of this, the hospital, run by the Salvation Army, is planning to open an in-patient hospice.

Regions in most provinces are moving, sometimes tentatively, towards integrating palliative practice with home care and cancer clinics. Studies and pilot projects receive government funding, but the impetus is coming from private citizens and medical professionals who refuse to tolerate continuing negligence. Canada's College of Family Physicians and the Royal College of Physicians and Surgeons have joined forces to create a one-year accredited course in palliative care, and Dr. W. Gifford-Jones, having won his lengthy battle to legalize the medical use of heroin, only to see heroin rarely prescribed, has endowed a professorship in pain control and palliative care at the University of Toronto medical school. Dr. Larry Librach is the first appointment.

Mount Sinai Hospital found a patron for palliative care in 1997, and with this financial support Librach's team moved from their grungy quarters behind the hospital to the bright, spacious offices of the Temmy Latner Centre for Palliative Care on the hospital's tenth floor. In May 2000, they moved again, to a corner of the hospital's new third-floor obstetrics ward in the Ontario Hydro building up the street. The team has grown to thirteen doctors and two social workers, plus consultants and support staff. In 1999, the Temmy Latner Centre joined with the Toronto Region Community Care Access Centre and the Ontario ministry of health to develop a model for the delivery of home palliative care services. The pilot project, which includes hospices, ends in 2001, and if successful, it will create a template for every region in Ontario.

Home delivery makes me think of Eaton's, long ago, horse-drawn milk and ice wagons during the war, the man from Shell who fills our oil tank twice a year, our mailman, the Internet, e-mail, pagers, fax and phones. How many hospices and palliative care units advertise? How many have web pages designed to inform the general public? How many have e-mail? Hospice King-Aurora, founded in 1983 by a small group of eloquent, educated, and committed women, hasn't had a speakers' bureau for years, although many of these volunteers, now highly experienced, are still active in hospice and in the community. Public education would help eliminate the ignorance, misinformation, and false expectations that contribute to our fear of dying, especially if end-of-life issues were discussed in school when children are learning about the creation of life.

It's easy to assume there is no need or demand for a service if the public has no way of expressing it. I know that York Region's pain and symptom management consulting team is accessible to anyone who calls, but the number is not in the phone book. Under York Region, I find numbers for birth control and sexually transmitted diseases, long-term care, and plumbing inspection. In the emergency numbers, I find, in addition to 911, two numbers for the deaf, Crime Stoppers, the Ontario Provincial Police, Marine and Air Search and Rescue, the Poison Information Centre, eleven numbers for victims of sexual assault, a Kids' Help Phone, two Distress Centres, and the Ontario Problem Gambling Helpline.

Under the auspices of the Canadian Palliative Care Association, a national committee, spearheaded by Dr. Frank Ferris, is making progress towards achieving a consensus on standards of palliative care. Agreement on standards may, eventually, lead to a process of audit and accreditation. Family physicians, nurses, and volunteers throughout the country are being educated in palliative care, to the point where a small hospital may have a specialist or one within call, and the argument that the principles of palliative care should be applied to *all* health care doesn't seem as extreme as it once did. Why shouldn't every patient be treated as an emotional, spiritual, and social being who need not suffer from pain, the side effects of treatment, or needless interventions? Hospice Windsor, Canada's first community hospice, founded in 1979, has long been integrated into both hospital and community resources. Caregivers, the bereaved, volunteers, and staff join in hospice support programs. At Hospice Windsor, the terrifying great divide between "active" and "palliative" treatment for cancer patients has disappeared.

In two of her weekly support groups for adults, Windsor social worker and therapist Jan Dennis uses meditation, music, visualizing, drumming, aromatherapy, and the resources of the hospice's Snoezelen Room, a tactile electronic playground designed in Europe, and used here, to stimulate handicapped children. Adults are stimulated too, and while I find the whirling smiley faces projected on the wall scary, I could sit forever stroking a shimmering *aurora borealis* of fibre optic cables. The latest thing in meditation at Hospice Windsor is the labyrinth.

When I first heard about it I visualized a claustrophobic Minotaur's cave, but this $16,000 labyrinth, made in the U.S.A., is a canvas circle, about thirty-five feet in diameter, which can be easily rolled out on the floor of a large room. The convoluted path, painted with purple lines to match the medieval labyrinth at Chartres Cathedral in France, leads to a central, tree-shaped space, then out again. It is designed to encourage contemplation, and walking the labyrinth by candle light with Jan Dennis and the other members of the group, I find calm, inner space. Some find revelation, recognition, freedom from fear. Seen from a distance, the pattern of the labyrinth is a tree of life surrounded by an umbilical cord.

Hospice Windsor has a reputation for the experimental. At the 1999 Humber College conference on palliative care in early April, I make a point of going to "Exploring My Dying, Living the Present by Challenging the End," a fifteen-minute workshop by two Hospice Windsor social workers and therapists, Maggie Johnson and Stephen Brenner. Brenner, dressed head-to-toe in black, his face blackened with greasepaint, prowls in front of our chairs. "I am *Dying*," Brenner chortles, leaning towards us. "I am not Death. I am the *process*. I am going to be *in your face*. I take things. *You have no control. I have control.*"

I'm jumping out of my skin, but Maggie Johnson in whiteface, white clothes, responds brightly from the other side of the room, "I am a sister to Dying and we have a peaceful relationship. I am light, memories, gifts, connecting." White Dying challenges Black Dying, calling him arrogant, boastful, vainglorious. Dying's two personas argue like characters in a play, but they speak directly to the audience and look each of us right in the eye. I'm freaked, and I'm healthy. Isn't this a heavy trip for people who *are* dying?

No, apparently. Since 1997, Steve and Maggie, the friendliest people in the world in real life, have, by popular request, led four

Exploring My Dying groups with the dying, their wives, husbands, and caregivers. A few have become too ill to continue, but no one has quit. The group began with a conventional seminar format, experts who lectured on loss, grief, wills, funeral plans, family relationships, spiritual issues, until the participants responded, *Enough! Enough! We want to talk!* Steve, trained in a clown ministry (nothing seems weird to me any more) thought, "If we're going to deal with dying, let's cut through all this 'do this gently' stuff and go *Boom*, here's what we're here to deal with, *dying*."

Participants are told at the first of five weekly sessions that they will die, metaphorically, with the group, at the end of the five weeks. Stripping away their everyday clothes down to their hidden black and white, Steve and Maggie begin to apply their makeup. As they transform themselves, moving into a rhythmic counterpoint dance, they raise the issues nobody wanted to hear about from the experts.

"It's powerful," says Steve. Black Death, a frightening, but familiar, figure, arouses anger; White Death, unfamiliar, proposes generosity. Towards the close of the three-hour session, Steve and Maggie hand out individual "death shields," cotton fabric stretched over circular embroidery frames. The participants, using markers, shells, beads, feathers, and paint, are to create facsimiles of their psychic selves, much as ancient warriors decorated their shields with sacred personal emblems. They are to take their shields home, add to them what they wish, and bring them back every week.

During the next three sessions, group members, guided and challenged by Steve and Maggie in their street clothes, tell their stories, argue with each other, debate religious differences, reveal secrets, reflect, make friends. When they arrive for the last meeting, the two faces of Dying, black and white, male and female, are facing each other, still, silent, in a dark room lighted by candles. This time, Dying's face is half-black, half-white. Together, Dying goes around the circle, fixing each person in turn with a prolonged, intense stare, asking, "Are you ready to die?"

No one has gone to pieces, Maggie says. "They handle it amazingly well. They have chosen to be in the group. They are supported by one another and by us. There are people who aren't fazed at all. They know who they are and where they're going. Okay Dying, you're here. So what?" Steve and Maggie, gradually removing their own makeup, mark the participants' faces with white and black streaks, marks of passage, and ask them to surrender their death shields, a gesture symbolic of their willingness to die. A few refuse. Most ask for them back. Some carry their shields into their deathbeds, and have them buried with them.

I watch this graceful, provocative mime knowing that, with the wholehearted support of the Canadian government and the participation of our armed forces, NATO aircraft are bombing civilians in Yugoslavia. Nobody at the conference mentions this. We care for the dying, we kill people. The daffodils are blooming. I'm depressed. I'm glad I'm going to Ottawa. Hospice of All Saints is growing and moving. The May Court, a volunteer charity, has given the hospice its support and its former convalescence home on the Rideau River rent-free for five years. It will now be called Hospice at May Court.

I arrive to find that walls have been knocked out to create a spacious living room and dining area around a small glassed-in courtyard. A sunroom overlooking the lawn and river has been converted into a library, with a grand piano; a smaller sunroom is an all-purpose gathering place. The colours are sandstone and sage. Concrete is covered with soft, compressed wood flooring. The hall ceilings have twinkling lights.

The move has been undertaken with some trepidation among the day hospice patients that the homey environment of 18 Blackburn will become institutionalized, but Barbara O'Connor, Susan Smith, and Diana Conner still pad about cheerfully in loose skirts, sweaters, and comfortable shoes. When I ask after the women of the Fresh Air club whose company I'd enjoyed eighteen months earlier, they tell me that Bea and Zoe are so alive and well they've been discharged.

"We have to push some people out the door," Susan laughs. "'Go out and be *well*.' They can always call and come back." Some well patients feel so nostalgic the hospice is thinking about starting a weekly program for "graduates."

Sofas and armchairs in the living room have been arranged in conversation groups, with chairs set apart for people not up to talking. The floors are bare, and the room lacks a fireplace, but three weeks after moving here, the big gripe is: "We can't smell the food!" The kitchen, an industrial space, is isolated in the northeast corner. There is more freedom here, Susan says. People can move from group to group if they become bored or irritated, or go off by themselves to one of the quiet rooms. "We mix the more sociable with the less," Susan says. "It's amazing how well people mix. We have very few conflicts."

As people stream in, call greetings, and stake out their favourite chairs, I hear the sound of Ruth Charles's harp around the corner in the dining room. The tune is "Annie Laurie," a folk song that takes me back to my childhood, but when I go to investigate, it's not Ruth playing. The harp is lying flat on the table, and an elderly man with a beatific smile is leaning over it, picking out the tune. Bernard, who doesn't speak above a whisper, loves playing the harp so much Ruth has written the music on a sheet of paper he slides under the strings to see which one to pluck. Bernard has worked up a small repertoire, including "Lili Marlene" and "My Darling Clementine," and he's happy to teach me. Amazing! In a few minutes, I, who failed recorder, can pick out "Annie Laurie" on a harp.

Bernard carries on a conversation by printing his responses on scrap paper. He tells me he is an RCAF war veteran. He survived the Battle of the Atlantic and three years of Allied bomber raids over occupied Europe. Now he has cancer. He is eighty-one, and he has been married nearly fifty years. At hospice, he writes, "I paint, play chess, play the harp and bother people." His eyes twinkle. "Now I am a *new* music teacher," he writes. "I am not a musician. You can dith on the dither, you can harp on the harp. For us terminally ill, we have a head start on the harp."

Ruth hangs the harp by its strap around my neck. She encourages patients to touch or hold the harp and play random notes and chords. "You can meditate on the note," she says, "and you can feel the vibration of the strings through the sounding box. The single note can be very evocative, and it resonates in the body." I pluck a string. The sensation trembles from my fingertips to my toes, an erotic thrill, but invasive. "Music arouses very strong emotions," Ruth says. "Some people don't want to go *near* it." She finds the harp less intrusive than the guitar. "The harp is flexible. People can take the harp into their beds. They can hold the sounding board right on their chests. Even in hospital, that resonating note in the room makes a difference, for the family as well. It's important to watch, to be constantly checking. Is it okay? You don't know what the song will bring up."

Therapeutic music, I am relieved to learn, isn't a young woman with a guitar whanging out "This Land is Your Land." "I modulate the mode," Ruth says, "to be where the person is in their emotion, to go with them." When patients respond to the harp's mystical voice, Ruth will encourage them to talk about the images or memories the chords bring into their minds. "I'll say, 'Is there somebody there? What do you want to say to that person? What are you feeling now?'" Deborah Salmon, music therapist at the Royal Victoria's PCU, calls these "ventures into the *deep*, into the expanse of one's own psyche wherein lies great wisdom." When patients are dying and their breathing becomes agitated or irregular, Salmon tries to match her playing to the rhythm of their breaths: "It's not uncommon for the person's rate of breathing to change, usually becoming slower and more regular. Although one can never know for certain, it is my impression that music may facilitate this final stage of dying. It seems somehow to support the person in letting go of life and moving toward death. On one occasion, death has occurred during live music." Salmon helps patients compose their own songs, or sets their lyrics to music. One man wrote an angry, funny blues riff about shit, called "Sick and Full of It."

When Ruth Charles plays and sings to patients, she likes to suggest songs from their teenage years, rock and roll, music from the

1930s, a song like "Lili Marlene" that brings back war memories for Bernard. Some of the old chestnuts, "Danny Boy" or "The White Cliffs of Dover," send classical music purists through the roof. Ruth cautioned a composer in day hospice that he would find the pop songs *very difficult*. If so, he could retreat into a quiet room. Sometimes the whole crowd will sing. Sure enough, as Ruth and I talk, someone is playing "Cruising Down the River" on a piano. Women's voices are raised in song, and when I turn around, I see them gaily waltzing around the living room.

When your guests are sick and suffering, it takes sensitivity to maintain a mood of good cheer that is not false cheer. Many of the patients are on chemotherapy, with all its miserable side effects, and while some, full of energy and optimism, are benefitting, others are tired, depressed, and in pain. "It is very difficult to intervene with family physicians," says the hospice's medical consultant, Dr. Pippa Hall. "I had a patient with *a lot* of pain. The physician was away, so I phoned the doctor on call. He was very angry that I would get involved without a referral. You can't ask for a referral because it looks like you're asking for money. I wish people could think of just helping the patient." Pippa Hall has to counsel patients and families about who to call and what to ask for, but the patients are upset and families are tired, anxious, and prickly. "It's not a straight path," Hall sighs. "It's a very tangled wood."

Many of these patients are single, and the companionship of the day hospice, now expanded to three days a week, with its order, good taste, and good manners, helps them bear bad news. One woman has been told her tumour has returned, another, recently diagnosed, starts chemo next week. Her doctor has told her that without chemo, she has three months to live, with chemo, possibly three years. She is angry, agitated, a coiled spring of terror. Her whole body screams *I don't want to die!*

"Day hospice can be *intense*," says Susan Smith. There are occasional arguments, patients who huff off, never to return, and, as in any crowd, bores, grouches, busybodies, and people who can't stand each other. Patients who look tired are asked if they'd like to lie down in a quiet room. They may be too polite to leave the company, but one agitated woman sleeps for an hour after a few minutes of therapeutic touch. The massage room, with a professional therapist who specializes in reflexology, deep massage of the feet and hands, is well used, and Francine, a tiny, ashen-faced bundle of bones, insists on a whirlpool bath. Susan worries that Francine, so frail she has to be lifted from a chair to her wheelchair, may break a rib, but Susan gives her a bath and a hair wash. "You do what you have to do," Susan says. Snuggled under a quilt in a reclining chair, her eyes closed, her hair in rollers, Francine's expression is blissful.

It may be Francine's last visit to day hospice. At lunch (Deborah Hebert's pumpkin-potato soup, green salad, crisp vegetarian pizza, and chocolate eclairs), the mood becomes pensive as Susan reports on the people who are missing. No one has died this week, but most of those missing are in hospital. The downside of a day hospice is that at some point the dying drop out. It's a hard loss for them, and for their hospice friends. The second phase of the hospice's expansion in its new quarters will be to open the east wing as a ten-bed in-patient unit.

We talk about renovating bathrooms, summer vacations, a birthday coming up. I meet a civil servant who shares my interest in Canadian war art. She, like several women, is wearing jeans and a T-shirt; other women, fresh from chemo, are dressed immaculately in business suits, high heels, hats. It's an odd ambiance, part Rideau Hall, part Mad Hatter's tea party. "IT'S THE NARCOTICS" is the bold slogan on one woman's T-shirt. She has short, dark hair, a dazzling smile and a big laugh. Her name is Terry Penner. She painted the slogan herself, she says, as a joke to explain her volatile behaviour. "I can get very angry. I have bad days." Terry's breast cancer has spread to her lungs, liver, abdomen, bones, lymph system, and brain. Her body is swollen with fluid. "I feel bitchy today," Terry had announced when she arrived, but her grin gave her away. Later she said, "I am not going to live so I have nothing to get angry at."

At the art table in the activity room, Terry is working on another T-shirt. The slogan, green on red, reads ABANDON HOPE, ABANDON FEAR. Two other women at the table are painting a serene still life of a teapot and bowls arranged on a swath of sky blue silk. It's a quiet, congenial corner. We talk about the beautiful day, daffodils coming up, spring. "I live to garden," Terry says, telling us about having to clean out the goldfish pond. "With my big belly, I'm afraid I'll fall in," she laughs. "They'll find me floating upside down and never know whether or not I killed myself." A volunteer quips, "It's hard to wear a life jacket when you're gardening." We laugh.

Terry is going to wear her ABANDON HOPE, ABANDON FEAR T-shirt to the hospice's formal opening on Sunday. I'm impressed. Here is a young woman using art to make a provocative statement about dying. Terry says she would wear her Sheila na Gig shirt, but it got spoiled in the wash. Sheila na Gig? What's that? It comes from pagan religion, Terry explains. Sheila na Gig, a sculpture found over hundreds of old church doors in the British Isles, is a leering woman holding open her gigantic vulva with both hands, "Come and get me, guys!"

XXIV

THE MESSAGES ON Terry's T-shirts speak forcefully to me, but I don't understand them. Can we talk later in the week? I ask. Sure, she says. She lives only a few blocks from the hospice with her husband and two teenage children, and when I arrive on Saturday, it is, fortunately, one of her good days. Since she's had to quit work, Terry spends most of her time in the sunroom overlooking their spacious garden. It's almost a sunken garden, with sculptures and an overturned canoe, the grass turning from brown to green. Chickadees zip back and forth to the feeder by the window.

Terry, in her mid-forties, has had metastatic cancer for nearly seven years. She has had surgery, chemotherapy, and twenty-five radiation treatments. "I was *assured* that if I had radiation there would be no new cancer sites," she laughs. "Well, a new site burst through my third-degree burns in the middle of treatment." Terry phoned the hospice in the fall of 1998 for advice about controlling her pain after she had decided to stop going to the cancer clinic: "If you have end-stage cancer, they will continue to see you at the cancer clinic until you die of treatment if you allow them to do it. They'd love to, but it's not something I wanted to do. Besides, oncologists don't have any knowledge of pain control. I wasn't prepared to go through a lot of diagnostic procedures to find out where each tumour was that was causing me pain. They had offered to sever the nerve to my arm, for example, if I would like."

Terry found out about the hospice from a friend who was a volunteer. "Oncologists don't give you any advice about how to proceed. They don't say, Go to your GP and ask for a palliative care doctor. They drop you. 'You go home and die then.' They're not interested in you any more. You're not a cancer patient, you're a dying person." When her family doctor was unable to control her pain, he referred her to a palliative specialist who put her on tiny, but effective, doses of Dilaudid. Hospice arranged counselling for her husband and children, and Terry joined the Wednesday day hospice when it started in September 1998.

"I thought, well, I'll come once," she laughs. "It was really nice to be there. It's like a country club. I'm home alone all day, and it's not as if I can't make my own lunch, but it's a great thing to have a day when you don't have to. By the time evening comes along, you're really tired from taking care of yourself all day. It's hard. On hospice day, I still have resources by evening. It's also a day when my family doesn't have to think about me. That's a real relief. They know I'm taken care of. Even on days when I don't feel like going, I go so they can have their day off. We can schedule nasty things that have to happen to my environment here for that day. I'm picky about it because I'm stuck here. The cleaner comes on Wednesday."

Terry was relieved that day hospice was not a support group: "I had support groups, and I watched a couple of support groups where the women died off in the period I've been sick. I really don't want to watch another group of people die. There are friendships developing in the Wednesday group that are problematic for me. I'm finding that difficult. Watching them get sicker while I'm sort of stable is emotionally draining. That's a tricky thing. You become attached to these people, absolutely. I don't think it's their job to be supportive of me either. It's draining for them too. It's another issue to deal with on top of your own process of dying."

When Terry stopped chemo and started with hospice eight months ago, her cancer was spreading rapidly: "I spent a lot of the fall explaining to my family and friends that I was going quickly because I *was* going quickly, but I'm not getting better and I'm not getting worse so I have to explain to everybody that I'm still here. Here I am! What do I do now? I just hang out. What I've learned with my cancer is that we don't know squat about this disease and we especially don't know anything about it when it's not treated. If you don't have treatments, nobody is observing you. Nobody is observing me. How would they know how my disease responds to no treatment? I'm full of fluid, I need to nap every day, I have so much cancer in my body that I shouldn't be alive, but I seem to be doing quite well. So, how come? We don't know how much cancer a human body can take."

In a day hospice where cancer patients on chemo measure their lives by tests, treatments, and white cell counts, Terry's rejection of treatment is as provocative as her T-shirts. "We are not chosen for our philosophical sameness," she says. "I find it hard to watch a couple of people I feel fond of stagger back into the chemo decision, watch them lose ground, watch them suffer. I learned to keep my mouth shut. I hear a lot of angry people when I tell them I'm refusing treatment. They feel I'm criticizing them, that what's good enough for them isn't good enough for me. But they're wrong when they think this is going to extend their lives. It's going to extend their lives if their tumour responds to it. If it doesn't work, it is going to destroy their immune system, their appetite, and make their body so frail they will not have the life they would have had without chemo. People lose ground very quickly. They're not ready for it. They have their hopes up. They haven't thought it through. I'm lucky. I've had cancer for six years. That's a lot of time."

After consulting a naturopath about poor appetite and digestion, Terry is able to eat anything she wants. She has her chest cavity drained regularly, but she credits reflexology for reducing her edema. Her hair is thick. She is conquering her fears of dying in pain or getting stoned on narcotics. "It's more the fear than the actual pain," she says. "I know now it's only pain. It's just pain. My palliative doctor seems quite unmoved by the process of dying. That's what makes her so good. She'll be there for you, and I understand that at the end she's there every day, but when I tell her on a bad day, 'I'm losing ground and I'm frightened,' her response is, 'Oh, is that how you feel today?'

"At times it's a bit daunting. Can't you feel sorry for me or something? But it's not her job. She can't stop me dying. How does a tumour kill you? I am very interested in the process. Where's the point where the tumour is too big to sustain life? How come cancer hasn't killed me? I'm not going to bargain with it. It can be there and I'm not going to stop it, but when I find a new tumour, I mourn it. You have to deal with your own fear, that's it. The fear is what kills you. From her I get fearlessness. There's nothing to be afraid of. It's part of being alive."

Is this where abandon hope, abandon fear comes in? "It's a Buddhist philosophy," Terry says. "I spend a lot of time in meditation. The idea behind it is that hope and fear are two sides of the same coin. We tend to spend a lot of time in this society thinking of hope. But hope is a trap. Hope is a trap that pulls you into the future. If you want to live without fear, you have to live without hope because every time you let yourself go for hope, you find yourself in fear that it won't work out the way you hoped. It robs you of your present, and our present is all we have. We don't know what the future holds in store for us, but we do know what we have right now, this moment that we are alive. We in fact have nothing. They call it groundlessness. We have no ground under us at all. It's learning to live with that, rather than try to control, or resist, just to stay there on that slippery slope with the ground slipping out from under you and to do *nothing* about it, not resist it, not go with it, just be there and experience it. They call it being a warrior, because you're showing great bravery. A warrior who takes off all their armour and sees how much they can be exposed.

"It's a hard thing to do. It's about pain, because pain and suffering are what teach you. We're here to learn. You can learn as much as the pain your life gives you teaches you, and as much as your own bravery allows you to experience it. The more we can let go of hope and fear, the more we can be here on this slope right now and learn what it has to teach us. What it has to teach is about beauty and joy. I sit and look out this window five, six hours a day. I look at the birds feeding and I watch the plants coming up and I find that my life has a great deal of quality. Even if I were in a high-rise apartment, the sky would be beautiful. There is beauty everywhere, and when you sit there in fear, you can't see it. Then you've lost everything."

Her family, Terry says, strategizes to stay in the present. "That requires a lot of willpower, but that's what we're doing. It's a tricky time for us. We really don't want to anticipate anything. We don't want to wish me dead, but we know I'm not going to get better. That's one of the things hospice has been really good for. In the middle of the night, when things are bad, you don't know what you are supposed to do. Should I call my palliative doctor? Go to the hospital? It's hard to make the decision when you're in escalating pain, and I hate to bug my doctor in the middle of the night. The hospice has a twenty-four-hour pager, and they're often just a sensible ear. They'll say, call, that's her job, phone her, phone her now, or, no, you can probably hang on. That's a really important resource.

"We don't know how to deal with death. We're trying to die at home, the government would like us to die at home, and we don't know how to do it. So, well, now what do I do? Tell me what the system would like me to do now. The hospice is there for that. They know the red tape and the next correct move to make. They're guides, and that's really, really important. We don't know how to die in our society."

Terry has no deathbed plans. "We don't know how this will go for me," she says. "And we don't know how my family will be able to take it. Will they be able to take a long, drawn-out home death? We'll have to see how it happens." Her parents, she says, believe in an afterlife, "but they resist the thought of their own deaths so severely there's no way they can come close to accepting the thought of how sick I am. They can't. They just don't think about it. If they do say something, it's 'When are you going to start getting better?' They check up on me a lot but they don't want to know how I'm feeling. If I admit to them that I'm having a bad day, they need me to tell them for the next five or six days that 'I feel good today,' whether it's true or not. They can't live with the news that it's not."

She says her husband feels in limbo between the hospice's caregiver support group, which he found informative, and bereavement counselling. "When the course was over, it wasn't over for him," Terry says. "He's still dealing with me. He's not bereaved yet." Their fifteen-year-old daughter, Hannah, has been working through her anger and grief by writing short stories and poems. It was in one of Hannah's art books from the library, Terry recalls, that she saw a photo of Sheila na Gig. "Once I saw her," Terry laughs, "I saw her everywhere." What was the book? She can't remember.

Hannah shyly offers me two poems and a short story about her mother. She wants to be a writer. She already is.

The Lucky Ones

We are a family
Curled together on the bed.
My arms wrapped around my mother
Face pressed to her warm side
I feel my father's callused fingers
Lightly stroking my arm.
A sob shudders through my body
As I press my lips together
Taste salty tears;
An ache in my chest

Refuses to die.
"I wanted to see you grow up," she says,
"To see your babies,
Read your books.
You have no idea how much it hurts."
She's wrong.
I know pain.
I feel warm moisture against my temple
Where she is crying on me
For the chances we never had
And Dad trembles
Attempting to regain control.
I've never seen him cry like this before.
Mom insists, whatever I want from her,
Just ask.
I want her to live forever
But instead I wrap my arms
More tightly around her waist
Rest my tear-stained cheek against her soft hip
Feel my Dad's fingernails scrape softly
Up and down my arm
Keep my eyes closed
So as not to see them cry;
And I try to remember
We are the lucky ones.

XXV

IS GRIEF THE REAL taboo? We can see people dying on television, at the movies. Edmonton film maker Joe Viszmeg made a second film, *My Healing Journey: Seven Years With Cancer*, a sequel to *In My Own Time*, shortly before he died in 1999. That autumn, Toronto artist Gail Geltner bravely exhibited photographs of her mother, dying of Alzheimer's, at an art gallery, exposing a suffering human face behind the locked doors. We go to plays about dying, Tony Kushner's *Angels in America*, Tom Stoppard's *The Invention of Love*; we write books, memoirs, poems.

But grief, in others, seems to leave us cold. I am astonished at the prejudice I encounter among medical professionals towards people who lament openly and loudly. "They're Italians," is the whispered explanation I hear where I live. Employers give us an afternoon, three days, maybe a week to get rid of the corpse and get on with it. Palliative physician Frank Ferris thinks that grief may be "the largest undiagnosed epidemic" in our society. I wouldn't call grief an illness, but it can become one, and people diagnosed as suffering from stress, depression, exhaustion, and pain may be finding socially acceptable ways of grieving. In a poem, "Time Out," Hospice King-Aurora volunteer Evert Van Den Brink, a widower, writes about being "busy" grieving. "Grief work," as the social workers call it, can be so all-consuming the griever has no energy to do anything else. Grief may well account for the high rate of suicide among the elderly, and we may avoid the dying in order to repress emotions we have no permission to express. And we avoid the bereaved.

"When our daughter died of cardiac arrest at thirty, I felt an overwhelming sense of stigmatization," Dr. Paul Henteleff told me. "People were avoiding us because we meant death. We felt *abandoned*. Widowhood is worse."

Hospices are finding an escalating demand for bereavement support. These people are not suffering pathological grief, they're sad, shaken, *alone*. Grief, I suspect, is not something most people "get over," and as we age, we lose more and more friends, colleagues, and family members to death. Grieving may be a continuous, cumulative experience, and the preoccupation of grieving a single death can last a year or a lifetime. One friend of ours, a smart, successful young businessman, was weeping for his wife five years after she died. It's taken me five years to write this book. I will always grieve for my parents, and it doesn't help that, from what I now know, I believe that my mother's suicidal depression was caused by years of chronic, unacknowledged, untreated, intolerable pain.

The simple fact that the grief-stricken, like the cancer-stricken, have to seek the company of their fellow sufferers in an isolated social situation is proof enough of the stigma. Unlike Victoria Hospice's walking groups, most bereavement support programs last only six or eight weeks. Here, at least, participants can tell their stories to sympathetic ears, cry openly, and be reassured that they are not going crazy. The risk is that grief, like hope, will become a clinical symptom to be examined, codified, and treated. Grief is already a business. Funeral homes are rushing into bereavement counselling, chaplains talk about setting up in professional practice, and schools automatically call in grief therapists when students die. We may be grieving, but a therapeutic approach to bereavement reinforces the attitude that grief is abnormal.

It's our attitude towards bereavement that's abnormal. If we allow women to take months of maternity leave when our children are born, why shouldn't we all be entitled to "eternity leave" before and after someone close to us dies? Some people find the phrase offensive. I wish it were mine. Eternity leave makes sense. We might need a few days to keep watch at a friend's bedside, three weeks to settle an estate, six months to care for a dying parent or child. Why should this not be included in employee benefit packages or in medical insurance policies? When I was a kid, I grew up in a neighbourhood of mothers. Our mothers, a diverse, skilled talent pool of unpaid labour, were there for us, and they were there for their husbands, neighbours, friends, and our grandparents.

The mothers are gone. Nobody has noticed. If we want to be sick unto death at home, we are faced with the option of paying professional mothers, nurses and homemakers, or going to where they work, the hospital. But is a paid caregiver, however compassionate, a substitute for a child, a dear friend, a lover? Why do we get time off work only after people are dead? A man forced by his contract to work a twelve-hour shift until his dying wife is stone cold will do everything in his power to believe, however bald and bloated she may be, she is *not dying*. And she will reassure him, yes, she's fine. She gives him moral support, her final gift. He is given no time out for her.

Grief is supposed to end at the funeral. For many, it does. A few days before my father died, two of his best friends asked me about a memorial service. Harry had told me explicitly that he didn't want one, but he'd gone to everybody else's funeral, and his friends insisted, "A funeral is for the *living*." I thought about it, and I remembered a conversation my dad and I'd had a week or so before. It had puzzled me at the time. He had spoken emphatically about friends and colleagues he especially admired, some of whom I'd never met, and their names, like the opening lines of Coleridge's *The Ancient Mariner*, were engraved on my memory. Of course, he'd been giving me his speaker's lineup. Sure, we'll have a celebration of Harry's life, a gathering of the clan. Neutral space. No religion. Wine and cheese. Thirty minutes' service. Short, personal eulogies, Robbie Burns, and, if I can get through it, "The Lake Isle of Innisfree." Suzanne, the violist who lived next door, volunteered her string quartet. Bless her.

Jim Alward and I scheduled the gathering for late August, when everyone would be back from the lake, and while I was burying Harry's ashes, Jim worked on the logistics. As I packed up the remnants of my parents' lives that I chose not to discard (this is hard), I selected old photographs of my mother and father for a table display. It was a revelation. Even in old age, they looked so young, handsome, cheerful, in love. My mother, in her last cleaning, did not discard these pictures. She didn't want a memorial service, and she didn't have one, but I was determined to include her in this one.

There was a good crowd, a lot of my parents' friends I hadn't seen for forty years. They recognized me. "She looks like her mother," they said. I was happy to see them. The music was lovely, the speeches witty, full of good stories, lots of laughter. I was too spaced out and deaf from the noise in my head to talk much. Hosting a celebration of my parents' lives was not something I had planned on. However, only two years before, I had helped organize a creative memorial service for my brother-in-law, poet Tom Marshall, so I did have a good model to draw from. What do other unchurched people do?

This theatrical dilemma may explain why memorial services of any kind seem to be going out of fashion. Traditional funeral customs have been so savagely criticized we're afraid of doing something stupid, vulgar, or controversial. People can fight bitterly over funerals. Should a casket be open or closed? Do we invite guests to the cremation? Is it proper to display ashes in a box or an urn? Is it an imposition to expect relatives scattered all over the world to gather for a short ceremony? One irony of our desire for immortality is that if we live to a great old age without a multi-generational family or a circle of younger friends, we suffer social death – isolation, dementia, institutionalization – long before we die.

Lack of ceremony is hard on people who find comfort in congregation, but more and more I see in obituaries: *Cremation has taken place. Private family funeral. No funeral. No flowers. A donation to the charity of your choice would be appreciated by the family.* Since when has dying become a fundraiser? Perhaps giving money away is our way of putting coins on the corpse's eyes to pay the ferryman.

We put stones on graves, it is said, to keep the dead from coming back, but they haunt us in our dreams and memories. We don't always get to choose our grave, and if we end up in some unexpected place, it might be best to leave us there. When Swissair flight 111 crashed into the Atlantic Ocean off Nova Scotia in September 1998, killing all two hundred and twenty-nine people on board, thousands of rescuers spent weeks fishing bits and pieces of decaying human flesh out of the water. Why? After the first few days, there was no expectation that anyone would be rescued alive. Some body fragments were ultimately identified by DNA evidence, but their ghoulish task left many of the rescuers so sickened they had to seek professional help. On the other hand, when an avalanche swept Michel Trudeau into British Columbia's Lake Kokanee and RCMP divers failed to find his body, the Trudeaus were content to let Michel rest in peace.

Public mourning is theatre, and if the death is dramatic, it's made for television. The prototype is the period of mourning following the assassination of President John F. Kennedy in 1963. Days of tolling bells, the swearing-in of a new president, and the murder of the alleged assassin ended with a solemn televised procession to Arlington Cemetery, Jackie, head-to-toe in black, walking erect behind the gun carriage that carried her husband's coffin. Television then was black-and-white, and while the British royal family used a similar scenario for the funeral of Princess Diana in September 1997, the gay colours of the television picture spoiled the funereal effect.

Diana's funeral itself was an anti-climax to the astonishing week of public grieving that followed her death in a car crash in Paris, France. As Diana's body lay in state in St. James' Palace, tens of thousands of weeping mourners converged on London. They waited hours in silent, shuffling lines to sign the guest book, and left mountains of flowers, teddy bears, cards, and candles by the walls of Buckingham Palace. Elton John's song "Candle in the Wind" became an international sensation, and in the media, the phenomenon of mass grief became a bigger story than the circumstances of Diana's death.

This "griefathon," as one commentator called it, seemed so excessive, so disproportionate to Diana's tarnished image and marginal role in public life, that the British appeared to be in the grip of mass hysteria. Even the taciturn old Queen was forced to make a hollow statement of sorrow, and to yield to public pressure for a state funeral. A year later, when Diana mania had all but disappeared, London-based Canadian writer Michael Ignatieff recognized the shock, guilt, and anger that had been triggered by the death of the "people's princess."

"When we mourned her death, we mourned our own," Ignatieff wrote in the *Globe and Mail*. "People wept for their own mothers and fathers, for lost children, as if all the unconsoled losses of private life had been suddenly allowed to seek public consolation. Her death became the catalyst for these suppressed emotions because we knew she had felt them herself. Her often confused expressiveness gave us permission to break the Windsor code of stoic reserve."

We adore idols and icons because, as Ignatieff says, they allow us to express taboo emotions. But these emotions are ours, not theirs. Diana's mourners knew her only through her graven images, photographs, and the ambiguous utterances her oracles leaked to secret sources. They grieved her because she was smashed. Their pilgrimage paid homage to a smiley-face Barbie doll who, blessed with narcissism, immense wealth, and innumerable acolytes, perpetually reincarnated herself as shy virgin, bride, madonna, madwoman, bulimic, spurned wife, single mother, New Age freak, fitness fanatic, whore and corpse, Britannia, the Faery Queen.

When Diana's brother, Earl Spencer, converted a stable at the family estate, Althorp, into a museum and gift shop and charged visitors $24 for a distant view of her grave and a chance to buy Diana souvenirs, the Church of England rapped him for creating a "Diana cult." The church, a wealthy and powerful cult in itself, knew a goddess when it saw one, and when it came to tackiness Spencer had to compete with the Diana memorial fund which licensed her signature, its logo, to be used on tubs of margarine. Sales of authorized Diana books, photographs, stamps, and CDs of "Candle in the Wind" raised more than $100 million for her charities in the first year after her death. Donations contributed another $100 million.

I balked at paying almost $20 to see an exhibition of Diana's dresses in glass cases when it came to Toronto – they reminded me of the glass cases full of human hair at Auschwitz – but I don't blame Diana worshippers for forking out money. Because we see ancient temples as ruins, we forget that peddlers once hawked magic potions, charms, amulets, and images of the deity in the temple's marketplace. African traditional healers are wiser about fetishes than we are.

In another five hundred years, Princess Diana might be as forgotten as Sheila na Gig. After weeks of fruitless searching through dictionaries, encyclopedias, and histories of Celtic and Stone Age cultures, I had almost decided that Terry was putting me on, when, in the gift shop at the Art Gallery of Ontario, I found a photograph of a Sheila na Gig in *A Little Book of Gargoyles* by British photographer and geographer Mike Harding. A gargoyle! Poor Inanna, so cruelly desecrated. She's still smiling, though, and while she's as bald as a breast cancer patient on chemo, she looks you in the eye and holds her huge vagina open wide in invitation. There are stone-carved Sheilas all over the British Isles, Harding says, and the signs of rubbing around their vulvas suggest that for centuries women wishing to conceive have touched them for good luck.

Now that I have found my ancestral deity, I have no difficulty finding her consort, the fertility god. His portrait by Andy Warhol, a small, cheap print that Andrew, my husband, bought years ago at the Art Institute of Chicago, is hanging in our downstairs hallway. Gunslinger pose. *Two Elvis*, 1963. Andrew and I will make a pilgrimage to the temple of the King of the Dead, Graceland, Tennessee.

XXVI

EARLY SPRING, 1956. A pubescent thirteen, nearly fourteen, growing like a weed, boyfriendless, I wondered why I seemed to be the only person to find our newly televised world boring. Precision tap dancers, lounge lizards, ventriloquists chatting with empty boxes, sweater gals in pointy bras singing oooah backup for Perry Como's hit song "Hot Diggity." Doris Day and Rock Hudson, Rosemary Clooney, the Andrews Sisters, the forced jokes and verbal violence of "I Love Lucy" and "The Honeymooners." Winnipeg radio stations were playing, at what seemed to be half speed, waltz tunes and oompah band music I'd been listening to all my life. *Is this all there is?*

Then on the radio I heard a new song by an unknown kid from Tennessee with the impossible name of Elvis Presley. The record was "Heartbreak Hotel" and if ever a song was written for me, that was it. I wasn't alone. "Heartbreak Hotel," Elvis Presley's first gold record, made him the most famous man in the world.

My girlfriends and I gathered in Virginia's rec room one evening early that spring to watch Elvis's first television appearance on the Dorsey brothers' variety program, "Stage Show." I can't remember what Elvis played and sang. It may have been "babybabybabybbbbaby-babybabycummonuh*baby*cummon, Iwannaplay'ousewithyooou," but the words were lost on me as Elvis flailed at his guitar, wailed, gyrated, rolled his eyes back, sneered, pouted and laughed, *Hit it!* The rhythm and tempo were unlike anything I'd ever heard, and Elvis, blond then, was so young, raw, *real*, like a girlfriend's dream-date older brother. I floated home, ecstatic.

It was a great year to be fourteen: "I Was the One," "Blue Suede Shoes," "I Want You, I Need You, I Love You," "Don't Be Cruel," "Hound Dog," "Love Me Tender." I didn't need a boyfriend when I listened to Elvis. Beautiful, sexy, Elvis was playful too, mocking, make-believe. When Elvis later hit *The Ed Sullivan Show*, my girl-friends and I pounded the floor in front of the TV and screamed. My parents, like parents everywhere, were aghast. But as soon as Elvis left the building, we bacchantes shut up and went back to our homework.

Boys screamed too. They imitated Elvis's ducktail pompadour and, with pelvises thrust out, Elvis's wide-legged, guitar-thrashing stance. Geeky guys with brushcuts became greasy, slouchy, pouting Elvii. It was wonderful. The romance ended in 1958 when Elvis was drafted into the U.S. Army. I went to university and, in 1963, dis-covered Bob Dylan. Folk was big, girls screamed for the Beatles, rock went electric and drowned in noise. Elvis made corny movies, played Vegas, sang gospel, got fat. Still though, that voice, and when I needed cheering up, I'd listen to my old Elvis albums.

Not long before his death, during one of his desperate comeback concert tours, Elvis was booked into an arena in Niagara Falls, New York. Andrew and I were living in Toronto, and we figured this would be our only chance to see Elvis in the flesh. The arena, crammed with metal folding chairs, was packed. Elvis, looking bloated in a white stretchlimo jumpsuit, his hair shoe-polish black, staggered on to the makeshift stage. He didn't seem to know, or care, what he was singing. When he forgot or slurred the words, he wiped his sweaty neck with silk scarves and tossed them to the women screaming at his feet. I thought of them, and my teenage self, when I heard on the radio on August 16, 1977, that Elvis had died at Graceland. I felt strangely guilty, as if, years before, in some mysterious way, Elvis had been torn apart by hordes of screaming pubescent girls. And I was one.

Twenty years later, on August 16, 1997, in *The Globe and Mail*, Frank McEnaney analyzed the cult status the King of Rock 'n' Roll had achieved in the posthumous years of his career. In 1957, at thirteen, McEnaney had been part of the adolescent pandemonium at Elvis's Toronto concert. In 1977, when McEnaney heard that the King was dead, he played Elvis's songs from his own youth for his three-year-old son. "I started reading about the early life," McEnaney says.

It was a story of mythic resonance. Born in a manger in Tupelo, Mississippi, the true King remains unrecognized until he reveals himself in glory at age twenty-one. For two short years he blazes forth like a comet in the sky. Then the false king Herod takes the census and the true King is shorn of his locks. For ten long years he remains imprisoned in a bland imitation of himself and then slowly struggles to set himself free. The struggle with the flesh – the thing that makes Elvis so beloved to us all – brings him down to the depths. He is a god crucified by hamburgers, ice cream sundaes, fried peanut butter and banana sandwiches, burnt bacon, waxy tubs of yogurt and a craving for Mars bars. A jealous god who blasts the graven image of Robert Goulet off the TV screen. A wrathful deity given to uncontrollable rages, a benevolent deity who hands out Cadillacs to strangers. Weak, strong, humble and arrogant, a spontaneous presence that gives Voice to all that we love and fear.

When McEnaney moved to the town of Collingwood, Ontario, on Lake Huron's Georgian Bay, in the 1990s, he was unaware that it was a world centre for Elvis sightings:

One evening, as the sun set, I looked up to see three Elvises hurtling headlong, flaming from the ethereal sky. What a vision: the famous Flying Elvises, alight with magnesium flares, parachuting out of a small plane. ('Oh Lucifer, thou Son of Morning, how hast thou fallen.') Turns out the mayor of Collingwood, a former president of the Elvis Presley Fan Club, had organized an Elvis convention that grew into an annual festival.

It was an Elvis impersonator who, on a dismal afternoon a day or two before Christmas 1998, persuaded me to go to Graceland. I fear Christmas. Heartbreaking things happen to me at Christmas. Ghosts haunt me at Christmas. Hospice is a refuge, and I was churning my truck through filthy brown slush on my way to Hill House when I heard, faintly, from the next corner, *'s all right, mama, any way you. . . .*

As I turned off for the hospice, there he was, an Elvis, short, smiling, pudgy, all in black with a pompadour and a booming amplifier. Cars honked as they passed, and the Elvis waved and shook hands with those who slowed down. I would have waved and said hello but I was in the outside lane. After I parked, I stopped and listened. Elvis, after all these years, was still singing to me.

In August 1999, Memphis, Tennessee, a dry, dusty midwestern city on a big muddy river, looks and feels a lot like my old midwestern hometown on a muddy river. Winnipeg, with its crypto Greco-Roman Victorian banks and warehouses, is the tomb of King Wheat, and Memphis, with its pseudo antebellum mansions, is the tomb of King Cotton.

I find King Cotton's photos and costumes in the Memphis museum, the Pink Palace, a garish mansion of pink stone built by the bankrupted founder of the Piggly Wiggley supermarket chain. Elvis, the King of Rock 'n' Roll, had adapted his glittering stage outfits from the embroidered silk and satin costumes worn by the King and Queen of the annual Cotton Carnival, just as he had bought Graceland in 1957 from the Old Memphis family that had built it in 1939.

There are now two Gracelands on Elvis Presley Boulevard, the estate and the plaza across the street. To tour the house, Andrew and I have to buy tickets in the plaza. The plaza has the *Lisa Marie*, the plane Elvis bought not long before his death, a museum with some of his cars, a chrome fifties-style diner selling Fat Elvis junk food, and stores full of Elvis souvenirs. I look around for the Swinging Elvis wall clock, the Graceland snowglobe that lights up and plays "Love Me Tender," the gold lamé Dancing Elvis *Hound Dog* phone I had seen for sale in the catalogue, but most of the shirts, jackets, mugs, fridge magnets, portrait buttons, and tote bags feature a gloomy, airbrushed picture of a Soulful Elvis in dark blue on black. Elvis, his image trademarked, licensed, and marketed by Elvis Presley Enterprises, has become Corporate Elvis.

We buy Graceland tour tickets for the next day, Sunday, August 15. Elvis's grave in the Memorial Garden is part of the tour, but we will have to line up for the candlelight procession that will begin to wind past his grave at 9:00 p.m. We grab the Sun Studio shuttle bus to visit the birthplace of rock 'n' roll, the grungy storefront studio where Elvis recorded "That's All Right" in 1954. I am not surprised by the number of middle-aged couples, like us, on the bus, but I wonder about the chubby little girl in shorts and a halter top sitting across from me, her long blonde hair held back with barrettes. Isn't she a little young for B. B. King, Johnny Cash, Roy Orbison, Elvis? The woman next to her, about my age, is bebopping along, tapping her foot in time to "That's All Right" blaring from the bus's loudspeaker. She is wearing a T-shirt with a portrait button that reads Young Elvis. I haven't seen this button before, and when I ask her about it, she points excitedly to the little girl.

"That's *her*! She's the youngest girl Elvis impersonator in the world! That's *her*. She's *nine*."

"Nine-and-a-half," Child Elvis pipes up.

Child Elvis and her grandmother are from Hamilton, Ontario,

and they have come here for Elvis Week to watch the other impersonators compete. Child Elvis, her grandmother says, got into it when she saw a video of a Canadian who won the Elvis impersonators' championship. Child Elvis is too young to compete, but she sings, tap dances, and she's here to pick up some performing tips. There are so many Elvises in competition, Grandma says, they were up until 3:00 a.m. last night. Child Elvis has slumped in her seat, sound asleep.

It's a slow Elvis Week this year. The Europeans, it is whispered, have been siphoned off by Princess Diana at Althorp. Graceland plaza, with no high-class restaurants, no cool, shady places to sit, is a hound dog. Crowds at the plaza are small, subdued. On Sunday, a van runs a dozen of us across the road for our tour of the Graceland mansion. The tour does not include Elvis's second-floor bedroom with its mirrored walls, monster bed, and the bathroom with the red shag carpet where he died, face down in a pool of vomit, twenty-two years ago. That's too bad. A black cabbie had tipped us off that we should visit the Lorraine Motel on Mulberry Street where Martin Luther King had been shot and killed in 1968. It's now the National Civil Rights Museum. The museum, we find, not only displays the bus where Rosa Parks refused to take a back seat, and the diner where the first black sit-in took place, but it projects on its walls life-size, continuous film footage of police breaking up 1960s civil rights demonstrations, violent, horrifying film I have never seen before.

In the meticulously preserved Lorraine Motel, the balcony where King was standing when he was shot looks exactly as it did on all the television footage I'd watched during the days after his assassination. Looking out from inside the motel, Andrew and I saw the boarded-up window on the next street where the assassin had aimed and fired. Martin Luther King's room, with its rumpled, unmade bed, dirty dishes and half-eaten meal, is arranged as it was when he walked out on the balcony.

Graceland is more tomb than shrine. The rooms are small, the ceilings low. Strip away Graceland's stone facade and oversized classical portico, and you have a suburban, two-storey, stucco-and-stone North American home. Not my house, a rich man's house, but it looks so familiar: the beige broadloom in the living room, a black grand piano, off-white upholstery, walls lined with velvet drapes in gold and peacock blue, Louis xv and Queen Anne reproduction furniture, a mirror over the fireplace, chandeliers, dining-room cabinets for china and knick-knacks, a country kitchen with appliances in avocado and harvest gold (I, too, have owned a fridge and stove in harvest gold), a vinyl padded bar and sectional furniture in the basement TV room, a 1974 billiard room draped, tentlike, with four hundred yards of brightly patterned pleated cotton fabric. Even the "jungle room," featuring armchairs carved with animal heads, fake-fur upholstery, and green shag carpet on the ceiling, was not all that uncommon in 1977.

What distinguishes Graceland from typical suburban houses is the absence of sunlight. Keeping the drapes closed on the main floor to prevent the sun from fading the furnishings gives the effect of darkness at noon. Elvis's two favourite haunts, the yellow-and-black TV room and the billiard room, appear to be without windows or ventilation. The TV room has three television sets, all in a row, which Elvis watched simultaneously, changing channels, when he felt so moved, by blowing out a screen with one of his enormous collection of handguns.

Suburban Elvis. Do we forgive him his excesses because his business manager cheated him, his wife left him, his film career failed, and because, by forty-two, he was fatally addicted to prescription drugs? In Graceland plaza, Elvis's voice floats out of loudspeakers, but he's been programmed to sing sentimental ballads. I miss the hurtin' songs, and so many of Elvis's early hits were about heartbreak, unrequited love, separation, solitude. *Are you lonesome tonight?* "Everyone shares a common element with Elvis," reads a sign in the plaza's Elvis Museum. "He encompasses the daring, the familiar, the spiritual, the dangerous, the sexual, the masculine, the androgenous, the eccentric, the traditional, the god-like and God-fearing, the liberal and the conservative in all of us." As Peter Guralnick says in *Careless Love: The Unmaking of Elvis Presley*, "in the end, there is only one voice that counts." And John Lennon said, "Before Elvis there was nothing."

After the long dark tunnels of Graceland's trophy building, with its rows of glass cases displaying gold records, guitars, costumes, jewellery, badges and plaques, it's a relief to come out into the sunshine. The Presley family plot in the Meditation Garden is on a little knoll to the south of the house, sheltered by a curving brick wall. The gravestones are arranged in a semi-circle in front of a small pool with fountains. The stones lie flat, their inscriptions engraved on full-length sheets of bronze. Elvis Aaron Presley. It was years after we'd named our son Aaron that I realized we had named him for Elvis. The grave is surrounded by wreaths and bouquets of flowers, teddy bears, Elvis photos and homemade signs reading "Artist of the Century." It's a pleasant idea, to be buried in your garden, as we all used to be, and the gravestones complement the stone walls of the formal flower beds so well it's almost as if Elvis had built the garden with that in mind.

Memphis is a mortuary theme park, its early history so dominated by epidemics of malaria, cholera, and yellow fever the settlement was nearly abandoned. The temples to the sick, including Baptist Memorial, the hospital where Elvis was pronounced dead, are monumental. On the riverfront, a new sports-arena-and-convention-centre has been built in the shape of a grey, steel-clad thirty-two-storey pyramid, The Pyramid. On Beale Street, birthplace of the blues, the only sign of life on Sunday is a black pick-up band playing in the park, a bunch of old guys jiving around, pretending to sing. The official Elvis restaurant, Elvis Presley's Memphis, is decorated like a funeral home, dim light, red upholstery, white pillars, black tabletops. On one wall, a dark blue curtain with twinkly multicoloured stars pulls back from time to time to reveal colossal, flickering Elvises from videos of his early black-and-white television shows.

Elvis is projected on walls. He sings from ceilings. He is reincarnated in impersonators, carried around as purses and tote bags. He glitters in jewellery, stares out of posters, CDs, and T-shirts. Elvis, ambiguous, ubiquitous, protean, reproduces his image to infinity. As twilight falls and we pilgrims gather in front of Graceland for our candlelight vigil, we wear images of Elvis in all his manifestations. Some young women have set up votive shrines at the edge of the sidewalk, pictures and figurines of Elvis arranged around burning candles. Elvis impersonators stroll around, pretender peacocks in gold silk, black leather, and makeup, each nodding to a knot of family admirers.

More pilgrims arrive, on foot. The police have cordoned off the road in front of Graceland, but apart from red cruiser lights whirling in the distance and the faint whack of a helicopter overhead, they keep a respectful distance. We are a quiet, orderly crowd, two thousand or so ordinary people shuffling in a double line towards the gates. We are almost exclusively white, but to my amazement we are not overwhelmingly old or middle-aged. In front of us, a couple in their late twenties have brought their two young children. The kids are falling asleep on the sidewalk, but they are not whining to go home. These parents wouldn't have been more than seven or eight themselves when Elvis died. There are hundreds of people here, including Child Elvis, who weren't born when Elvis lived. Elvis lives through artefacts, images, imprints, stories, sacred sites. Will scholars two thousand years from now be debating the existence of an historic Elvis?

It grows dark. The sky, with a crescent moon, is a luminous cobalt blue. Shadows appear, the line lengthens. We stand, shifting from foot to foot, in the dim glow of street lights, the odd guttering candle. Candles will be given out at the gates, but many people have brought their own. I notice how every square inch of Graceland's stone wall is covered with love notes, signatures, scratched and written. Conversation is muted. The mood is intimate, companionable, like a summer bonfire.

Peace in the Valley, Elvis sings from somewhere in the black trees on the Graceland grounds. Elvis, if he had lived, would be sixty-four, and today, August 15, 1999, my parents, aged ninety and eighty-seven, would be celebrating their sixty-first wedding anniversary. Unthinkable. Impossible. *I'll stay with you until it's time for you to go*, Elvis sings from the trees.

"Light your candles!" A snapping of matches and lighters and our faces are illuminated by a thousand little points of flame. A young woman, president of the Elvis Country Fan Club, tells us over the loudspeaker how much we love Elvis, and he loves us. Elvis sings, *I can't help falling in love with you*. So okay, this is the South, and I'm feeling so mellow I could handle "Old Shep." A ghostly procession of torch bearers in white shirts winds down the driveway from the house. The gates open, and in a few minutes, a long line of twinkling lights begins to flutter like fireflies up the driveway towards the Meditation Garden. The gates will stay open until the last pilgrim has passed through, morning if necessary. Morning. Her star glows in the west.

XXVII

HAVE I BUILT MY ship of death? I'm working on it. I have made a pilgrimage, and I have uncovered a mythology, wacky as it may seem to others, that enriches my life. I am hoping not to embark soon, but I have learned wisdom from the dying and from those who care for them. Hospice King-Aurora is part of my life, and a ten-minute drive away there is Hill House Hospice, Dr. Brian Berger and York Central, a hospital with palliative care beds.

My ship will be a canoe. I'll place a Sheila na Gig in her bow, and I'll pack in morphine, champagne and caviar, Moosehead beer, a fibre optic spray, a drum, my favourite CDs, a tape Andrew made when we were young of water lapping and loons calling, and, for sure, the collected poems of W. B. Yeats. "The Wild Swans at Coole" is the greatest resurrection poem I've ever read, but I may need someone to read it to me. Who's going to be my crew? Will they be strong, and row together?

My navigational chart has been drawn for me, unexpectedly, by my mother's younger sister, Elinor. All my childhood and adolescent life in Winnipeg, Elinor lived in Vancouver, then in West Vancouver. I rarely saw her. Elinor and my mother, the proverbial Grasshopper and Ant, did not see eye to eye, but when as a girl I was toiling, antlike, over my boring studies, Elinor, a vivacious executive secretary, seemed to me to be the epitome of sexuality, independence, and *joie de vivre*. Elinor had gorgeous clothes and swarms of boyfriends, some younger than she as she grew older, and she was always travelling to some exotic place, Death Valley, Sante Fe, Acapulco, or to her friends' dude ranch in the Cariboo. She was my glamorous Auntie Elinor. Her friends called her Swede because she was so blonde.

Elinor never grew old. The older I grew, and the older Elinor became, the younger she looked. Elinor didn't tell me how she did it, and I never asked, but over the years Elinor travelled so far back in time she looked younger than photographs of her youthful self in our family album. At seventy-five, Elinor's personality, her interests, her infectious giggle appeared to me to be the same as they had been all her adult life, and she looked younger than I did at fifty-two.

Elinor and I seemed to have almost nothing in common except our giggle and girlish voice, but after Harry died, we began to phone each other on Sundays to keep in touch. I was pleased that Elinor took the initiative, but I was taken aback when, in the spring of 1996, she invited me to visit her in West Vancouver for a week. In the past, I'd let Elinor know when I'd be in town and she'd take me out for a fabulous dinner. These occasions were infrequent, and I'd felt that for Elinor entertaining her "little niece," as she jokingly called me since I had grown so much bigger, was something of a family duty. On the phone now, Elinor sounded lighthearted, as always, but the tone of her voice told me she wasn't asking me, she was *ordering* me. Yes, Elinor, I will come. She insisted that I bring her a Blue Jays baseball cap she could wear to watch the games on TV. Her medications, she said, made her eyes sensitive to glare from the window.

More than twenty-five years before, Elinor's heart had been damaged by a viral infection. She'd had to go on a disability pension, but retirement, she'd said, only gave her more time to have a good time. She rarely talked about her health, although she had told me about her near-death experience from a massive cardiac arrest three years earlier. Elinor said she could hear the voices of the medical team working to resuscitate her. In her mind's eye, she saw them bathed in blue light. When the light turned to pink, she knew she was going to live. Elinor had made an amazing recovery. I had never thought of her as being sick.

What would Elinor and I find to talk about for a week? I needn't have worried. Elinor had summoned me to discuss her ashes. Years before, Harry had promised to sprinkle her ashes on our lake. Elinor had vacationed there often as a girl, and occasionally when I was small. Would I undertake to do this? Of course, I said. I can do ashes. I would be honoured. Bronze nameplate on the boulder? I asked. No, absolutely not. The First Memorial Society, she said, would take care of the cremation. If I heard that she was in the hospital, I was *not* to jump on a plane. There would be no funeral. She had appointed a trust company as her executor. She had discussed everything, in person, with the trustee. He would make all the arrangements. Everything in her bachelor apartment would go to the Salvation Army.

Elinor had travelled light all her life, as indifferent to possessions as she was to husbands and children. Would I like her grandfather's old tobacco jar? I brought it down from a shelf, covered with dust. Cleaned up, the jar had an elegant art nouveau design in navy and orange. Yes, I'd like it. She also wanted me to have a framed photograph of her mother, Bella, my grandmother, an indomitable strength in both our lives.

Elinor blinked back tears when I told her how much I had always admired her. No one had told her. My mother didn't see Elinor's insouciant lifestyle as resourceful. "Elinor," she'd say, "You've got a good brain, *use it*." To Elinor, her sister Margaret, married, with no need to earn a living, was an intimidating intellectual who spent her days reading scholarly books. I was dumbfounded. I recalled my mother as being thoughtful, critical, a moralist, but I assured Elinor that, to the best of my recollection, when Margaret wasn't resting in bed she was cooking, reading recipes, washing, and knitting. Her favourite book was *How to Eat Right to Keep Fit*.

That cleared the air, and when Elinor told me more about their unstable, unhappy childhood, I understood better the sources of Margaret's anger and Elinor's need for friendship. Elinor introduced me to her circle of strong, loyal women with whom she went out to dinner and the theatre, and she phoned up a lost cousin, my mother's favourite, who took us out to lunch. Elinor had also been in touch with her only living nephew, Bill, a cousin I barely knew, who worked in Southeast Asia. Bill and I were the last leaves on this dying branch of the Duncan family tree. Elinor could only walk short distances, pausing to catch her breath, but every day she was up and out of bed, impeccably dressed, smiling, her makeup perfect.

During my week in West Van, Elinor and I got to know each other, a little, and while we had sharp differences of opinion on some subjects, we made each other laugh. Elinor joked about how the nurses' jaws dropped every time she walked into her doctor's office, What, you're still *alive*? Elinor, one of the miraculous minority to survive CPR for years, was dying. She knew it. Her cardiac specialist, a superb doctor and a forthright man, expressed absolute amazement that she had lived this long. Elinor wasn't a candidate for surgery. Her wounded heart was wearing out. Some day soon it would stop.

Heart surgeons and cardiologists may think that a heart attack is a nice, clean way to go, but the prospect didn't cheer Elinor. Her smile was as bright as ever, but she sighed at times and her eyes filled with tears. "Old age is hell" was the only complaint I heard her utter.

We had a good time, and I was pleased when Elinor invited me back for another week's visit in March 1997. I stayed in an excellent bed-and-breakfast up the street from her apartment. It was near the ocean, and I could walk for miles on the sea wall. But Elinor was more tired, her breathing laboured and shallow. Her ankles were swelling. Her hair had thinned. She'd had, like me, a ruddy complexion, but now the skin drawn tight over her face and skull was white and translucent. Elinor had fainted in a restaurant in the fall, and she had been going back and forth to hospital for tests and treatments.

Her lungs were filling with fluid. She took a bewildering array of pills. She was as thin as a will-o'-the-wisp.

Yet Elinor could still mix a mean Caesar, and she was determined that we would do lunch and eat out, including dinner at the home of friends up the mountain in North Vancouver. My misgivings must have shown in my face, because Elinor promised she would give me the high sign to leave as soon as she got tired. The meal was delicious and our hosts understanding when we asked to be driven home, but sitting in their car as it snaked around the black mountain roads, I realized, with a feeling of panic, that we were climbing up, not down, Grouse Mountain.

"Where are we going?"

"We want to show you the city lights," our hostess replies. *Lights! I've been seeing Vancouver's bloody lights since I was five years old! I hate seeing lights! I hate mountains! You're supposed to be taking Elinor home! She's tired! Elinor is dying! Can't you see? Turn around, go down the mountain, I need to get Elinor home!*

"Shouldn't we be taking Elinor home?"

"I'm fine," Elinor pipes up from the back seat. I turn around. Elinor gives me an enigmatic little smile.

By the time we reach the lookout at the top of Grouse Mountain, I am ready to hurl everyone here over the edge. There is a crowd. We have trouble finding a parking spot. Shadowy figures in parkas mill about, carrying telescopes. I am freezing. I stand dutifully at the railing. Oh, there's Stanley Park, I say. Oh, Lion's Gate bridge. Oh, a ship on Burrard Inlet.

Heather. Elinor's voice. I turn. Elinor, in a black raincoat, is standing some distance behind me, pointing to the western sky behind the mountain. I look up and see a golden dragon flaming through the starry night lashing its fiery tail. Halley's comet. Of course. That's why we have come up Grouse Mountain. I smile. Elinor smiles. Our eyes meet. *That's me*, Elinor is saying. *Good-bye, Heather, good-bye*.

Elinor died a week later, five days after I returned home. It buoyed my spirits to picture her rocketing through space. The day after I was told of her death, her trust company called. I was one of four beneficiaries named in Miss Duncan's will, was I not? Yes. Her estate was small. Yes. The trust company would have to charge a $5,000 executor's fee. Fine. It was a large fee, given the size of the estate. Yes, go ahead. *Why are you calling me?*

The trust company was calling me because, now that their valued client, Elinor Duncan, was dead, her estate wasn't worth their time and trouble. I, her eldest next of kin, was to take charge. I saw Elinor flaming through the sky, red with rage. I was red with rage. But I wasn't alone. Elinor had, quietly and without ceremony, introduced me to her circle of friends in Vancouver. I immediately called her best friend, Noreen. Elinor had trusted Noreen with her life, and I knew Noreen to be loyal, able, and experienced with paperwork I knew nothing about. Noreen settled Elinor's estate in no time, and I was glad that not all of Elinor's things went to the Sally Ann. Noreen sent me a jewelbox full of Swede's lockets, bracelets, and gold chains.

My own responsibility was Elinor's missing ashes. Elinor, where are you? Did you make it to the crematorium, or did the untrustworthy company toss you in False Creek? *Pipe down little niece. I'll let you know.* Weeks later, as I walked across our rural road to the mailbox, I noticed a big, white cardboard box sticking out. What could that be? The mail sticker said, "Elinor Duncan." I thought, Elinor can't be sending me a package, she's dead. Then, as I picked it up, I realized *This is Elinor.*

I laughed and cried and laughed. I think Elinor would have laughed too. Imagine, a memorial society sending ashes through the mail to an unconfirmed destination. So cool. So West Coast. Such inconceivable anguish if the mail had failed.

I buried Elinor in July in my sacred place, the deep cleft in the sheer granite cliff at the south end of our lake. I waited for a morning when the water was glassy, then, not long after sunrise, I paddled over in the old red canoe, the black box holding her ashes at my feet. Resting my canoe in the pale, lichen-covered cavern, touching its soft walls, I opened the box. Elinor's ashes, in a plastic bag, were light and white, and as I slowly dribbled them into the cave's reflection on the black water, they rose, like clouds, to infinity.